The Master Scratchbuilders

Their Aircraft Models & Techniques

John Alcorn
General Editor

Schiffer Military History
Atglen, PA

Book Design by Ian Robertson.

Copyright © 1999 by John Alcorn.
Library of Congress Catalog Number: 98-89832

All rights reserved. No part of this work may be reproduced or used in any forms or by any means – graphic, electronic or mechanical, including photocopying or information storage and retrieval systems – without written permission from the copyright holder.

Printed in China.
ISBN: 0-7643-0795-9

We are interested in hearing from authors with book ideas on related topics.

Published by Schiffer Publishing Ltd. 4880 Lower Valley Road Atglen, PA 19310 Phone: (610) 593-1777 FAX: (610) 593-2002 E-mail: Schifferbk@aol.com. Visit our web site at: www.schifferbooks.com Please write for a free catalog. This book may be purchased from the publisher. Please include $3.95 postage. Try your bookstore first.	In Europe, Schiffer books are distributed by: Bushwood Books 6 Marksbury Road Kew Gardens Surrey TW9 4JF England Phone: 44 (0)181 392-8585 FAX: 44 (0)181 392-9876 E-mail: Bushwd@aol.com. Try your bookstore first.

Contents

ACKNOWLEDGMENTS 4
LIMERICKS FOR MODELLING 6
INTRODUCTION 8
GEORGE LEE: A FOND DEDICATION 10

CHAPTER I:	VACUFORMING AND BASIC MODEL STRUCTURE 16	
	by John Alcorn	
CHAPTER II:	HOW I BUILT MY CURTISS HS-2L 28	
	by Bob Davies	
CHAPTER III:	HOW I BUILT MY SHORT SINGAPORE III 39	
	by Alan Clark	
CHAPTER IV:	HOW I BUILY MY DE HAVILLAND DH9A 49	
	by John Alcorn	
CHAPTER V:	HOW I BUILT MY GLOSTER GAMECOCK 78	
	by Ron Lowry	
CHAPTER VI:	HOW I BUILT MY GRUMMAN TBF-1C AVENGER 89	
	by Arlo Schroeder	
CHAPTER VII:	HOW I BUILT MY MITSUBISHI G4M "BETTY" 96	
	by Bill Bosworth	
CHAPTER VIII:	HOW I BUILT MY AVRO LANCASTER 104	
	by Peter Cooke	
CHAPTER IX:	MODEL RESEARCH AND PHOTOGRAPHY 116	
	by Clark Macomber	
CHAPTER X:	FINISHING 126	
	by Peter Chalmers	
CHAPTER XI:	TOOLS, SUPPLIES, MATERIALS, SERVICES & WORKPLACES 142	
	by John Alcorn	
CHAPTER XII:	TRIO DIVERSO 152	
	• Mauro Cescutti 152	
	• Kevin Clayton-Greene 156	
	• Dr. Dennis Collins 163	
	EPILOGUE 164	

Acknowledgments

For MSB, I owe primary indebtedness to the several fellow scratchbuilders who have contributed HOW I BUILT MY... chapters, plus Pete Chalmers for FINISHING and Clark Macomber for MODEL RESEARCH. I am also grateful to the other fine modellers who kindly provided (mainly) "portrait" photos of their creations. "Thanks!" go also to elder son Stewart's wife, Sue, who typed most of my DH9A chapter; and to my wife, Francie, who typed certain other sections, scanned in much "hardcopy only" material, and endured my never-ending questions regarding the computer.

In a broader sense, however, we owe the debt for the context of our hobby to IPMS. Without this focus, we would be far fewer modellers, plying our craft in isolation and without collective inspiration. This is pretty much how it was in the "old (pre-IPMS) days," when our bonding elements were simply the few journals which pandered to us, such as MODEL AIRPLANE NEWS in the USA, the kit and materials suppliers, and such buddies as we happened to acquire. Even so, we static builders were a mere sidelight to the flying model crowd.

But all is very different now, what with the stimulus and comraderie of IPMS chapters, regions and national organizations; each hosting periodic meetings, contests, and conventions. This is sustained by the astonishing and synergistic infrastructure of kits, aftermarket items, supplies, and subject reference material. Let's take a single example: the 1/48th scale Hasegawa Macchi C.202 kit; supplemented with the Jaguar or True Detail cockpit interior package; the various Floquil and other paints of the appropriate colors; and the Aeromaster, Tauro, and other decal sheets. AERO DETAIL#15 covers the Macchi C200/202/205 series in detail photos and line drawings; while Ali D'Italia's Aer.Macchi C.202, and SQUADRON/SIGNAL#41 outline its development/operational history as well. This reference largess extends, of course, to scratchbuilding.

I am moved to end ACKNOWLEDGMENTS on a note of appreciation to my recently acquired modelling buddies of the IPMS/ USA Seattle chapter. They are one great bunch! I came here in Summer '96, not knowing a soul except Bob La Bouy. But, it wasn't long before I was one of them, and soon felt as though I had been so forever. Not only are they friendly, great fun, knowledgable, and fine modellers, but they have taught me—an old George Lee-trained practitioner—numerous tricks of the trade. Most notably, Bill Johnson induced me to abandon my old diaphragm air compressor in favor of bottled CO2. Thanks, Bill. Thanks, group.

SIKORSKI S-38: This lovely S-38 amphibian, to 1/24th scale, was built for the Johnson Wax Company corporate offices by Bob Rice, of Tucson, Arizona. A good, profusely illustrated "HOW I BUILT MY S-38" article appeared in the June 1997 issue of SCALE MODELER (heh, heh, along with "CATWOMAN On the Prowl").

Rumpler TAUBE#1. This lovely TAUBE was made by Dr. Raleigh Williams, also of Tucson, during the period 8 August 1996-97. He states that he recommenced modelling in 1990, following a 55 year pause! At the 1998 IPMS/USA Nationals, it took first place in its SCRATCH BUILT 1/48th SCALE class, and the DETAIL AND SCALE award.

Rumpler TAUBE#2. This model depicts one aircraft of an incident which took place in the early months of W.W.-I, related by Marshal of the RAF Lord Douglas of Kirtleside in his autobiography YEARS OF COMBAT. To quote: "We were...north of Neuve Chappele when I suddenly espied a German two-seater...just below us. The German observer did not appear to be shooting at us. ... We waved a hand to the enemy and proceeded with our (observation) task. The enemy did likewise. At the time this did not appear to me in any way ridiculous...there is a bond of sympathy between all who fly, even between enemies." The BE.2a was flown by Lt. Harvey-Kelly of the RFC, as well as by Lt. William Sholto Douglas. Dr. Raliegh Williams' inspiration was the painting by Paul Lengelle of the incident: one of a series for Aviation Week and Space Technology magazine, 1979.

Acknowledgments

Limericks for Modelling
by John Alcorn

T'was a sniffly lad of Kilkrankie,
    Who eschewed the use of his hankie.
He put paint up his nose,
    So that when he snoze,
His models would be finished quite swanky.

There once was a basher named Crocker,
    Who finally went off of his rocker.
As they took him away,
    I heard him to say;
"It's the kit sellers you should put in the locker."

T'was a superdetailler named Flynn,
    Who at the Nats was determined to win.
The subject he chose,
    Just won by a nose;
Five Blue Angels on the head of a pin.

An ecology zealot from 'Frisco,
    Built his models from dough and Crisco.
"So, after they're made,
    They can biodegrade;
Or, I can sell the rights to Nabisco."

There was once a hacker named John,
    Whose NINAK went on and on.
He was young when he started,
    But by Hari Kari departed;
Upon seeing the RE-8 made by Ron.

There was once a builder in Texas,
    Who, though single, had several exes.
He had treated them right,
    But, stayed up all night;
Mixing paint instead of the sexes.

T'was a shy figure crafter from Spree,
    Who made one whose charms you could see.
When asked into which class
    He wished to enter this lass;
He said:"It's a fantasy subject to me."

There once was a talented Lapp,
    Who fashioned his gems from scrap.
"When I build 'em up here,
    Mid the snow and reindeer;
I'm spared all that peer pressure crap."

There once was a duke from Paducah,
    Who smoked Green Stuff in his hookah.
His models were nutty,
    Doubtless due to the putty;
That had become lodged in his snookah.

There was a young builder from Kent
    Evicted for non-payment of rent.
"I can live on the streets,
    Eating turnips and beets;
So long as I have kits and cement."

T'was a Da-Daist builder from Chartres,
    Who favored mixed-subject art.
He built a cathedral
    With too much dihedral;
And cried "Merd!"when it all fell apart.

There once was a dioramist from Spain,
    Who inclined toward subjects arcane.
When he fashioned in clay
    An Auto-de-Fe;
He was tried, and died in great pain.

"I like to build planes out of plastic;
    The feeling I get is fantastic.
I love the mood
    Of quiet solitude;
But, when I drop parts, I get spastic."
    -submitted by son Stewart Alcorn of his Dad

The Group had a grouser named Jack
    Citing skills which they all seemed to lack.
Superglued to a wall
    In front of a mall;
They said;"Be grateful we glued you in back."

Scratchbuilder George was having a fit
    Choosing a subject not found in a kit.
He considered a Gotha,
    and a Blackburn Botha;
Then, decided a C.O.W. Fighter was it.

There was once a young Scot named Moran,
    Who kept model paint in his sporran.
But, he fell on his face,
    'While engaged in a race;
Now, his privates are schwartzgrun and tan.

A compulsive builder named Ted
    At last went out of his head.
Off to Bedlam he went,
    Which he didn't resent;
"Now, I'll see Mustangs and Camels in bed."

T'was a ribald constructeur named Poirot
    Who fancied the avions d'Amiot.
Why he chose a 'Bus
    Was a mystery to us;
Until we saw what was going on below.

A scruffly scratchbuilder named Babbit
    Never bathed, and lived with a rabbit.
In his case, he built kits
    In his odiferous knits;
The term "scratch" simply referred to his habit.

T'was a light-wielding judge named McKnight,
    Whose light into a cockpit took flight.
When Butch, who was no nerd,
    Learned the fate of his bird;
You wouldn't care to share McKnight's plight.

There once was an Egyptian named Phut
   Who was chief ship modeller for Tut.
When Tut was entombed,
   Poor Phut was doomed;
With Tut they put Phut when Tut's hut was shut.

T'was a wonderful bird of Katroo,
   Who wished a perfect birthday for you.
You got a Zero on floats,
   Borne by funicular goats;
Hippo-Heimers brought Buffaloes too.

McTavish, of great ship modelling fame,
   Built Cutty Sark in a bottle of same.
One night he forgot,
   And swallowed the lot;
The inquest said the distiller's to blame.

In order to be fair and effective,
   Judges must be ruthlessly objective.
But, this doesn't ensure
   That they won't endure
Some indignant loser's invective.

T'was a conversion builder named Dow,
   Who's P-40 on floats caused a row.
He said:"My uncle had heard
   That they once built such a bird."
The category entrants had a cow.
His entry was rejected as spurious:
   "To our contest it would be injurious."
Dow replied in a huff:
   "I've had quite enough;
You people are dumb and imperious."
There's a moral to this fable;
   That unless you are quite able
To show documentation
   Of your contest creation;
Don't put it onto the table.

This closeup of the NINAK's nose region emphasizes the type's DH4-like engine area, the fabric covered propeller (of the actual aircraft), the Hucks Starter Dog on the propeller hub, the orthodontic flying and landing wires, the piano drag wires, and the split-axle undercarriage of DH9As in '20s service. (Michael Cole photo)

Introduction

While MASTER SCRATCHBUILDERS (MSB) is a sequel to the gratifyingly well-received SB!(-I), the format and content are almost entirely different.

CONTENT

In order to provide a broad coverage of scratchbuilt techniques, seven HOW I BUILT MY... chapters are included, authored by as many credentialled, well-known modellers. In fact, their selection was based in part upon their differing methods of construction and finishing, as well as subject matter. In addition to construction detail ("how to") shots and line drawings, each HOW I BUILT MY... chapter features one or more large format color portraits of the featured subject, plus portraits of other models built by the author.

While these seven chapters comprise the core of MSB, several others are included to round out coverage of the scratchbuilt topic. For example, Clark Macomber of ACCURATE MINIATURES has kindly provided a thought-provoking chapter on model subject research, a vital prerequisite for most scratchbuilt efforts. This, because many scratchbuilt models are of arcane, "off the beaten track" subjects, usually entailing considerable research and often requiring "scratch built" plans. However, as he emphasizes, commercially available drawings of even the more popular subjects should be thoroughly verified for accuracy, by comparison with published dimensions from reliable sources and careful scaling, where possible, from photographs. A complex, time-consuming scratchbuilt model should not just be a tour *de force* of craftsmanship: it should also represent its subject in the most authentic manner possible, as regards configuration, detail, finish, markings, and "weathering" as appropriate.

Although MSB is not an update of its predecessor, it must perforce include some material from SB! if it is to be a "stand-alone" compendium of scratchbuilding techniques. For this reason, a separate chapter is included on VACUFORMING—one of the foundations of the genre.

The chapter on FINISHING is primarily an explanation of the methods employed by Peter Chalmers of Charlotte, North Carolina. Although not a scratchbuilder, he is a highly knowledgable aviation enthusiast, whose 1/48th scale renderings of (mostly) W.W.-II subjects are superb. His finishing techniques well complement those explained in the several HOW I BUILT MY... chapters. There is also a chapter on TOOLS, SUPPLIES, MATERIALS, SERVICES, and WORKPLACES.

The chapter TRIO DIVERSO features the handiwork of three scratchbuilders having very diverse modelling interests—and living in even more diverse corners of the world: Dr. Dennis Collins, of England (vintage British racers); Mauro Cescutti, of Italy (W.W.-I and earlier); and Kevin Clayton-Greene of Tasmania (W.W.-II). Finally, you will find "portrait" photos of models by other outstanding scratchbuilders, including Tony Clements and Robert Rice.

Even with all of this largesse, however, MSB cannot possibly cover the entire gamut of scratchbuilding techniques, since no two modellers build exactly alike. Nevertheless, we hope that it inspires a younger generation of talented modellers to tackle subjects be-

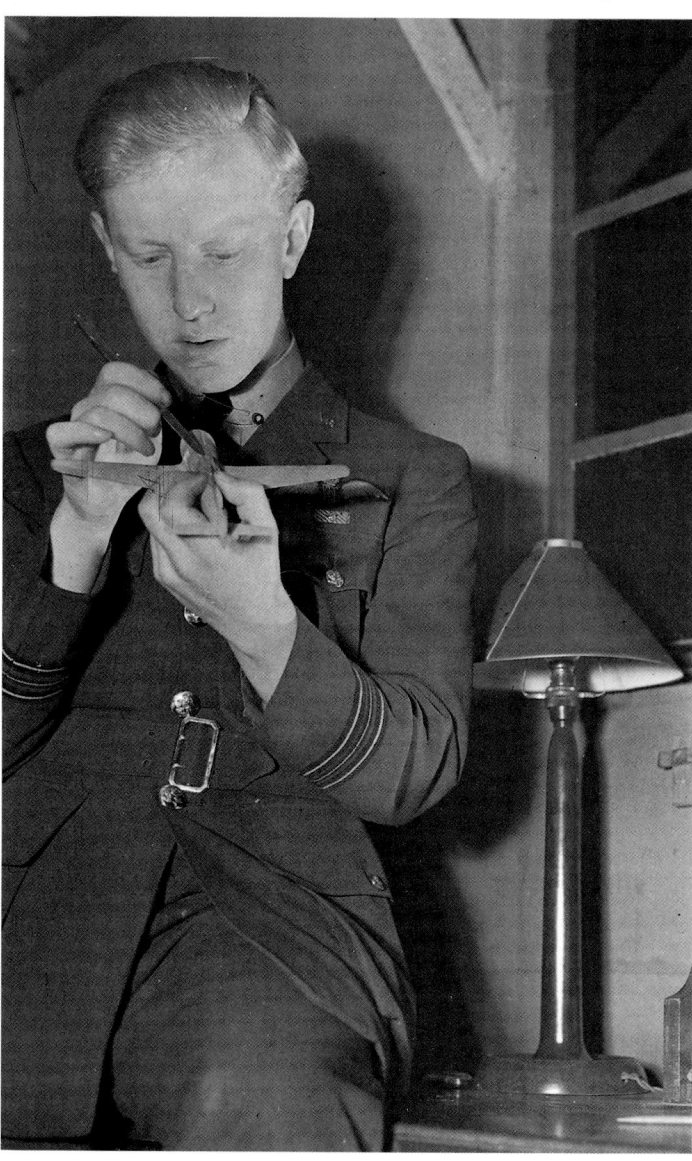

In SB!, I included a facsimile of the 23 March 1942 LIFE cover, showing an earnest high school lad, intently sanding his 1/72nd scale SPITFIRE, made for the U.S. Government sponsored identification model program. This time, we have James "Ginger" Lacey, who, as a Sergeant with No.501 Squadron flying HURRICANES, was one of the top-scoring RAF pilots during the Battle of Britain (shown here later, as a Squadron Leader). Not having access to state-of-the-art modelling tools, the ever resourceful Lacey is nonetheless superdetailling the cockpit of his Fw190 using a kitchen knife from the squadron mess. Or, possibly, he is simply tormenting the Luftwaffe pilot of his Fw190 "Voodo Doll." - photograph courtesy of the Imperial War Museum, London: Neg. No. CH8457

yond the admitted plentitude of kits, providing them with a wide choice of construction methods. Who's for a 1/24th scale Curtiss F8C-4 HELLDIVER, Westland WAPITI, Nieuport-Delage 29, Aviatik C.I, or Aichi D1A2?

STYLE, UNITS, AND TERMINOLOGY

Since each HOW I BUILT MY... chapter was written by a different modeller, their styles of writing, emphasis, and amount of detail vary considerably. As general editor, I made no attempt to bring them into conformity. I simply corrected any misspellings, punctuation, and syntax errors (no doubt making a few of my own in the process): in addition, I occasionally urged the author to expand discussion of certain topics felt to be of especial interest to modellers, and to clarify ambiguous passages.

They say that Britain and the USA are two countries separated by a common language. I made no attempt to rationalize this, including spelling. Nevertheless, my own spelling has gradually become Anglicized in certain cases; the result of reading so much aviation and general historical material from the Mother Country. You'll note an example in the title of this book. Still, I draw the line at "colour," "whilst," and "aluminium." Also, you'll find unashamed use of the British system of units, perpetrated upon us by our forefathers, whose native land has even abandoned it.

Despite all of the fine rhetoric above, I have attempted to standardize a few specialist terms, in the interest of clarity and readability. Even in SB!, we used the term "vacuform," in leiu of the rather awkward "vacuum form." Similarly, herein the word "thou" denotes thousandths of an inch, rather than "thou." or the possibly misleading "mil." Also, note that "high impact polystyrene sheet" has mercifully been replaced by "plasticard," itself a blatant Americanization of the British expression "plastic card" (same number of syllables, but easier to say—and write). And scratch built has become scratchbuilt.

SCRATCHBUILT SUBJECTS

Scratchbuilders are, as a rule, strongly inclined towards constructing models of arcane, "off the beaten path" subjects—some would say, to a fault. Aside from our natural proclivity toward unusual subjects, it does seem like carrying coals to Newcastle to scratchbuild a 1/48th scale SPITFIRE Mk. I, Bf 109E, SBD-3, TBF-1C, or P-51D, in view of the superb kits of such subjects now available.

So, as if to ensure a clear playing field, Alan Clark selects the Short SINGAPORE and Blackburn FIRECREST; Bill Bosworth the McDonnell XP-67 "MOONBAT"; Bill Davies the Curtiss HS-2L; I the DeHavilland DH9A; and George Lee the Curtiss "CARRIER PIGEON," Keystone B4A, and Vickers C.O.W. Fighter! But, honest folks, we usually make our selection based upon an innate fondness for the subject.

But, this is not to say that we eschew the more popular subjects: witness Peter Cooke's SPITFIRES, Arlo Schroeder's TBF-1 AVENGER, or Bill Bosworth's Mitsubishi G4M. Here the difference is usually one of scale, and the lavishing of detail which can—indeed, must—be evidenced in larger models. Another viable motive is that of accuracy: to faithfully replicate a common subject which has never been rendered correctly in commercial kits, at least to a given scale. Arlo had an even better motive: he flew two tours of duty in the SWPA riding backwards in TBF's.

Bristol BLENHEIM "MK.II" in Finnish service, scratchbuilt to 1/32nd scale by Robert Karr, who painted the backdrop and took the photo.

George Lee - A Fond Dedication

It seemed obvious that this volume should be dedicated to George Lee. Not only was he the Grand Master of the static scale airplane scratch builders—at least in the USA—but he was revered by all who knew him: as a modeller; airplane enthusiast; mechanical designer *par excellence*; wood carver; husband; father; grandfather; and friend. They just don't come any better.

His capsule "autobiography" was included in SB!, so needn't be repeated here.

What does need emphasizing was his aviation knowledge, which was encyclopedic; his modelling skills, which have yet to be excelled; and his willingness to share his modelling "secrets" and aviation lore with anyone who was demonstrably earnest in their desire to learn or gather reference material.

As a modeller, George was of the "time is no object" school—getting it right was what mattered. If it took him 15 years to complete his epic Keystone B4A, so be it. (He did build other models during that time, but the Keystone was always underway.) This project was also a measure of his almost incredible patience. Obviously, he had exceptional manual skills and keen eyesight for such work, honed over the years as he became better and better, right up to the end. (So much for this ridiculous idea of a "seniors" category, to allow for their failing faculties.) An asset of his which always impressed me was his resourcefulness in finding solutions to new modelling challenges. This was, to some extent, a manifestation of his professional training as a designer of complex, demanding structures, mechanisms, and systems for a vast melange of exotic de-

GEORGE LEE AND KEYSTONE: So, here we have George, understandably looking pleased over his magnum *opus,* or perhaps more accurately, over having it finished.

vices required by his physicist leaders. This talent went hand and glove with his penchant for pushing his skills to the limit with each succeeding model. While the Keystone was his *magnum opus,* he didn't rest upon his laurels from it for long. Soon he was hard at work on a 1/16th scale Vought O3U-3 floatplane, which was going beyond the Keystone in certain respects: just for example, the control surfaces were to be movable from the cockpit!

The Aviatik D.1 BERG, Keystone, and Vought O3U-3 were in the mainstream of his airplane interests. But we, his fans, ever delighted in his proclivity for undertaking some arcane subject, just because it was so fascinating, bizarre, and even amusing to him. It was with more than a little humor that George undertook his Curtiss CARRIER PIGEON mail plane, Vickers 161 "C.O.W. Fighter," and Westland PTERODACTYL. However, when he expressed his intent to scratch build a Mk. VIII INTERNATIONAL TANK, we began to get concerned. But, as he said: "I just want those armor guys to know that we can do 'em, too." His complex, articulating tracks errr... broke new ground, as did the rivet detail on the armor plate body.

But, mainline interest or slightly tongue-in-cheek diversion, authenticity was always his first priority (Workmanship wasn't even an issue: it was instinctively his best—he was incapable of doing otherwise.). He gathered configuration material on the COWFIGHTER, PTERODACTYL, and CARRIER PIGEON as for his Keystone; although much less was perforce obtainable, due to the obscurity of these birds (bovines). As a matter of fact, it is remarkable what he managed to dredge up on the Keystone, which isn't exactly the most well-documented of airplanes. I recall that he began with the Paul Matt drawings, but modified them considerably in certain respects—primarily in the nose area—based upon factory documentation eventually obtained. For his O3U-3, he gathered a veritable mountain of material, including facsimiles of factory drawings and many fine photographs. He was also on solid ground for the fuselage markings of "1 - 0 - 10" of the battleship Pennsylvania: he had the actual fabric of this machine for these numerals, plus the Pennsylvania logo!!!

Incidentally, based upon his testimony and material gathered, two models on his "must build" list were the Douglas WORLD CRUISER and the Curtiss NC-4. We only wish that they had come to fruition.

All of us who knew and loved George miss him a great deal. But, his presence remains in our hearts, memories, and in those magnificent models which he left to posterity, both as inspiration and visual documentation of historic aircraft which have long been extinct. So it is with his Keystone, now in the U.S. Air Force Museum; his Sikorski S. 39 CS "SPIRIT OF AFRICA" and Verville-Sperry R-3, in the NASM; and, hopefully in the not-to-distant future, his Vought O3U-3 floatplane, in the U.S. Naval Aviation Museum at Pensacola.

KEYSTONE B4A: This closeup conveys as well as any the exquisitely fashioned detail of this wonderful model. It Mark Spitzed the 1988 IPMS/USA Nationals at Dayton, Ohio.

AVIATIK D.1 "BERG": This lovely 1/32nd scale model of the Austro-Hungarian fighter was George's first plastic scratchbuilt effort. It took "Best of Show" at the 1971 IPMS/USA Nationals in Atlanta.

Vickers 161 C.O.W. Fighter. This "Humor in Modelling" subject is, in fact, one of George's finest models.

Westland PTERODACTYL Mk.V.

I decided to include photos of all his scratch built models, from his first all-plastic Aviatik D.I BERG on, excepting those in the NASM. Even though most appeared in SB!, I felt that this tribute to George's talents would be appreciated by one and all. Besides, whenever possible, I used different photos; others were presented to much larger size; and one, ROSAMONDE, was not included before.

Curtiss "CARRIER PIGEON." George's penchant for building arcane, even bizarre, subjects reached its peak with this LIBERTY-engined contraption. Aside from the Keystone, I believe that this was his favorite model.

"ROSAMONDE." O.K. fans, here's one George Lee model which I'll bet you've never heard of, let alone seen. Unfortunately, I wasn't able to find the letter from him explaining its identity and circumstances. Then, just today (13 June '98) at our Seattle IPMS chapter meeting, I said to Jim Schubert, one of our finest modellers, and a veritable font of aviation knowledge: "O.K., Jim, I'll bet I finally have you on this one."; followed by a brief description of it. To which he replied: "Oh, you mean ROSAMONDE, the one-off biplane constructed in the Republic of China in the '20s. At home I have a long article on it, including three-view drawings." Jim Schubert, the Gerard Darrow of airplane lore.

Jim was referring to the fascinating feature by Dan Abbot in the May 1993 W.W.-I AERO. As he explains therein, Dr. Sun Yat-Sen's Republic of China government in Canton had realized the need to develop an aviation capability, for both military and economic development purposes. They had engaged the services of several Americans, including Dan Abbot's father, to acquire aircraft and facilities, and to train Chinese pilots and maintenance personnel. Several aircraft were indeed purchased, including five Curtiss "Jennies," two Curtiss H16 and two HS-2L flying boats. Among those placed under contract was a certain Guy Colwell (a former Bristol employee), who they directed to design a "light reconnaissance bomber" for indigenous manufacture.

"AIRPLANE No.1," a conventional biplane of the era, powered by a Curtiss OXX-6 engine, was completed in June 1923. On 10 August, it was christened—with a bottle of Champagne, no less—by Dr. Sun Yat-Sen, being named for his Wesleyan-educated wife, Rosamonde. Dan related that he was present at the ceremony, although incognito—he was born two days later!

Four such aircraft were manufactured, and one—named ROSAMONDE, but doubtless a composite—now resides in the Peking Air Museum. George's model is in a Taiwan museum.

Vought O3U-3 "In the Jigs." With this awesome 1/16th scale model, George was moving even beyond his Keystone.

Pratt & Whitney R-1340 for the O3U-3.

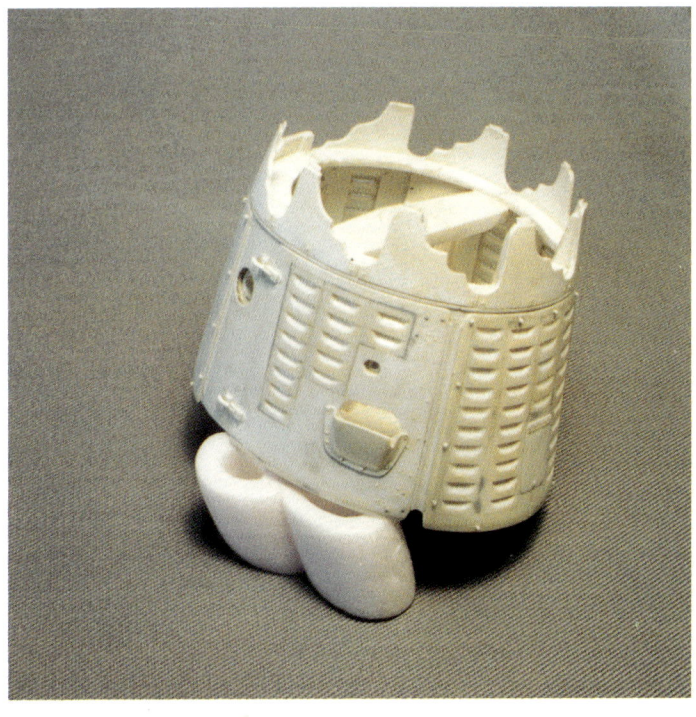

Forward Fuselage Coaming of the O3U-3. This amazing piece belongs in the Louvre.

George Lee - A Fond Dedication

CHAPTER I
Vacuforming and Basic Model Strucure
by John Alcorn

INTRODUCTION

While this chapter contains material from SB!, it is included here in order that MSB will provide comprehensive coverage of basic scratchbuilt techniques.

Vacuforming is, of course, only required for producing curved, usually double curved, elements in plasticard and clear plastic sheet. It is therefore primarily applicable to streamlined, all metal aircraft from the early 1930s onward. However, many 1920s, WW-I, and earlier aircraft featured curved metal panels, and some featured entire formed plywood fuselages which lent themselves to vacuform replication.

Preparation of vacuformed fuselage, wing, and various smaller components is the very essence of scratchbuilding, yet this crucial stage represents but a small fraction of the total "manhours" required for the project: and the vacuforming operation itself requires but a few hours at the most; far more effort and skill is required to prepare the forms.

Part 3 of this chapter covers THE BASIC MODEL STRUCTURE. Again, for "stand alone" completeness, a discussion of wing and fuselage structures for subjects having vacuformed shells is included.

Part 1: PREPARING THE FORMS

For us old solid modellers, carving the fuselage, wing, nacelle, cockpit, etc., forms from hardwood is very satisfying, taking us back to our modelling roots. In other words, the first actual construction step is to build a solid model. It often looms as the most daunting hurdle to anyone lacking such background. For this reason, it is worth dwelling upon the specifics in some detail.

MATERIAL: The most commonly used form material is basswood (from the Linden tree). It is hard enough to permit inclusion of complex, crisp detail without being unpleasantly difficult to carve. Its best characteristics are a very even texture with minimal grain, and lack of sap in properly cured specimens—in contrast to, say, pine.

FUSELAGE OUTLINE: Let's use the example of a 1/32nd scale Douglas A-20A, based upon my (Alcorn) Scale Models drawings. The 18" long fuselage side view is traced (on a light table or against a window) on stiff manila paper, which is then carefully cut out using a sharp #11 X-Acto type or surgeon's blade. Using this template, the side view is then marked upon the mating surfaces of

Douglas A-20A. This 1/32nd scale model represents a strafer modified aircraft of the 89th Squadron, 3rd Attack Group, 5th Air Force, operating from the Port Moresby, Papua, New Guinea, area in late '42/early '43. It was awarded "Best of Show" at the 1974 IPMS/USA Nationals, in Anaheim, California. I invested around 2,400 hours in its construction. Badly damaged by the cretins who moved us from San Diego to Williamsburg, Virginia, in 1988, its repair is yet another retirement project. Sad to say, during that episode, its flex-mounted twin .30s simply vanished. Construction of this airplane is emphasized in this chapter. (Joe Faust photo)

two good quality basswood blocks—each of an appropriate plan view thickness to form one side of the fuselage.

The side view of each half is then rough cut out, using a knife or jigsaw. If a knife is used, the perpendicularity of any given cross section can be maintained by periodic checking with a small carpenter's square. The side contours are brought into final shape using wood files, and finally, sandpaper blocks. At some point in this process, allowance must be made for the as-formed thickness of the polystyrene shells: that is, the fuselage contour must be appropriately undersize all around (use 30 thou in the case of 40 thou sheet). This can perhaps best be achieved by drawing and cutting the heavy paper template with this allowance. Incidentally, marking the side view on both sides of each block—registered by carefully scribed lines across the front, back and top—will facilitate the process of achieving accuracy across the faces.

Now, the two fuselage halves are lightly glued together by running a bead of wood glue along their mating edges. (Don't glue over the entire surface, or you'll later have great difficulty separating the halves for the molding process.) Once glued, the top and bottom surfaces should be given a final truing with a sandpaper block. This ensures that the two halves are an exact match and that perpendicularity of the edges to the sides is maximized.

At this point, the top (and bottom) views are marked on the block, again using heavy paper templates—registered to the joint between the two halves and to fore and aft marks or edges. Sure, the side view contours mean that fore and aft repositioning of the template will be required as marking progresses. Now, rough out the top view with a knife; followed by filing and block sanding to bring in the top/bottom contour. Again, make allowance for thickness of vacuformed shell, so that the final product won't be "fat" by that amount.

CONTOURING: This is the most satisfying portion of the entire form-making process, as well as the most demanding. But, George Lee insisted that it's (Peking) duck soup: just cut away everything that doesn't look like an A-20.

First, "female" cross-section templates are cut from heavy paper, having first traced them from the plans on a light table. Again, remember to make allowance for thickness of the plastic sheet. For the A-20, there are eight cross-section locations, which must be defined by some appropriate means. One option is to separate the fuselage halves by the solvent and prying method described above. Mark the cross section locations from the side view template and then carefully reglue the halves. Take this opportunity to give a final check of the side view contour—typically, a little truing here and there will be appropriate.

Now, unsheath the old carving knife and begin whacking away. At first, caveman tactics are appropriate, since there is lots of material to remove. Incidentally, the time-honored X-Acto type whittler's blade in the fat, hexagonal holder is fine, although at first you may prefer to use some more robust weapon, as long as it's sharp. Generally, the cuts should be fore and aft, shallow and elongated: this is efficient and minimizes the chance of accidentally removing a divot from the mold volume lurking beneath.

Eventually, you'll have removed enough material that it will be appropriate to begin test-fitting the templates. Initially, you'll be quite a way off—the cross-section will still be "too square." Now, it's time to sheath the assault weapons and abandon the power grip (the X-Acto type whittler's blade may still be appropriate, though possibly now held in a smaller handle). Free whittling cuts have given way to shallow slices, with the blade guided by the thumb of the piece-holding hand. You're now making the transition from wood butcher to craftsman.

By now, you're carefully pecking and checking. At some point, the wood file will begin to supplement and then replace the knife as your basic tool. It, of course, has the great advantage of generating smooth transitions from one cross-section contour to the next, and of replacing the chiseled surface with one that is "rough machined." Now, aside from nose contours, about which more later, the A-20 fuselage is straightforward. Basically, one fuselage section contour blends into the next, with no concave regions.

Finally, even the file and occasional knife sliver will give way to sandpaper: folded, rolled, or block-mounted as appropriate. As you proceed to finer grades of sandpaper, you're entering the final phases of form preparation. Inevitably, during this tedious and time consuming phase, you'll occasionally revert to file or knife and—yes—despite all precautions to the contrary, to application of a dab or two of "plastic wood."

In the case of the A-20, and of many other aircraft, it is now appropriate to perform major yet delicate surgery upon your fuselage form—namely, removal of the nose and tail region. Such amputation is necessary for one or both of the following reasons: to provide a separate form for molding the nose section in clear plastic, and/or simply to divide the fuselage into sections which can be accommodated by your vacuforming rig. This can be accomplished with an X-Acto type (or equivalent) saw blade. The crucial thing here is to accurately mark the cross-section to be cut on the form surface—it must be perpendicular to the fore and aft centerline and to the parting plane.

FORMS FOR SECONDARY FEATURES: Engine nacelles, tail booms as for a P-38, or large floats are made just like fuselages. Certain shallow bumps, lumps, and gentle surface anomalies are best vacuformed integral with the primary element. Such features can be produced in one of two ways on the wood form: by carving integral with it, or by carving separately and gluing onto the larger element (with the help of glue or plastic wood edge filleting, as appropriate). For large lumps and/or those with angular cross-section and main surface intersections, it is best to carve a separate form, vacuform the item, and fit it in place later. Below some critical size, just carve the item in plastic and glue it on: or, if angular, build it up from plastic sheet.

MOUNTING THE FORMS: First, the completed fuselage forms must be separated, by solvent painted into the seams to loosen the glue, followed by running a knife blade into and along the joint to break it apart—if the knife blade breaks instead, you'll know that you used too much glue.

In order that the vacuformed sheet plastic pulls down clear to the centerline of the wood form, it must be mounted upon a base of suitable height—1/4" is about right for large forms such as a fuselage. Balsa is an adequate and convenient material for the base, which must be carefully trimmed and lightly block-sanded to be flush with the edge of the hardwood form. Once done, a scribing tool can be run around the seam, indenting a "parting line" into the balsa: this leaves a convenient centerline trim mark on the polystyrene shell.

No vertical "cliffs" should be left exposed on the hardwood form, such as that created by the severed nose portion. So, a balsa block should be glued in place and carefully faired into the form. In this manner, the styrene sheet won't be pulled thin as it passes across the end of the form. This feature is shown in the accompanying photo, illustrating the mounted fuselage form.

Incidentally, even though you may never need to remove it, it's a good idea not to glue the base too extensively to the form—you may later want to reassemble the form segments for some reason.

Over extensive form surfaces, especially where concavities exist, it may be advisable to drill several 1/32nd diameter holes into the form and clear through the base, in order that good vacuum is experienced over the entire forming surface of the polystyrene sheet.

PART 2: VACUFORMING

THE VACUFORMING RIG: The archetypal personal vacuform rig was that produced by Mattel in the early sixties. It was a self-contained device, embodying the platen, heater, and vacuum box features. Unfortunately, it was of modest size, and worse, is no longer produced, being something of a collector's item by now.

We have always used a "custom-built" model, whose plans are shown here. Making it is no problem if your workshop includes a Bridgeport Mill—otherwise, it helps to have a machinist friend with access to such a device. The rig is really quite simple, consisting of a vacuum box, a set of various sized platens, and an adapter plate to accommodate the larger ones.

The vacuum box is simply an electronic can, or equivalent: modified by replacing the top with a perforated metal cover and a sidewall hole to receive a vacuum fitting. Perforated 1/16" thick plate is cut to size and matching holes drilled in the box top flange and plate. It is attached by flush screws, with a thin sealing gasket trapped between plate and box flange. For "system vacuum" we use the family tank type cleaner (Electrolux, Eureka, or equivalent) with its hose snout inserted through the box vacuum fitting.

The platens are where the Bridgeport comes in, to machine the frames from plate stock. Either structural aluminum (2024, 6061, 5083, etc.) or 300 series stainless steel will do. Our machinist-friend bent up the ends of the upper platen elements after machining holes therein, to form handles. But, separate handles could of course be made and screwed on. A crucial element for proper function is a series of studs attached to the lower platen and projecting through matching clearance holes in the upper plate. The studs can be attached in any of several ways, the important points being: firm attachment so they don't pull out; reasonable vacuum tightness; correct alignment; and bottom ends flush with the frame. For the resourceful modeller lacking either a Bridgeport or a machinist friend, other platen options are surely available—after all, the requirement is simple enough.

VACUFORMING TECHNIQUE: For demonstration purposes, we'll form a fuselage half for the 1/32nd scale A-20. Since the form, including end blocks, is 12 inches long, we must use the 18" long by 7" wide platen and adapter plate.

For a large component such as this, 40 thou plasticard should be used. With a mat cutting knife and long steel straight edge, cut out from commercially available 48" x 48" sheets several pieces which just fit within the studs of the lower platen: 6" x 16-1/2", in our case. Place one such piece between the two platen elements and dog them together using the wing nuts.

Fire up the kitchen oven to 250-275 degrees F: hopefully, it has a window and inside light. Set the vacuform rig nearby on a stool or counter. Plug in the vacuum cleaner and place the form on the rig. Have a good, clean pair of heavy cotton work gloves at the ready. Now, put the loaded platen in the oven, on a rack, with the handles down so that the drooping plastic can't touch the rack. Watch

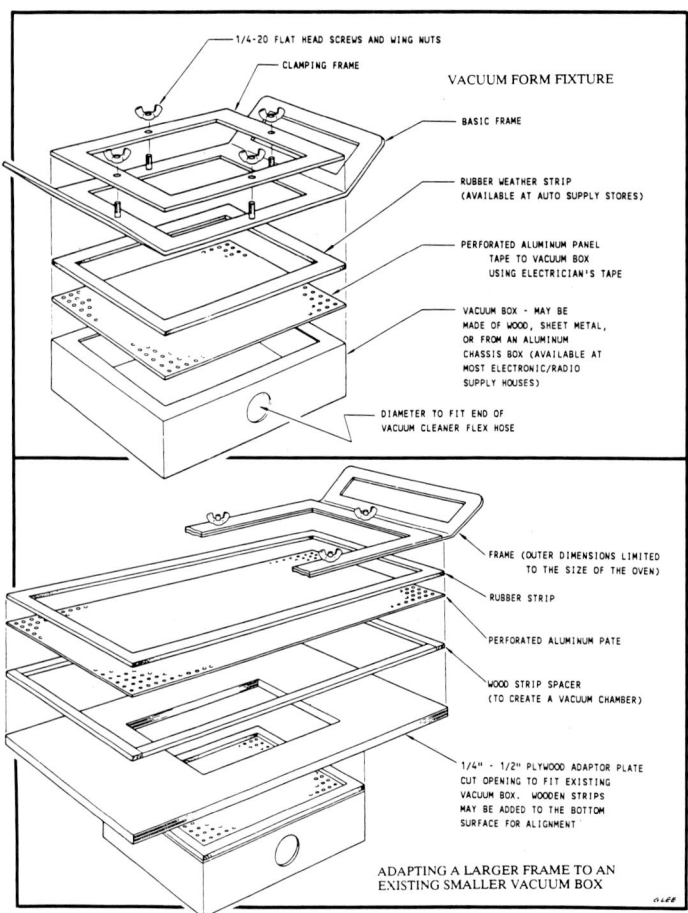

VACUFORMING APPARATUS. George Lee drew this "exploded view" of the vacuforming apparatus which he, and I, had made by a machinist friend.

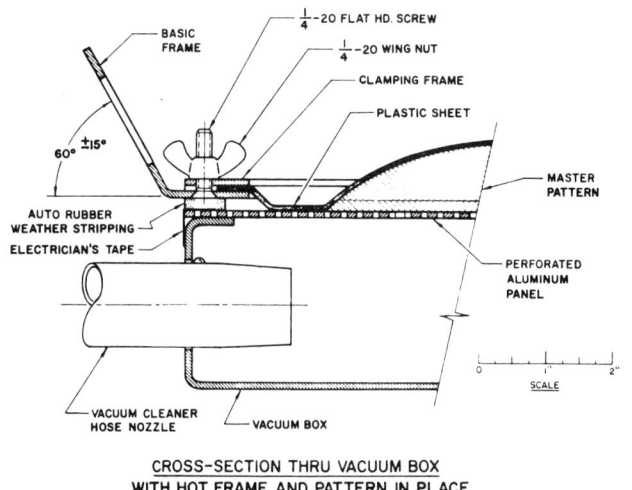

**CROSS-SECTION THRU VACUUM BOX
WITH HOT FRAME AND PATTERN IN PLACE**

This cross-section through the vacuum box, also drawn by George, reveals further details of our equipment. Unfortunately, not shown is a plastic adaptor in the vacuum box opening, into which the vacuum cleaner hose nozzle is inserted. Without this, it would leak too badly. It can be seen in the next illustration.

it closely until the plastic has sagged 1/2 inch or more. Turn on the vacuum cleaner and (with gloves on) quickly open the oven, grab the platen, turn it over and bring it down smartly and squarely upon the rig. Yreka! You have an A-20 fuselage half—or ...

• the platen wasn't brought down squarely upon the vacuum box (or its adapter plate), so that the wood form is too near one edge of the plastic. Further, if the mismatch is too great, vacuum may be lost due to a gap between platen and seal. Mismatch is a common error, which simply requires practice to avoid;

• the plastic didn't pull down past the centerline (base) of the hardwood form. If the plastic was hot enough, no time was wasted between oven removal and placement, platen registration over the vacuum box (or adapter plate) was good, and full vacuum (suction) was obtained, then the fillet radius at the base of the 40 mil plastic should be about 1/4 inch. A significantly larger fillet radius usually means inadequate vacuum, which usually results from leakage through the seals, or through seams in the vacuum box;

• you tripped over the vacuum cleaner cord.
  - *Erare Humanum Est*

Incidentally, the plastic from a faulty pull can usually be re-used at least once. Simply put the platen/plastic back in the oven, making sure that the shaped plastic doesn't touch the rack. As it heats, the plastic will recover its unformed (but droopy) shape, as if by magic.

Once a good shell has been obtained, it's an easy matter to trim off the excess sheet—so long as the form-to-base seam line is visible on the inside surface. For final trimming, rub the shell on a piece of #220 (or so) sandpaper, laid upon a flat surface. Accuracy can be assured by fitting the shell over the wood form periodically to check registration with the center plane edge.

This having been accomplished, it is necessary to produce a datum line along each fuselage half. I usually locate this using cross-section templates, each having the datum point marked thereon.

CANOPIES: In a very real sense, this is where the gentle art of vacuforming plastic model airplane components began. Certainly, they were the first such items to appear in kits.

I (Alcorn) have tended to vacuform canopies for larger scale efforts from the real thing—Plexiglass (Lucite, or Perspex if you prefer) sheet. Its advantages are that it is very strong, and hard enough that its surface can be worked after forming and then polished back to high optical clarity; also, it is not attacked by lacquer thinner. Its disadvantage is that it is very hard to cut—it must be sawed and the edges then sanded to final shape. Also, I've never found sheet thinner than 1/32", thus limiting its use to larger scale models—if any reader knows of a source for 10 thou stock, please tell me. Plexiglass must be oven heated to around 300 degrees F. After vacuforming, the inner surface can be sanded to eliminate surface blemishes: you can work down from #400 grit, if necessary, eventually converting to aluminum oxide rouge and finally to auto polish.

Peter Cooke typically uses optical, UV grade 10 thou PVC sheet, heat formed over a shape whose surface is also "optical grade," so that nothing beyond fine polish is later required. But, for canopies, turrets, etc., having extensive framing (such as his Lancasters), he casts in clear epoxy, using techniques described in Chapter VIII.

Incidentally, two useful articles on modelling canopies appeared in Fine Scale Modeller: August 1986, Vacuum Forming Canopies, and February 1988, How To Install Canopies and Clear Parts.

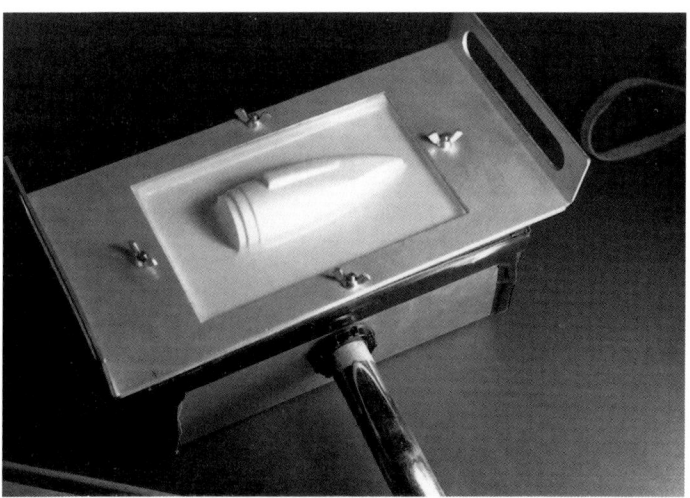

Here is the Lee/Alcorn vacuform rig, showing vacuum box (with vacuum-cleaner hose tube inserted through the plastic adaptor), and aluminum platen. An inboard A-20A nacelle half has just been formed (circa 1972).

PART 3: THE BASIC MODEL STRUCTURE

INTRODUCTION

In this part we discuss the internal structure of a scratchbuilt model whose exterior is primarily vacuformed shells. Structures of models having slab-sided fuselages and fabric covered wings are discussed elsewhere.

The internal structure of a scratchbuilt static scale model serves three basic roles: it supports the thin vacuformed shells against gross and local distortion; provides hard points for component assembly; and simulates visible structural elements of the actual aircraft. This vital and time consuming structure constitutes a fundamental difference between scratchbuilt vacuformed and commercial injection molded models, since the latter have thicker skin and integral structural features.

FUSELAGES FROM VACUFORMED SHELLS

Still using the A-20 as an example, the structural work begins when the shells have been trimmed to their centerline marks. This aircraft was of monocoque construction: in any case, interior features are visible only in the crews' compartments. In nonvisible regions, it is only necessary to place sheet stock bulkheads for rigidity; and wing/tail assembly attachment features.

Our preference is to build up fuselage halves for later centerline assembly: in this case, half bulkheads are installed—about 1-1/2" apart. In the visible crew compartment areas, bulkheads, formers, keel beams, stringers, decks and such which comprise the actual structure must be simulated. First though, smooth the inside surface of the shell with sandpaper, to remove any evidence of the form. Where light fore and aft stringers are present, they should be added first, with appropriate slots cut in the intersecting formers and bulkheads. In constant cross sections where the stringers are parallel, they may be trued by running a slotted former back and forth before the liquid glue attached stringers have set permanently to the shell. At about this point, with perhaps a temporary bulkhead or two for rigidity, each knife-trimmed shell can be trued over its centerline parting plane by gently dragging it back and forth across a big sheet of sandpaper (say 220 grit) laid upon a flat surface. While taste and circumstances may vary, generally the canopy and other areas later to be cut away should be left in place until the shell has been well stiffened by its internal structure, but before proceeding beyond this point.

In crew compartments especially, many secondary features should be added integral with the shell structure. These include brackets and shelves for equipment, and perhaps even a "black box" or two. Then, after careful cleanup with knife edge scraping, fine sandpaper and the like, the visible interior is airbrush-painted in the appropriate color.

Wing/fuselage attachment demands careful planning and execution in order to ensure accuracy and strength of fit. Location, dihedral, angle of incidence, plan and transverse alignment, as well as strength and method of attachment are factors which must all be considered before adding the fuselage features. The technique to be employed will depend upon specifics of the aircraft, as well as personal preference.

In certain cases, it is appropriate to terminate the wings at their root interfaces, perhaps as on the real thing. Tubular brass sections could be built into the fuselage to receive wing spar extensions of the next smaller size. For wings with heavy, rectangular spar extensions, sockets can be constructed within the fuselage center section. Some jigging and fixturing may be required to properly align these features.

The basic alternative to wing root joints is to provide a well stiffened cutout for later insertion of the complete wing. Such might well be the best choice for low winged aircraft such as Bf-109 or P-51 (a Spitfire, though, is probably best served by wing root attachment, due to its extensive fillets). However, shoulder and mid-wing aircraft can also be assembled in this manner. I (Alcorn) chose this method for my 1/32nd scale Douglas A-20A. I accurately cut out the wing/fuselage junction airfoil on the two shells and then reinforced the area. Since the tapered wing was larger at the centerline, I assembled the two fuselage halves over the wing. The cutouts automatically produced correct wing positioning in all but plan view perpendicularity. A wing with constant central region cross section can, of course, be inserted through cutouts in the assembled fuselage.

Full wing assembly for mid-taperwing aircraft can also be achieved by the solid modeller's time-honored method of removing the fuselage section above (or below) the wing and later reinstalling it with appropriate seam filling.

Before joining the fuselage halves, any interior details which cannot be conveniently reached later should be added. This can be frustrating since, at this point, the emotional sentiment is to get on with major assembly. Just about any feature attached to the sidewalls falls into this category, including control units and myriad "black boxes." Control cable runs should also be added.

Transverse elements which cross the centerline demand some premeditation. These include visible bulkheads, decks, and instrument panels. Despite your best placement efforts, you're lucky if preattached bulkhead halves match exactly at assembly—even if they do, there's still the seam to contend with. Nevertheless, this is

Here are some of the wood forms for my 1/32nd scale Douglas A-20A. Note that this fuselage side has been cut into three elements, each of which has been mounted upon a balsa base, with balsa "fairing" pieces as appropriate—see text.

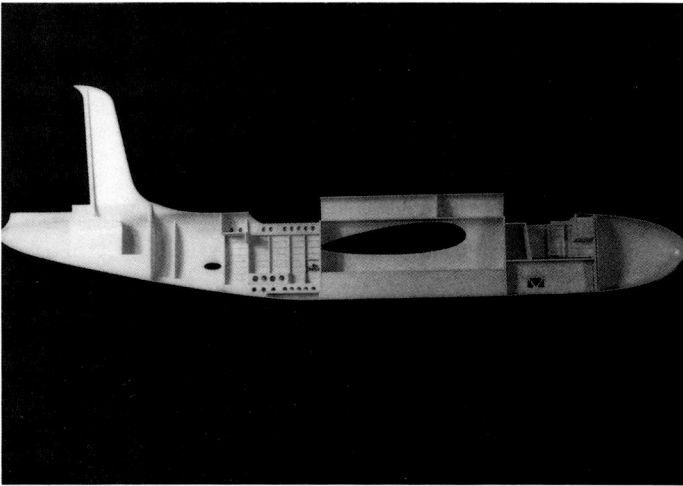

A carefully contrived study, showing the profile-contoured white pine fuselage of my 1/24th scale Bf109E, resting upon Doug Carrick's MAP plans. All of the work to this point was performed by the knife and file shown, plus a carpenter's square. If all of these illustrations seem familiar, you must have SCRATCH BUILT!.

An "inboard profile" of my 1/32nd scale Douglas A-20A. This includes three vacuformed sections: nose; main portion; and tail.

usually what must be done. Seam matching and joining is facilitated by placement of an overlapping, full height strip behind one of the halves. Unless they are badly mismatched, this will provide alignment and a surface for glueing—by the simple expedient of painting the visible seam with MEK and letting it capillary onto the strip behind.

WINGS

There are at least three basic methods of wing construction available to the static scale scratchbuilder: solid; vacuformed shell over internal structure; and the rib, spar, and embossed skin techniques.

SOLID: For small models, or aircraft with very thin wings, it is not unreasonable to carve the wings from solid polystyrene stock. The only concern is possible long-term droop of long cantilevered wings.

A variation is to build up a solid wing by gluing sheet stock together, with embedded brass tubing for rigidity. But, this too has its pitfalls: I (Alcorn) laminated the upper wing of my 1/32nd scale Rumpler CIV in this manner, using MEK. Unfortunately, within a year after completion, the wing acquired a pronounced droop, despite the presence of two brass tube spars. Doubtless, residual stresses within the laminate, in concert with the underwing camber, possibly aggravated by rigging tension, was responsible for the problem. While this could perhaps have been avoided by longer "curing" of the laminated blank with weights atop to assure straightness, I recommend not using this method.

Probably the most efficacious method for producing solid wings is to carve them from basswood, over which is applied a skin of plasticard. For wings with single curved surfaces, such as a Messerschmitt Bf 109, plasticard can simply be attached by contact cement or epoxy. In this case, a plastic leading edge should first be affixed to the basswood core: the tip would also be of plas-

tic. For double curved wings, such as for a Spitfire, the top and bottom skins could be vacuformed over the basswood forms, their tops and bottoms later glued together to become the permanent core. The plasticard skin serves a dual role: unlike bare wood, it can be scored for panel lines, etc.; it is an ideal painting surface, which will not crack as the wood core gradually dries out—a fate which almost always eventually afflicts models made entirely of wood.

For vintage aircraft, one must simulate the fabric-over-rib surface contours. Our preferred method is to emboss the rib locations on the inside surface of each wing plasticard skin, which is then glued down to a basswood core, or to a rib and spar structure. This procedure is discussed in the chapter HOW I BUILT MY DE HAVILLAND DH9A.

Yet another solution for solid wings is to cast them from epoxy resin, using Peter Cooke's technique as described in Chapter VIII. In this case, the above comments regarding rib simulation apply to the wood master form, rather than to the final wing itself.

SHELL OVER STRUCTURE: For modelling thicker, metal skinned wings such as the 1/32nd scale A-20, a good technique is to vacuform the skin, which is then mounted upon a built-up plasticard structure.

Making The Forms: Since both the upper and lower surfaces have airfoil, it is necessary to prepare forms for each. The procedure is generally similar to that for the fuselage. Select hardwood plank, hopefully of thickness appropriate for the upper and lower surfaces (if the source block is significantly thicker than necessary, have it planed to size, or do it yourself if you have the tools). Then, make the planform template, carve or bandsaw to rough shape, file and block-sand the leading and trailing surfaces, and lightly glue the upper and lower planks together. Once glued, give a final sand-block truing to the edges, to ensure that the final products match exactly.

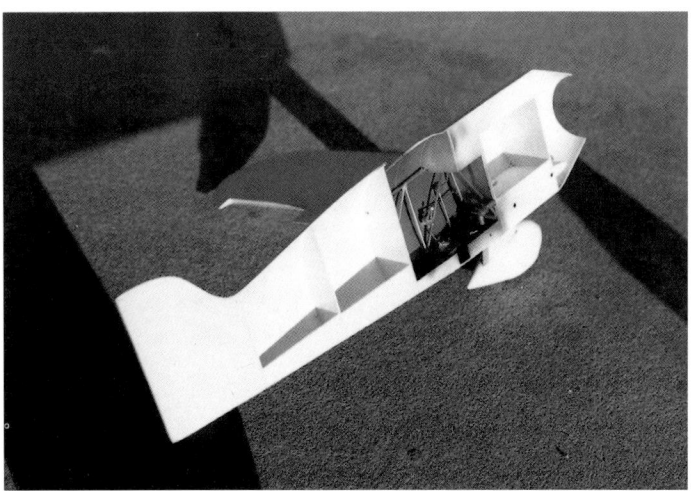

This, and the following two shots, depict my construction approach for the W-W#44 model. I attached the wing and landing gear leg to each fuselage half, prior to joining the two. Why? Why not.

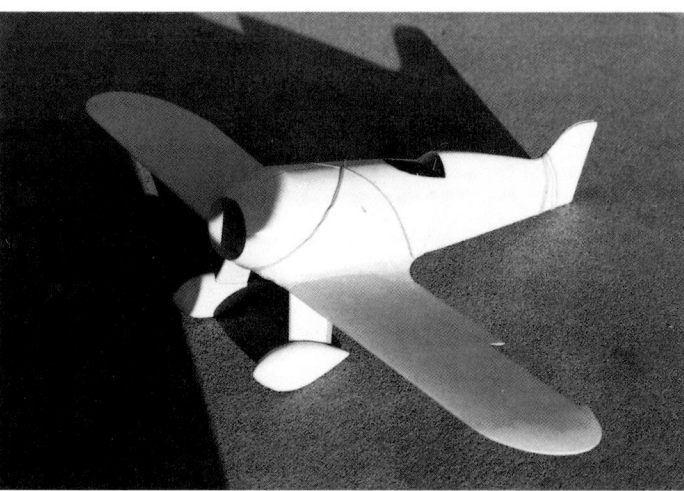

Here the halves are temporarily joined with stout rubber bands, for test fitting.

Wing thickness as a function of span (front view taper) must next be generated. Large, relatively flat, wide chord surfaces are difficult to carve: a small plane can be a handy tool for this job.

Now, using the airfoil templates as guides, carve, file, and block-sand the wings to their proper cross section shape. The outer wing panels of the A-20 presented a special problem, since the airfoil featured "washout"; from +3 degrees at the root to -1 degree at the tip.

The wing forms must, of course, be appropriately undersize to account for final thickness of the shells. Twenty-five to thirty thou is the proper allowance for 40 thou sheet stock: some slight thinning occurs during vacuforming—around 5 thou is typically removed later during block sanding of the surfaces (see below).

Also, the planform (chord) size of the wing should be undersize, to allow for runout of the shell beyond the trailing edge, as well as for leading edge thickness. Trailing edge runout is a function of both shell final thickness and of the terminal angle of incidence of the upper (or lower) airfoil section. Be somewhat generous here, since you don't later want to run out of chord during final planform truing. So, use the initial sheet thickness (say 40 thou) for your calculations. Conversely, since it's being pulled straight down during vacuforming and since considerable final edge block sanding will occur, allow about half of the sheet thickness for the leading edge.

Internal Structure: For making the polystyrene wing structure, several important factors must be considered:

• Proper dihedral, rigidity and dimensional stability are achieved by one or more main spars at appropriate locations, typically those of the actual aircraft. Main spars should be fashioned from thick polystyrene stock, say 1/4 inch. (For my A-20, I used basswood, through fear of long-term droop: but I now believe that this was an unnecessary precaution, which, in fact, caused problems.)

• It is challenging to assemble rib elements to the spars so that correct airfoil is maintained. This is because the ribs must perforce be segmented, with portions removed for the spar(s). Female airfoil templates, of Manila paper, should be used for this purpose.

Here (*right*) the halves have been permanently joined and surface detail added to the fuselage. The engine, cowl, and tail elements are being test fitted. The large cutout behind the upper firewall is for later installation of the tensioned monofilament nylon rigging wires: having been passed through holes in the wings, they will pass through holes in the fuselage centerline panel and be set in place with crimped metal ferrules. At this point, the entire model will have been finish painted, decal markings added, oversprayed with clear lacquer, and rubbed down. Thus, attachment and painting of the cover panels will be an onerous chore. "Why would anyone do it this way?," you may ask. You tell me how else was I to anchor those tensioned rigging lines or finish painting the model after they had been installed. In fact, it all turned out quite well: to this day, my W-W#44, at least, shows almost no evidence of the patched-in panels. Needless to say, however, I had to patiently await full drying of the patch seam filler (probably polystyrene paste), and of the subsequently applied black paint before rubbing out.

Wedell-Williams #44. Here is my 1/16th scale model, finally completed, 15 years after its debut at the 1983 IPMS/USA Nationals in Phoenix, Aridzona (where it was awarded "Best Aircraft"). Only in June 1998 did it acquire Hamilton-Standard logos on its propeller blades (courtesy of Lloyd Jones) and a pitot tube: the latter feature at the urging of John Amendola, our local wizard aircraft (and automobile) painter, who otherwise spoke favorably of the model. But, Jim Schubert points out (correctly) that, even now, it lacks the propeller data plates. Maybe someday. (Paul Ludwig photo)

• Various wing features requiring cutout areas, penetrations, and hardpoints must be accommodated. Cutouts include ailerons, flaps, and wheel wells. These require careful placement of edge "closure" pieces for fit, strength, and neat, correct simulation of the area if later visible (as for wheel wells). In the case of ailerons (and flaps) it makes sense to install edge strips to either side of the seam, so that when the flying surface is later removed, it will have its own structure. For multi-engined aircraft with nacelle wheel wells, the underside wing skin is often removed, exposing structure and gear attachment points: this of course must be anticipated as the wing structure is planned.

• The wing skin must be reinforced sufficiently to prevent local distortions (sagging, waviness) after completion. This requires a rather extensive internal structure, including ribs and secondary spar elements. Typically, unreinforced shell cells should have characteristic dimensions of about 1 inch on a side or less. For some models, though, wing structure should show subtle evidence of ribs, etc., beneath. In such a case, ribs should be placed in correct locations, without skin bracing in between. I (Alcorn) built the wings of my 1/16th scale Wedell-Williams #44 racer in this manner to simulate the appearance of the plywood skin undulations evident in numerous photographs of the real aircraft.

While the complete wing structure could be made independently, it is usually convenient to add some of it after attachment of the upper shell. Most of the secondary stiffeners can be "custom" shaped and fitted as you proceed, rather than attempt to predetermine the geometry by layouts. In fact, the entire wing structure can be assembled into the top shell, airfoil templates being used at two or more locations to ensure that the shell has not become distorted. In this case, the upper shell must be carefully trimmed beforehand, as described below.

Shell and Structure Preparation: The trailing edge of the completed wing must be straight, sharp, strong, and accurate in plan view. Achieving this result requires considerable planning and effort, to wit:

• After trimming (slightly oversize in chord), the vacuformed wing shells should be block-sanded over their supporting wood forms, in order to begin the process of truing the surface.

• Then, the shell trailing edge is beveled on its underside with a large sanding block, while supporting the outside edge with some appropriate straight surface, such as a thick block or table edge. In order to ensure that the beveled surfaces of the upper and lower shells mate at assembly, each should be flat: that is, lie in the wing split plane. This can be achieved by lightly rubbing each shell on a large, flat piece of sandpaper from time to time. This technique shouldn't be used for primary beveling, though, since it's tough to retain uniformity of material removal along the wing. A trick way

This model represents the W-W #44 in its September 1933 configuration, sporting a newly-installed 800hp Pratt and Whitney R-1340 WASP engine, with which it set a landplane speed record of 305 mph at Chicago on the 4th, piloted by Jimmy Wedell himself. The sobriquet "Miss Patterson" refers to Patterson, Louisiana, the home base of W-W #44. By the next racing season, Jimmy Wedell had been killed—ironically, in a dual-control training crash. Doug Davis, now flying #44, edged the landplane speed record up to 306 mph, but was killed in it during the Thompson Trophy Race when he stalled out after cutting a pylon. This model is a near twin to the one in the NASM, which represents #44 in its 1934 Bendix-winning configuration, when fitted with a 550 hp R-985 WASP Jr. During its construction, I had become so enamored of the airplane that I had to have a model of it for myself. This photo shows well the stringer simulation on the rear fuselage, using the technique described in the text. (Edmund Smith photo)

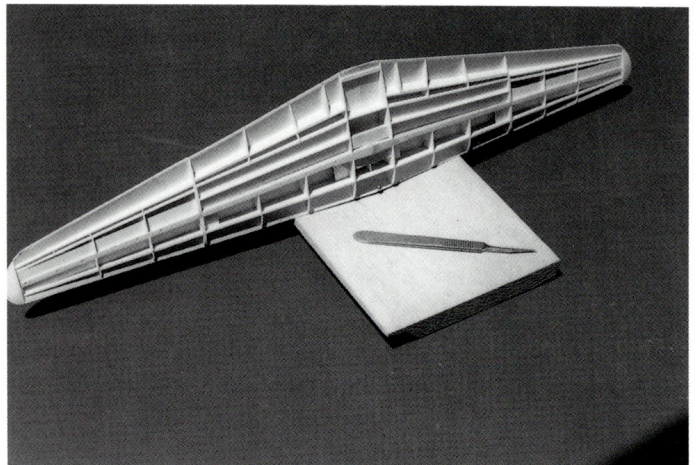
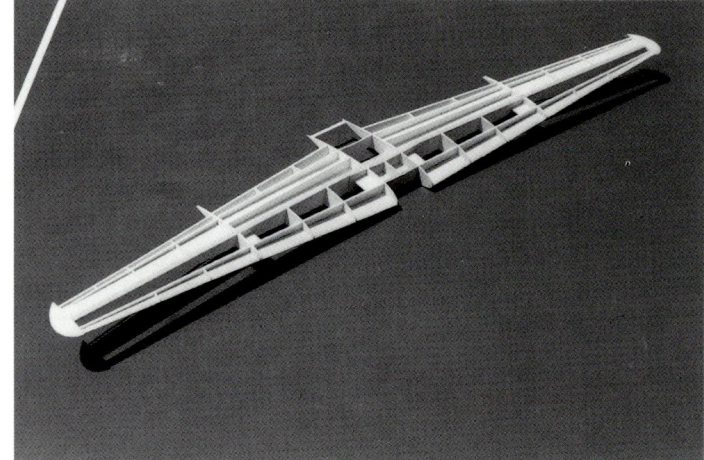

This, and the next figure, show the structure of my 1/32nd scale A-20A wing. Notice that some of the secondary rib elements were added after installation of the wing upper skin. On this model, I used a basswood mainspar, due to concern over possible long-term droop. In retrospect, this was unnecessary, and caused some problems. For one thing, it was difficult to get the plasticard skin to adhere to the wood: if it doesn't, the skin is somewhat spongy in this region.

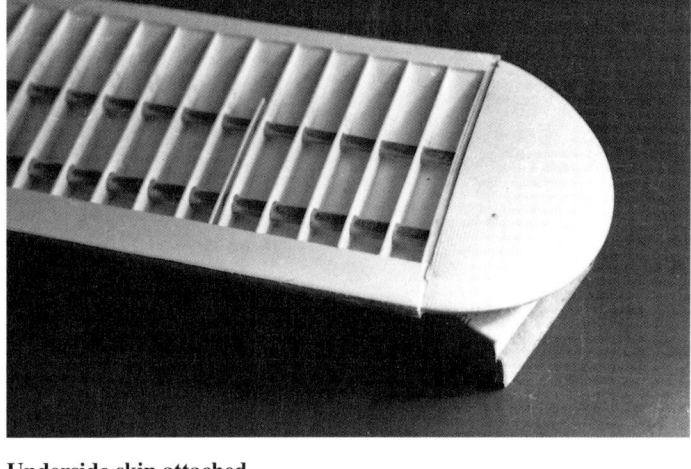

Underside skin attached.

Wings: Rib/Brass Spar/Embossed Skin Construction. While this technique is described in the chapter HOW I BUILT MY DE HAVILLAND DH9A, these three sequential photos show this approach as used on my 1/16th scale Laird SUPER SOLUTION for the NASM. Perhaps they're worth three thousand words.

of trimming the shells to the split plane is with their wood forms. Simply separate the form from its base, insert it into the roughly trimmed shell, and carefully block-sand until leading and trailing edges of the shell are flush with the base of the form.

• The completed wing internal structure (ribs, etc.) must "feather out" at the forward edge of the top shell trailing edge bevel. Also, the overall structure must be smoothly contoured so that it will mate to the lower shell without gaps or humps. This is achieved by block-sanding the structure underside in spanwise strokes, taking care not to damage the trailing edge bevel or leading edge of the top shell.

Upper Shell Installation: This step is comparatively straightforward, since the shell to structure interfaces are accessible from beneath for gluing. Nevertheless, the shell should be test-fit over the structure beforehand to ensure good contact at all appropriate locations. Then, after the shell has been attached, but before the glue joints have dried, carefully check for any distortion. To assure straightness of the trailing edge, it should be held firmly down upon a flat surface until the glue has thoroughly dried.

Lower Shell Installation: We are now at the point of installing the underside shell of the wing. This is rather challenging for large wings, since the mating elements aren't accessible for liquid glue brush/capillary application except along the leading and trailing edges.

The first step is to carefully test fit the lower shell to the structure/upper shell. A fair amount of such fitting and minor trimming may be required to assure yourself that all elements are in contact when the lower shell is pressed into place. For larger models, such as the 1/32nd scale A-20, the wing panels are in two pieces: inboard and outboard. This facilitates the process considerably.

Plastic cement from a tube should be quickly and liberally applied over the mating edges of the structure and the lower panel pressed into place—it must, of course, be held there until the glue

has set. Then, fuse the leading and trailing edges together with liquid glue. Sight down the trailing edge to see if it is straight. If some minor waviness is evident, press it down firmly against some straight surface. Now, despite your best efforts, the lower panel may not be firmly attached to the structure over some areas, as evidenced by "squishiness." All you can do is drill a series of small holes through the shell where you know that structure exists beneath, such as the spar. Then, dab liquid glue into each hole until things stick together, and later fill the holes.

Final Shaping: While the wing is now structurally complete, some fairly serious final truing of the upper and lower surfaces may be required. First though, check the planform, which should be slightly oversize at the trailing edge and will probably need some minor truing along the front. Carefully block-sand these edges until the final shape is achieved. Now, with a large, flat sanding block, coated with rough sandpaper (say, 220 grit), work both surfaces using spanwise strokes. Airfoil templates can be used for checking,

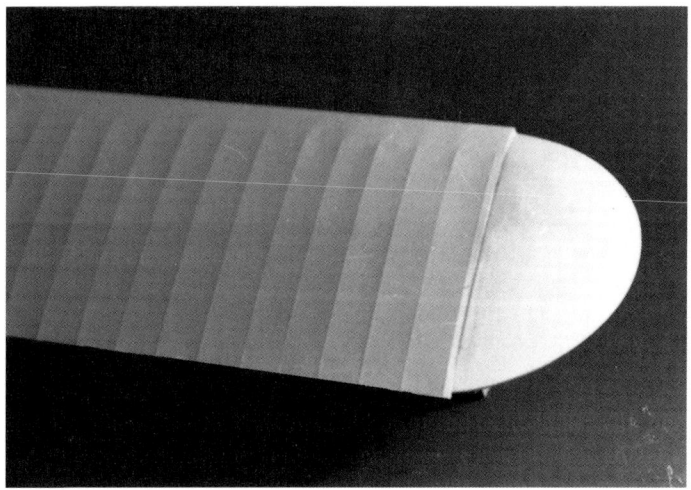

Upper, embossed skin attached.

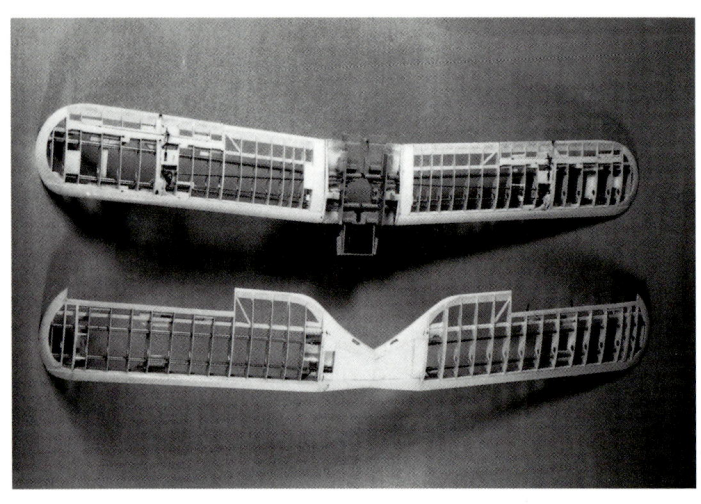 

Wing Structure of George Lee's Vought O3U-3. Note that by this time, he was including working control surfaces!

Fuselage Structure of George Lee's O3U-3. What is there to say?

Here we are given a preview of Alan Clark's magnificent Short SINGAPORE III, which is featured in Chapter III. (Manny Cefai photo)

although at this point only minor corrections can be made. The main thing now is to get the surfaces straight spanwise, smoothly contoured chordwise, and the trailing edge straight, even, and thin. Naturally, progress to finer grades of sandpaper as these goals are approached.

Removal Of Flying Surfaces: Now carefully mark the aileron and flap locations. Using a small metal straight edge (such as a 6" pocket rule) cut away these elements with a #11 blade. Cleanup and shape the edges with small sandpaper blocks—some minor repairs may even be in order. Further, one of the mating surfaces may require the grafting of a plastic strip in order that, when reinstalled, the flying surface is flush with the wing trailing edge.

RIB/BRASS SPAR/ EMBOSSED SKIN: This technique is described in Chapter IV, in the WINGS section of this name.

SURFACE FEATURES
Creation of numerous surface features, such as panel and rivet lines, fabric wrinkling, and plywood warping, is covered in the various HOW I BUILT MY... chapters.

For his Vought O3U-3, George Lee produced fine surface detail, including rivet lines, upon 10 thou skin elements, which were then attached to the basic fuselage and float shells. While I never discussed this with him, I believe that he attached the outer panels after having painted, or perhaps airbrushed, liquid cement on the shell region. Many of these skin elements had perforce been vacuformed, obviously over the same molds as used for the thicker shells. You'll see no finer example of this technique than the central float of his O3U-3. I (Alcorn) now intend to skin all exterior "metal" surfaces of any future model in this manner, possibly using 10 thou PVC, as recommended by Peter Cooke.

Not covered elsewhere, however, is simulation of fabric-over-stringer areas, such as the rear fuselage of my Wedell-Williams #44. The challenge is two-fold: to achieve smoothly-flowing stringer lines, which are evenly spaced at any given fore and aft location; and to obtain adequate stringer sharpness, with realistic interstringer catenary (sag). My preferred approach is the thread-on-shell method, as described below, and in the captions of the accompanying figures.

The vacuformed surface is first airbrush coated with grey auto primer. The stringer locations are then sketched on with a pencil: you'll doubtless erase repeatedly until the correct "flow" and spacing is obtained. Anchor each thread (with a dab of lacquer thinner) at its forward end and work aft, laying the lightly tensioned thread down over the pencil line, and gently mashing it into the primer, which has been softened with brushed-on thinner. As the threads converge toward the rear, frequent adjustment must be made before adequate spacing and contour is achieved, despite your best pencil work.

Once they are all in place to your satisfaction, begin laying on thick grey primer, using the brush and forefinger method. Eventually you'll have enough buildup (filleting) that sanding is in order, to begin forming the interstringer contours. This is performed using a tight roll of (initially) 220 grit sandpaper, held with thumb and forefinger, running along each interstringer "ditch"—you'll need to use progressively tighter (smaller diameter) sandpaper rolls as you move aft. While this procedure is tedious, a beautifully sculptured pattern will begin to emerge. Additional primer must inevitably be added here and there, brush applied and forefinger smeared, as before. Towards the end, you'll need to add several airbrush coats of primer—partly to obtain full coverage of the threads.

Simulation of Fabric-Over-Stringer Rear Fuselage-#1. Thread has been applied to the vacuformed shell of my 1/16th scale Wedell-Williams fuselage. The stringer locations were marked on the bare plastic with pencil and the thread stuck in place with brush-applied MEK. Brush and finger application of unthinned grey lacquer auto primer has begun, to provide filler for the interstringer contours. When enough primer has been laid on, the contours will be developed using tightly rolled sandpaper. Later, grey auto primer will be liberally airbrushed on, followed by spot filling and final contour truing with rolled sandpaper. I first employed this technique on a 1/24th scale HURRICANE solid model. The end result can be quite convincing: the stringer lines are much crisper than for a shell vacuformed over a form to which the threads have been applied.

CHAPTER II
How I Built My Curtiss HS-2L
by Bob Davies

INTRODUCTION

When John Alcorn first asked me to contribute a chapter for MSB, I was, I must say, honored to be included with such an accomplished group of modellers. Then I began to have second thoughts about showing my work, since I was still modelling in relatively small l/48th scale. Most of the other scratch builders would be describing their work done in scales ranging from 1/32 to 1/16, which allows them to use a much broader range of materials and methods. I first started modelling scratch aircraft in the early 1930's, at what we then called 1/4"=1'. I have stayed loyal to that scale ever since, even when other scales became more popular, at least for scratch building.

So, after thinking it over, I decided to give it a try, hoping to maybe encourage some of the more accomplished younger modellers to venture into scratch building. Many of these modellers are into super detailing and replacing many out of scale kit parts with scratch built assemblies, so it is but a small step to go all the way. I will try to describe some of my more basic, less complicated methods. My models, for the most part, are still basically 95% plastic construction, without some of the more involved procedures of resin casting, metal turning, mould making, etc.

My first recollection of building models was when I was eight or nine years old. The first examples were made from white pine wood from apple boxes. (Yes, apples did come in wood boxes back in the good old days). The models were quite basic, but the Kid was proud of them. I think that I first started to pick up "Model Airplane News" in 1935. From these pages came plans to work from and advertisements for HAWK solid wood kits for the large sum of Twenty-Five Cents. Later on, when William Wylam's plans started showing up, I was thrilled with their detail, which was great considering what was available at the time. I used his plans extensively for building balsa and basswood models. When we think about how far the hobby has come in the past sixty years, it is amazing!

After about a fifteen year layoff from modelling, I was introduced to plastic models in the mid sixties. I learned about I.P.M.S. in a local Dallas hobby shop and went to my first meeting in 1967. I joined I.P.M.S. on the spot and have been a member ever since. I met George Lee at the 1968 National Convention in Los Angles, and later John Alcorn in 1974. I owe a great deal of gratitude to them both, for all the help and encouragement they have given me over the years.

I have had a long love affair with Curtiss Aircraft through the years, as many of my fellow modelers will attest. They always seemed to know that if it was a Curtiss, it was my model, and the razzing never let up. As a Flight Instructor during World War II, we flew P-40s in Transition Training.

RESEARCH

After securing Peter Bower's book "Early Curtiss Aircraft," some of the early flying boats took my eye. The book has good line drawings of most of the aircraft. But where was I to get good background details? Voila! The Canadians, in their advance material for the 1992 I.P.M.S. Convention in Ottawa, had a pamphlet on restored Aircraft in the National Aircraft Museum. The one that I wanted was there in all its restored glory: the only remaining example of the Curtiss HS-2L.

So it was off to Canada, where I spent three glorious days at the musuem. The people in the museum Library were most helpful. First off, I was able to secure good drawings in 1/24 Scale and was allowed to browse through a file of photographs taken during restoration. I then was able to take photographs of the restored aircraft, located on the museum floor. I took six rolls of film, of every conceivable detail including rigging, fittings, engine closeups, cockpit, etc. I owe a deep debt of gratitude to all the fine people at the museum, for without their help, the Curtiss HS-2L would have been just another project left unfinished.

The first step upon arriving home from Ottawa was to have the museum drawings reduced to 1/48th scale and develop the six rolls

Bob Davies. "At age 77 as of this writing (July 1998) and on the verge of becoming a great-grandfather (achieved on the 28th), my goal is to become *one* of the oldest *active* modellers in IPMS/USA (31 years continuous membership). I am a (semi-) retired architectural designer and W.W.-II pilot/flight instructor, who still enjoys modelling, along with other interests, including woodworking, gardening, and thrice-weekly workouts."

Curtiss HS-2L: This wonderfully crafted 1/48th scale model of a fascinating but demanding subject earned the George Lee Memorial Judges Grand Award at the 1993 IPMS/USA Nationals in Atlanta: also Best Aircraft and Best Detailed Aircraft. (Partain photo)

When we reflect upon the USA's meagre contribution of combat aircraft in "The Great War," only the Dayton-Wright built DH4s, and perhaps the Curtiss H-12/16 flying boats, usually come to mind. But, the much smaller Curtiss HS boats were out there, too, performing antisub patrol from France, as well as training. However, of the 1092 HS boats constructed (mostly -2Ls), only 182 made it to France (all but about 20 being -1Ls), entering service from June 1918. Postwar, they gave long and faithful service in the U.S. and Canada, serving with the U.S. Navy until 1928. (Partain photo)

This closeup emphasizes Bob Davies' fine replication of the HS-2L's 400 hp LIBERTY 12 engine, and 2+2 four-bladed propeller. The fan drives a wind-driven generator. (Partain photo)

of film. I now had good reference for designing the masters for photoetched parts. Drawings were made of each individual part to be photoetched 8X, or at 2"=1'0". The reason for such a large scale for the Master Drawings was to capture as much detail as possible. Some of these parts in finished scale are very small. A typical turnbuckle is 1/64 X 3/16 actual size. These parts included control horns and guides, inspection plates, strut base plates, turnbuckles, engine parts and mounts, fan blades propeller boss, etc.

Each part was designed and then inked with an OO Rapidograph Pen. For multiple parts, I made positive prints on a Canon Copier. The next step was to arrange all the parts on a large piece of white bond paper 20"X 32" with a 1" black border around the edge. Each drawing was affixed with a glue stick. This master sheet was then taken to a blueprint shop for reduction to a 1/24th scale positive print. I was then ready to send my work to FOTOCUT for the final steps in the process. From this 1/24th scale positive, Fred Hultberg makes a 1/48th scale negative for working up the final brass product. This was my second time at using my own designed photoetched parts, having first used them on an Aeromarine 39-B with an exposed OXX5 engine, scratch constructed.

FUSELAGE CONSTRUCTION

First off, for methods of fuselage construction, I would like to refer you to Chapter III in Scratch Built! for John Alcorn's very complete description of the carving of basswood masters and the vacuforming process—and to the similar discussion in Chapter I of this volume. My method varies from John's only in the following way:

My fuselage master is made up of four blocks of basswood, with each mating surface painted black. The two pieces making up each half section are permanently glued together. This line between the two half sections gives me a reference for the horizontal center line. I now have a block ready for carving that shows both vertical and horizontal thrust lines depicted by a fine black line. I prepare carving templates from 20 thou plasticard. Each one shows the horizontal thrust line for reference during the carving and sanding process—as per Chapter III of SCRATCH BUILT!. When I am finished with sanding, a single edge razor blade is used to part the two half fuselage sections. I am now ready for vacuforming. For work in 1/48th scale, I find that 20 thou plastic sheet stock is suitable. I block the two half fuselage sections up about 1/8" off the platen, to insure a good pull, and this also gives me a little leeway in trim-

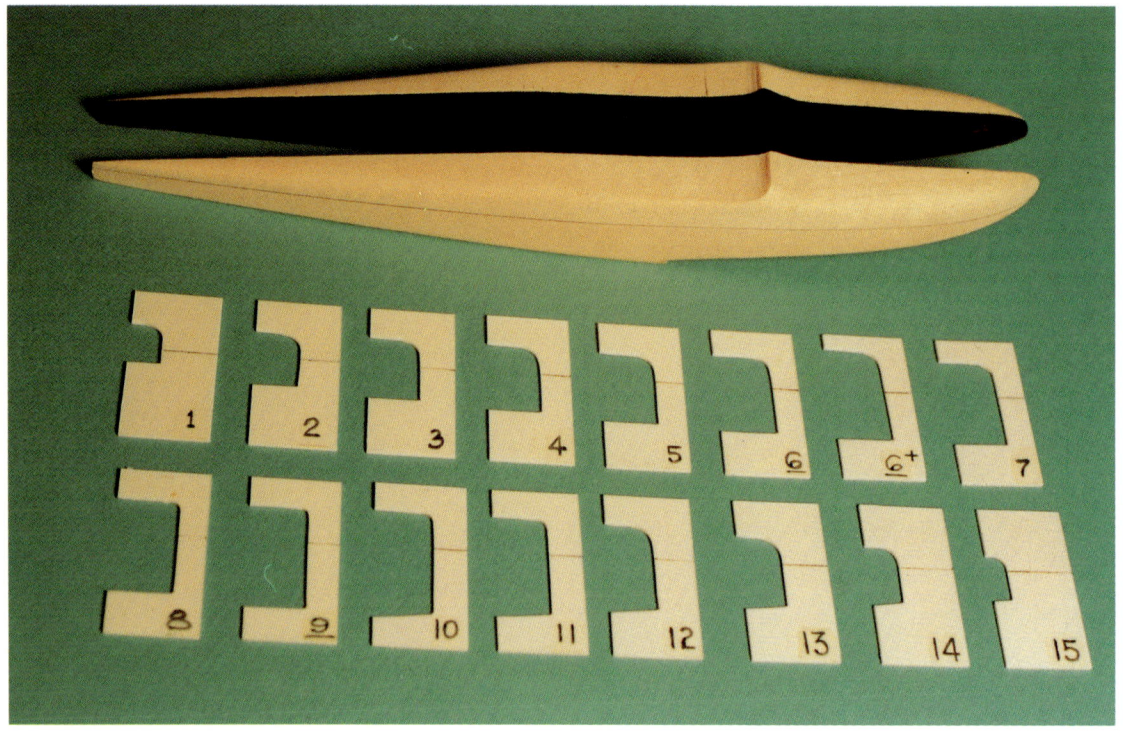

Here are the basswood forms for the basic hull, with their cross-section templates—made of 20 thou plasticard.

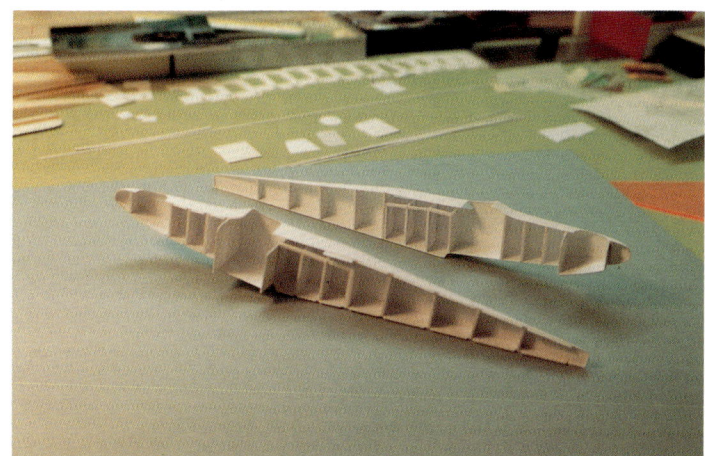

In this view, the hull shells, vacuformed from 20 thou plasticard, have been fitted with bulkheads.

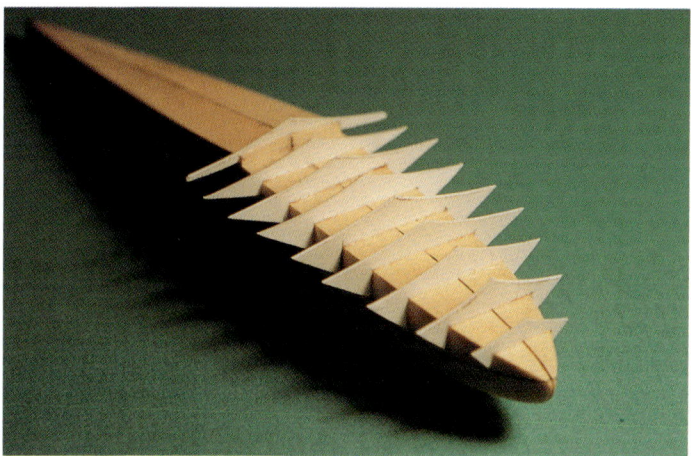

Here we see 20 thou plasticard bulkheads for the sponson added to the vacuformed hull. The sponson will be "planked" with strips of 15 thou plasticard.

ming and sanding against the wood master. I am now ready to detail the interior of the fuselage.

After the fuselage (hull in the case of the HS-2L) was completed, the sponson was then added. Bulkheads were cut from 20 thou styrene and glued to the hull at a scale 18"o/c. From nose to the hull step, planking of 15 thou plasticard was applied to the sides and bottom to complete the sponson. I have constructed fuselages in one of the following methods: first, where the vacuformed shell acts as a closure around a completely detailed framework representing either metal tubing or wood framework, with all the detail work completed within the so called cage; second, where solid bulkheads are used for lateral strength and as dividers between the detailed areas, such as the cockpit; the third method is good for a model that has many openings for viewing all the interior detail. In this method all the structural detail is applied to the vacuformed shell. Bulkheads, stringers, truss detail, etc. are detailed from nose to tail section. A good example would be an A-20, in which I can think of at least six areas where interior detail may be observed.

The second method was chosen for the HS-2L. Lateral bulkheads were placed about every three scale feet, except in the cockpit and observer's nose station. These two areas were then detailed as per photographs taken of the restored aircraft. Bulkheads, stringers, etc. were placed as required. The flooring in each area was of slatted wood construction. These items were constructed using plasticard and strip stock. The interior painting was done to represent varnished wood and Naval Gray. The seats were vacuformed plastic with seat cushions of carved plastic. (Chapter VI pp 87 of SCRATCH BUILT!) Rudder bars and control wheels were of photoetched brass. A rather sparse instrument panel was constructed with switches, pulleys, control cables, etc. All controls were dual with the pilots sitting side by side. The observer's station was detailed as per photographs. This included a Scarff ring and twin-mounted Lewis machine guns.

Curtiss R-6L Fuselage. Just to prove that, for some models at least, beauty isn't just skin deep, here is a peek into the fuselage of Bob's 1/48th Curtiss R-6L.

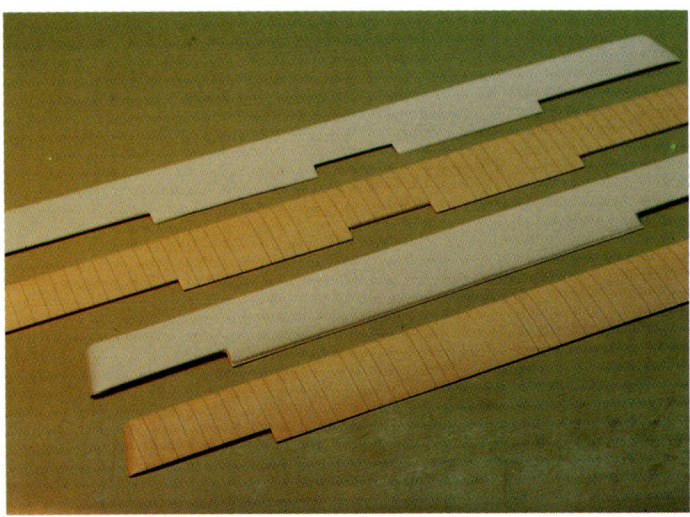

Wings-1: For his HS-2L, Bob made basswood core wings, the core first serving as a mold for vacuforming the skins. As can be seen here, he wrapped thread over each rib location prior to vacuforming (the continuous thread proceeding from one location to the next on the underside).

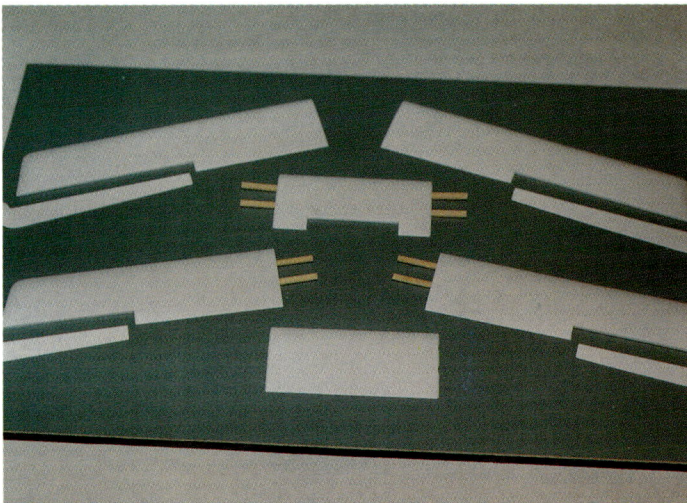

Wings-2: Here we see all of the completed wing elements. While contact cement is a more commonly used bonding agent for attachment of skin to wood wing cores, Bob used Testors liquid cement—applied progressively to the skin only (see text).

WING CONSTRUCTION

I wanted to vacuform the entire wing with one pull, but with a wingspan of 18 1/2", this presented a problem. None of my vacuforms were large enough. The only way was to design a platen to fit in the oven diagonally from one rear corner to the opposite front corner. The problem was solved by giving the platen an angle at each end.

The wings have a relatively thin airfoil section with a distinct camber on the underside. Basswood plank 3/16 x 2"x 24" was used for each wing master. After cutting out the wing to outline form on a band saw, I proceeded to work the plank down to airfoil shape. I have various sizes of homemade sanding blocks with graduated grits of sandpaper glued to each side. I find it helpful to place the wing in a simple holding jig at the front of my workbench. This allows both hands free to control the work. After finishing the top airfoil, the wing was reversed in the jig in order to shape the camber on the underside. This was accomplished using a slightly rounded sanding block, carefully sanding from end to end on each pass, until I had the correct camber. The wing was then removed from the jig for final sanding. NOTE! I leave a small square edge, approximately 1/32" at the trailing edge at this time, to facilitate the next procedure.

Many methods have been used to duplicate the wing rib effect on fabric covered surfaces. Again, we come back to the scale in which the modeller is working. In larger scales, such as George Lee's Keystone, even the wing rib stitching was embossed from the under side. For 1/48th scale, I use the following method. After the wing master has been finish-sanded and several coats of sealer applied, I mark the locations of each rib. I then take a single edge razor blade and make a slight cut on the leading and trailing edge at each mark. The slight nick holds a wrapped thread in place. The aforementioned 1/32" thick trailing edge keeps the wood master from crushing or splitting under the tension of the thread. Thread

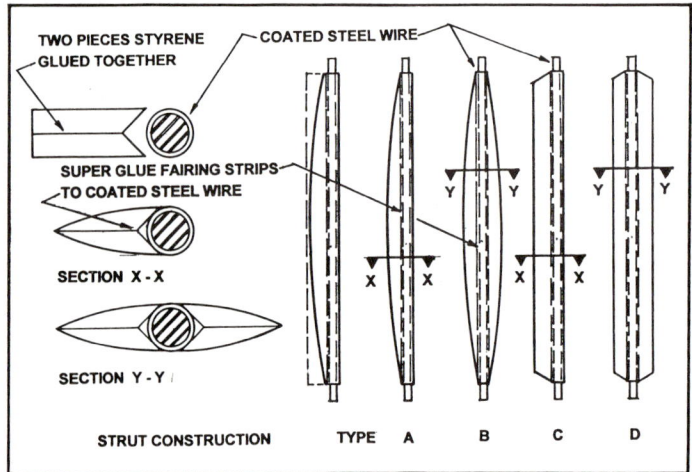

Struts. Bob's line drawing complements his text explanation for producing streamline, steel wire core, longitudinally tapered struts.

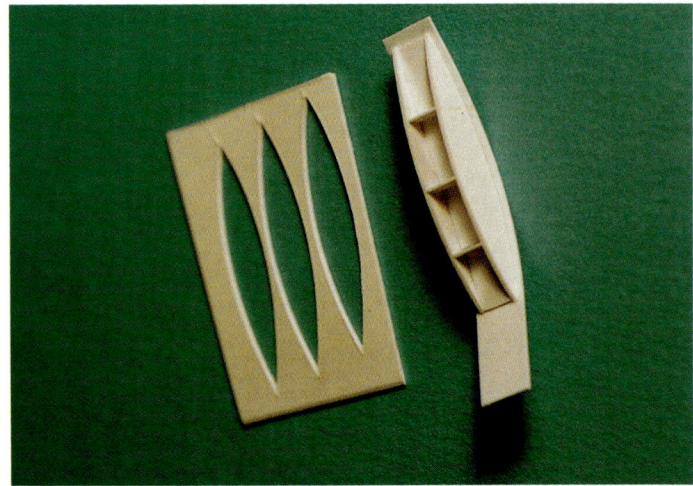

Wingtip Floats. This photo nicely illustrates how such an element can easily be scratchbuilt in flat plasticard.

transition from rib to rib is made on the reverse side. For models with thicker airfoil section and rounded tips, I dope the thread after it has been positioned to prevent movement or sag, toward the tip during vacuforming. For wings with a camber on the underside (as on the HS-2L), this presents a problem in that I cannot correctly obtain a rib simulation by vacuforming over the camber. To avoid this, I use a flat piece of basswood with same plan form and rib spacing as the master. I stretch the nylon thread over the blank and vacuform as in the above top section. The description of gluing will follow later.

For vacuforming the wings, the same procedure is followed as for the fuselage. I block up the master with a piece of 1/16" cardboard cut slightly smaller. Again this gives a distinct line to trim and sand to.

The next process is to mate the plastic skinning to the basswood core. I prefer to secure the top skin first. Align the skin and core and hold in place temporarily with masking tape. Various types of glue have been used by modellers in the past, including double stick tape and contact cement. I prefer Testors Liquid Plastic Cement. I start at one wing tip and work my way down the length of the wing, applying the cement with a brush only to the under side of the plastic. Any cement applied to the wood core will cause later softening of the plastic skin and ruin the effort. For the bottom, remember that the plastic was formed over a flat wing surface. The camber to the plastic occurs when I glue the plastic to the wood core. A little rubbing with the fingers will bond the plastic nicely. A little more touch-up sanding, trimming, and filling any defects with gap filling superglue, and I have a finished wing ready to use.

OTHER COMPONENTS

RUDDER AND STABILIZER: For the smaller scales, I have found it is hard to get a sharp trailing edge on the rudder and elevator by the vacuforming process; however, it can be accomplished with patience and a little effort. Another method is to use a sandwich of two layers of sheet plastic stock equal to the thickness of the finished rudder and stabilizer. I rough up one side of the sheet stock with sandpaper, then apply red food color to this surface. When dry, I glue the two pieces together with liquid plastic cement. I now have a center line to work to. Sanding and shaping of the plastic is done in much the same manner as shaping basswood. Care must be taken when wet sanding the plastic to remove all scratches. For duplicating the fabric covered structure, thin strips of 5 thou plastic styrene are glued at rib locations and lightly sanded.

STRUTS: The method that I use for construction of all interplane and engine mounting struts gives me the strength of straight steel wire, along with the versatility of being able to shape plastic fairings. When observing biplane wing struts, you will note that there were a number of ways the struts were shaped. I start with plastic coated wire found in "PLASTRUCT" displays found in most hobby shops. The wire is cut to length to include an adequate amount to anchor into the wing structure. The wire is then stripped of the plastic coating at each end equal to anchor length plus the thickness of the anchor plates. Plastic fairing strips are then glued to the plastic coating. Again, I use two pieces of plastic stock with food color applied to the adjoining sides and then glued. The plastic stock is beveled on the side to be glued to the rod. The next step is to shape the plastic to plan form and then carefully sand to the correct airfoil shape using the red center line as a guide. Some filling may be required at the juncture of the rod and the shaped fairing. I use superglue and find that any rough spots can be corrected. Prime the strut and you will be pleased that you not only have an accurate shape, but a very strong strut. Other bracing struts on the fuselage of the HS-2L were constructed from square brass tube. These were located from the engine to the fuselage and from tail assembly to the rear fuselage decking.

FLOATS: The floats were the simplest subassembly to construct. Vacuforming was not necessary, since they did not have a sponson shape on the bottom and were not rounded on the top. Two pieces of 20 thou, sheet plastic were shaped to the side plan view.

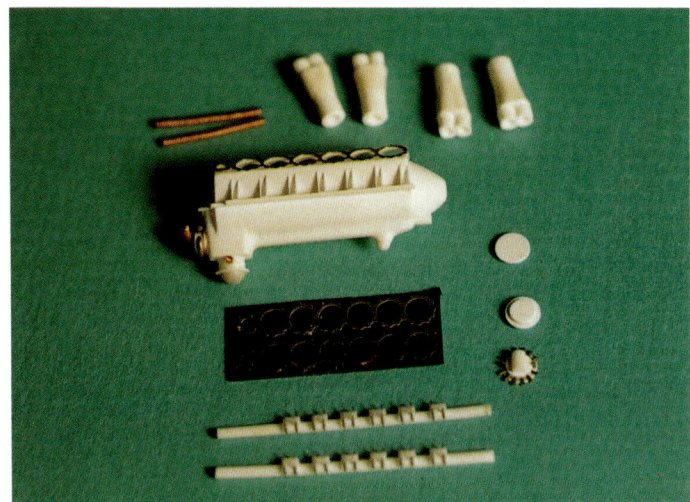

LIBERTY Engine-1: In this view, we see the three basswood forms, two of the vacuformed elements, and the assembled crankcase.

LIBERTY Engine-2: Here we see the completed crankcase, four of the twelve cylinders (each fashioned from EVERGREEN tube, no less!), and other components.

(A symmetrical tear drop shape). A center line gusset was glued between the two sides, with right angle gussets glued to the center line member. Skinning of 10 thou plastic was then glued to the framework top and bottom. Trimming and sanding followed. Attachment points were marked and drilled for the steel struts, which were quite small without any airfoil streamlining applied.

ENGINE: The background information required to construct a replica of the Liberty "Twelve" was obtained from drawings from Aerial Age weekly and Historical Aviation Album. Photographs were taken of a static Liberty engine on display in the Naval Air Museum at Pensacola, and were of special help for reference during construction. The crankcase was constructed in three pieces; A top and bottom section plus a nose cone. Basswood masters were carved for each section, to be vacuformed. A flat plastic plate was cut to shape to fit between the top and bottom sections. This became the support for the engine bearers. Twenty-eight mounting feet were shaped from 5 thou plastic. These were glued to the support plate and against the top section of the crankcase between each cylinder location. Photoetched brass cylinder gaskets were superglued to the top beveled surface of the block. The next step was to carefully cut and trim out the plastic within each gasket opening to receive the cylinders.

"Evergreen" plastic tube was used to construct each of the twelve cylinders required. The main cylinder barrel was 1/8" o.d. tube with two pieces of 3/32" o.d. tube flattened on two sides to represent the intake and exhaust portion of the cylinder. A simple wood and plastic jig was constructed to align the cylinders to the block and for attaching the exhaust stacks. The next step was to attach photoetched brass gaskets to each cylinder to receive the intake and exhaust ports. Fine copper wire was wrapped around a piece of piano wire to make springs for valve lifters. One spring was placed in the center openings of each intake and exhaust port. These would later be connected to the camshaft and rocker arms.

"Artwork" for photoetched parts. 8X scale pen and ink originals were replicated on a copier, and then assembled to obtain the requisite number of parts on one 20 by 32 inch sheet. A 2X scale photopositive was sent to FOTOCUT, who then made one 4x5 inch sheet, in 5 thou brass. Bob required two different sheets for the Curtiss HS-2L: these also contained the parts for three other models!

Other subassemblies, including tubular camshaft, intake manifold, generator, carburetor, distributor, cooling water pipes and pump, oil lines and pump, and oil filter spouts, were finished and painted before assembly. Materials for these assemblies are as follows: Stretched plastic sprue, plastic tube and rod, aluminum and brass tube, copper wire, photocut nuts and bolts, pins and plastic card stock of 5 to 20 thou thickness. The completed engine is made up of more than 375 individual pieces!

PROPELLER: The propeller was a four bladed type, but unusual in that it was actually two two-bladed propellers overlapped and bolted at right angles to each other at the hub. It was quite noticeable that the pitch of each blade was flatter than a normal propeller due to the stock only being about half the dual thickness. Clear basswood was selected to carve from, as the tip half of each blade was finished in a much lighter stain than that used at the center of the blade engine designed for the HS-2L project.

LIBERTY Engine-3: This shows two (!) crankcase assemblies, in a fixture for installing each bank of cylinders. Bob reports that his 1/48th scale LIBERTY contains 375 pieces!

Martin T4M-1#1: This fine 1/48th scale Bob Davies effort shared Judges Grand Award honors at the IPMS/USA Nationals in St. Louis. It also received the Verlinden Award for Excellence in Modeling. (Partain photo)

PAINTING AND ASSEMBLY: I refer you to the close up photograph of the HS-2L. The propeller boss was from the photoetched parts.

The HS-2L was assembled much like any other biplane, with most of the individual parts finished and painted before final assembly. The parts assembled before painting were the fuselage, lower wing, and tail surfaces. All other parts were painted and finished before assembly and included the top wing, struts, engine, and pontoons. This included marking and drilling for strut locations and any necessary decaling. The struts even had decaled numbers to show location for erection much like on the actual aircraft. The paint scheme chosen was for a U.S. Naval Aircraft, in the mid to late 1920s. The fuselage, pontoons, and struts were painted Navy Aircraft Gray F.S.16473. The top of the upper wing, top of the elevators, and stabilizer were painted orange yellow F.S. 13538. The bottom of the top wing and all of lower wing and bottom of the stabilizer-elevators were finished in aluminum dope. I used Model Master paints throughout. Decals were selected from Micro Scale

Martin T4M-1#2: (Partain photo)

Douglas SBD-3#1: Unlike some scratchbuilders, Bob harbors no phobias against kits. Here is his 1988 rendition of Monogram's. (Partain photo)

Douglas SBD-3#2: But, he went way beyond the kit in the cockpit, and other areas. The markings represent Profile#196's interpretation of Ensign J.A. Leppla's VS-2 aircraft following the Coral Sea battle. (Partain photo)

sheets for the national insignia, small lettering and numerals. The large numerals on the hull were cut from white decal paper. The rudder stripes were painted with an air brush.

A simple jig was constructed to facilitate assembly of the various finished sub-assemblies; one that I could add to and remove supports and braces as assembly progressed. After the fuselage, lower wing, and tail surfaces were painted and finished, they were placed back in the jig to receive the engine mount and engine. The wing struts came next, with the top wing to follow. Finally, the pontoons were added to the lower wing. This completed assembly of all the major parts.

RIGGING

The rigging was completed with the model still secured in the jig cradle, but with most of the jig bracing removed. I used the same nylon thread as described earlier. This was a slow, tedious process, but if a person can thread a needle it can be done. (Yeah, Bob; blindfolded, wearing workman's gloves. - ed.) All the rigging was secured through eyelets in base plates, turnbuckles, or wing and fuselage anchor brackets. As on the actual aircraft, some bracing wires between fuselage and wings had turnbuckles to control tension. This was carefully dupli-

Boeing P-26A. This began as the old Aurora kit, almost completely transformed by Bob in 1984. He vacuformed a new fuselage, cowling, and wheel pants; then scratch built an engine and propeller. This left the wings, stabilizer, elevators, and rudder, plus a few other parts from the kit; all of which required extensive modification. (Partain photo)

cated on my model with photoetched parts. Control surface rigging from the tail assembly and wing ailerons to the cockpit area was completed with the same nylon thread.

I secure the thread with superglue at one anchor location, trim the thread and proceed to the next eyelet, pull tight, glue, and trim again. Any sag in the thread can be drawn tight with heat from a hair dryer. Just a note to remember when using superglue—Never, and I mean NEVER leave a superglue joint without first touching up with semi-flat lacquer.

Above all, remember that scratch building requires a great amount of patience by the model builder and also the willingness to re-do work on parts and assemblies that one is not totally happy with. Many of the procedures described in the above text required maybe a second or third try before I was happy with the final results.

The HS-2L project required in excess of 800 hours over a period of a year and a half. It was defnitely a labor of love; with detail work on the engine, rigging, and use of many photoetched parts all helping to make for a very satisfying model.

My hope is that this review of "How I Scratch Built My HS-2L" will encourage modellers to make an even better model with their next project.

On 26 October 1922, Lt. Cdr. Godfrey de C. Chevalier made the first U.S. Navy carrier landing, in Aeromarine 39B, BuNo. A606, on the "covered wagon" Langley, off Cape Henry near Norfolk, Virginia. This 1/48th scale scratchbuilt model by Bob Davies won "BEST AIRCRAFT" and the "DETAIL & SCALE" awards at the 1992 IPMS/USA Nationals, in Seattle, Washington.

CHAPTER III
How I Built My Short Singapore III
by Alan Clark

ABOUT ALAN CLARK
Alan made his appearance into this troublous world on 23 July, 1933, in Hitchin, Hertfordshire. During the War years, he lived in Hitchin, seeing the occasional Luftwaffe raider.

He served his electrical engineering apprenticeship at G.W. King Ltd. (an automation company), after which he was for many years an electrical design engineer in the automation industry—primarily for automotive assembly plants in Italy, Sweden, France, Spain, and Germany, as well as in Britain. In this capacity, he traveled throughout Europe, and even to Moscow and Saudi Arabia. Alan served his two years of National Service (1954-56) in the RAF, servicing aircraft electrical systems at RAF Odiham Stations Flight. A special duty was responsibility for the electrical systems of Field Marshal Montgomery's personal DC3 (KN 645).

Later, he was engaged as a technical writer for Shell Oil, and British Aerospace (De Havillands) at Hatfield.

For the last four years of his career, Alan served as Exhibitions Officer for the Shuttleworth Trust at Old Warden—a kid in a candy store.

Alan relates that he has been modelling for well over fifty years, having acquired his basic skills building wooden solid models, plus the occasional "flyer." He was IPMS/UK National Champion in 1993 (SINGAPORE III) and 1996 (Blackburn FIRECREST). Between 1982 and the present, he has also won seven gold and four silver awards at the British National Model Engineer Exhibition. He and his wife Vivienne have lived together in the charming town of Hitchin, Hertfordshire, for 44 years. They have two grown children, Christopher and Angela.

INTRODUCTION
Building the SINGAPORE flying boat was, for me, the culmination of my modelling activities in that it combined my two main interests: aircraft and boat modelling. Also, the SINGAPORE has been a favorite ever since I received a "Dinky Toy" model of same as a Christmas present in 1938! A further impetus was the publication a few years ago of Harry Woodman's fine drawings in 1:72 scale (Argus plan No. 2988). These drawings were enlarged by a factor of two to give a scale of 1:36. Following a great deal of further research, the project began.

HULL
As with most aircraft models, the hull (fuselage) was commenced first. I used a plasticard plank-on-frame method as follows: a line drawing of the hull was draughted, in the manner of boat construction methods, from which 19 strategically placed formers were cut from 40 thou plastic card. The positions of these formers were selected to coincide with obvious changes in contours where possible, e.g. at the chine positions, known bulkhead positions, wing location strong points, between windows, etc. All the formers were then divided into their respective port and starboard halves, each half former then being heavily scored on its inside former line (about 1/4 inch from its outer edge, but not forgetting a flat at the bottom for the floor position). This scored line was to allow for eventual breaking away of the inner portion of the former at a later stage of the construction, after all outer planking had been completed. To assist in this breaking away operation, further scored lines were cut radiating from the inside former line to the vertical centre line of the former.

Two outline (handed) shapes of the complete hull profile were cut from thin plastic sheet (5 thou) and lightly spray-glued to a flat building board. Block board, not plywood, is recommended for this purpose, as it will always retain its perfectly flat surface with no tendency to warp. Thin plastic sheet was used for the hull profiles, as its function was simply to retain the formers in their respective

So, here we have Alan Clark, abeam over his Albatros DVa.

Short SINGAPORE III. This awesome 1/36th scale model was National Champion at the 1993 IPMS/UK convention. It is seen here over the Red Sea. Alan relates that, while the remaining 36 production SINGAPORE IIIs were doped aluminum overall, K3592—the first article—was left in bare metal finish—at least from photo evidence. -Manny Cefai photo

positions: these thin profiles would be eventually cut away and discarded.

The port and starboard sets of half formers were then cemented to their respective positions on the profiles, being retained in their vertical positions by means of small right angle wooden blocks which were temporarily affixed by means of double sided adhesive tape. As a further aid to retaining the half formers in their vertical positions a half inch wide strip of 40 thou plasticard was cemented at approximately water line level along the whole hull length from nose to tail (stem to stern!). Also at this stage a further strip of plasticard was cemented to the edge of the chine position, this being cut to conform to the plan view shape of the hull (see photo 1). After these operations the small wooden retaining blocks were removed.

Both hull halves were then planked with 1/4 inch wide 40 thou plasticard, much in the manner of planking a boat. After planking, the complete half assemblies were then liberally coated with liquid cement and allowed to dry out for at least a week. This made the assembly into a hard solid mass and allowed any possible distortion to take effect.

The two hull halves were then removed from the building board by the use of a slim knife blade and cleaned up generally on their exteriors. All imperfections on the exterior (and there were a lot of them!) were treated with GREEN STUFF body putty and rubbed down. This process was repeated until the surface was as blemish free as seemed possible. The thin plastic sheet profiles upon which the formers were mounted were cut away to reveal the inner surface of the hull halves; after which the previously scored sections of the formers were broken away by the use of long nosed pliers, thus leaving the basic ribs. The inside surface of the hull was then again liberally coated with liquid cement and generally cleaned up.

At this point the boat's floors (decks) were added (section by section), further false formers inserted, bulkheads were fitted, and all ribs were capped with thin flat MICROSTRIP. Finally, all stringers were fitted between the rib (former) positions, again using MICROSTRIP of suitable sections (not a very exciting job...). Port

Blackbum YA.1 FIRECREST: This magnificent 1/24th scale model understandably won a Gold Medal and the Scale Models Cup at the 1997 International Model Show and Model Engineer Exhibition, as well as being IPMS/UK National Champion in 1996. As with many of Alan's models, this one is represented in natural metal finish, using 10 thou aluminum litho printing plate, plus very malleable pewter sheet in certain difficult, strongly double-curved areas such as the propeller spinner. His technique for achieving this remarkably effective finish is described in the text of this chapter. RT 651 was one of two prototypes, completed in 1947 as a Torpedo Fighter/Bomber. -Manny Cefai photo

Even the five propeller blades were made of aluminum: hardened sheet, cut, filed, and twisted to shape; faired with Milliput body putty; covered with thin aluminium sheet; and painted matte black. Incredibly, at least to me (Alcorn), all of Alan's painting is hand brushed: even the propeller blade logos/stencilling!! - Manny Cefai photo

Alan faithfully replicated the fuselage girder structure using brass tube, rod, and channel; rivetted and soldered. This framework was mounted upon a brass floorplate, with brass bulkheads fore and aft: their edges were faced with 40 thou plasticard. The shells underlying the aluminum skin were vacuformed plasticard.

Bristol CENTAURUS: two row, 18 cylinder, 2825 hp radial engine. Alan's representation was built around two nine-faceted plasticard crankcase "boxes," with cylinders turned from 10mm plastic knitting needles! Alan reports that it took him two years to construct this model (the engine/cowl/propeller assembly would have taken me this long! - Alcorn). Incidentally, an excellent, well-illustrated feature of this model can be found in the July 1997 issue of SCALE MODELS International.

holes (scuttles) were drilled and reamed in their appropriate positions, glazing being left until much later. All furniture, e.g. wireless operator and navigation consoles, tables, swivel chairs, refrigerator, cooker, work bench with vise, various tables, bunks, and cupboards, were made and fitted. The whole interior was then painted and dry-brushed to a suitable weathered finish (see photo 2). Incidentally, whilst not a great deal of the interior fittings can be seen, they were all fitted as described. Here Murphy's Law comes into play—if any detail is left out, its omission will later become obvious. Anyway, I know they are all there!

Upon completion of the interior fittings, the two hull halves were cemented together, imperfections again being treated with GREEN STUFF and generally rubbed down to a smooth finish (see photo 3). Floors were covered using car body repair aluminum mesh, this being inserted and fixed to false floors via the cockpit area and gunners' positions. After this gynecology-like operation the cockpit instrument panels, seats, control wheels, etc., together with details concerning the gunners' positions, were made and fitted.

The instrument panel was made from two laminations of thin sheet aluminum, painted matte black; the rear sheet having the instrument faces scratched through the paint to the metal with a needle, the top sheet having holes drilled and reamed to match the instrument positions. After gluing the laminations together the instrument faces were covered by drops of DEVCON epoxy adhesive

De Havilland 95 FLAMINGO: This 12-17 seat airliner, powered by two 890 hp Bristol PERSEUS engines, was DeHavilland's first all-metal aircraft. G-AFUE, the prototype of 15 examples, first flew in December 1938.

Alan's 1/30th scale model was completed in about 1995, following a three-year research/ construction effort. The fuselage shell is epoxy/fibreglass, built up over a wood mould. The wings are plasticard over a wood spar and rib core. As usual for him, it is skinned in aluminium litho plate. He reports that the cockpit, passenger compartment and lavatory are fully fitted out. This model was awarded a Gold Medal and Scale Models Cup at the 1995 Model Engineer Exhibition.

Northrup DELTA 1A: This delightful 1/24th scale model was completed circa 1983, following an 850 hour effort. The fuselage was planked with plasticard strips over plastic formers. The wings are plasticard sheet, contact cement-applied over balsa cores. The cowling was turned from a plastic rainwater pipe fitting! In his inimitable fashion, Alan skinned it with aluminium litho plate, this being his first. -photo courtesy Aeroplane Monthly.

applied with a cocktail stick. This adhesive dries crystal clear in about five minutes. Side panels were fabricated with rows of switches and levers made from various sizes of pins and nails fixed into panels and then fitted to the side structures. Scarff rings for the gunners and other minor details are described later.

WINGS

The wings, of a convenient constant chord section, were constructed on flying model principles utilizing ribs and spars cut from 1 mm thick, 3-ply wood laminate, the spars being a double thickness of the same material glued together. Ribs were stationed at regular intervals along the spars to coincide with aileron positions and interplane strut strong point locations

It should be mentioned that 1 mm 3-ply wood can easily be cut with sharp scissors: no fret saw is necessary. Also, with the constant chord wings of an aircraft such as the SINGAPORE, the wing ribs can be clamped together as a block and sanded to an exact uniform shape.

The ribs and spars were then assembled on and glued to the lower wing surface which had previously been cut to the wing planform shape, again from the aforementioned 1 mm 3-ply wood, after which various strong points for joining and strut locations were added in the form of wooden blocks glued to the structure. (See photo 4.) When all glued joints were dry, the upper wood coverings were affixed, again utilizing 1 mm 3-ply timber. Both top and bottom wood wing covering was heavily scored to assist the curvature over the airfoil sections, the visible grain of the wood running spanwise. It will be seen from photo 4 that all the leading edges of the ribs have been removed, as it would not have been possible to take the wood covering around the leading edge of the wings; the leading edges being solid blocks of balsa wood glued on and carved to shape *in situ*.

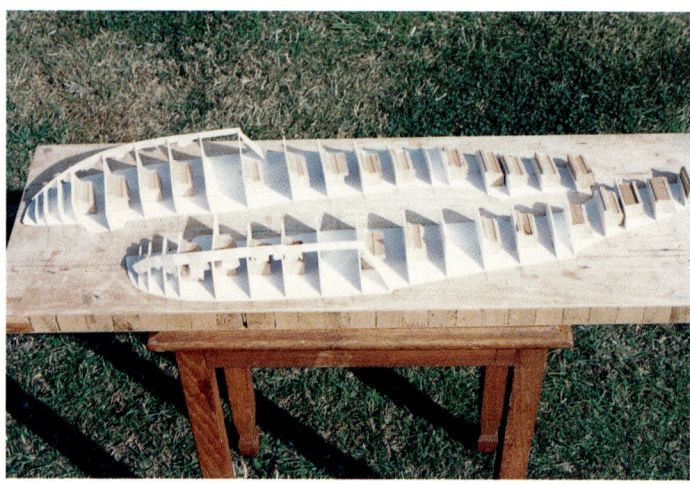

#1. Hull Construction. Note: This and the remaining construction/detail photos are numbered in accordance with their text descriptions.

#2. Hull Interior Details.

After cutting the ailerons from the outer wing panels, the complete wings were then covered in 5 thou special plasticard, gluing being via Dunlop THIXOFIX contact adhesive (or similar). The card used for this covering was of a type which cannot be cracked (obtainable in the U.K. from book binders and used as separator cards); therefore a sharp trailing edge can be achieved by folding and running a steel rule along the fold using considerable pressure. Each of the wing sections was covered in two pieces of card; the wrap round leading edge and the sharp folded trailing edge meeting at the main spar location at both the top and bottom of the wing section. A point of which to beware—this type of card cannot be glued with polystyrene cement! The ailerons were treated in the same way as the wings.

The lower wing centre-section proved to be a little difficult because of its complex shape and tapered curved root when viewed from the front. This was solved by first constructing the lower centre section in exactly the same way as for the top wing, boxing in the spar positions where they pass through the hull, then adding the extended and deeper wing-root ribs. These were then faired in using body putty of an epoxy resin nature such as MILLIPUT or ISOPON P38. (See photo 5: shown inverted.) The covered spars form part of the roof of the hull. The lower centre section was then permanently fixed and faired into the hull. (See again photo 3.)

Turning to the outer wing panels—a plasticard profile plan shape was added to each wing tip, the whole being filled with epoxy body putty, and when dry, shaped and sanded smooth. The three sections of the top wing were then joined together via stub spars. The lower wings were left unassembled to the hull at this stage for the sake of modelling convenience! (See photo 6.)

Wings and ailerons were finally given metal leading edges and tips. The methods utilized are detailed later in this chapter, in the FINISHING section. The fabric covered areas had their wing ribs simulated by strips of self-adhesive LETRATAPE, all being finally covered in light weight model tissue applied with aerosol spray glue and then given multiple coats of clear acetone dope. The silver fabric areas were then hand brushed using JAP-LAC silver lacquer, which approximates very favourably with doped fabric finishes seen on real aircraft. (Note: I'm afraid my expertise with the air-brush is not all it should be as I only finish a model at intervals of approximately two years!)

#3. Hull Halves Assembled.

#4. Wing Structure, With Lower Plywood Skin Attached.

44　The Master Scratch Builders: Tips & Techniques from the Master Aircraft Modelers

#5. Lower Wing Centre Section.

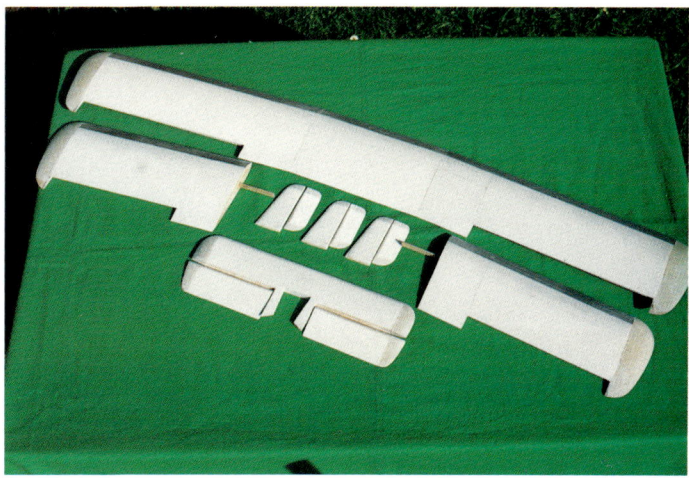

#6. Wing and Tail Components.

EMPENNAGE

Profiles for all flying and control surfaces which make up the tail feathers were cut from 1 mm, 3-ply wood. Balsa sheet to make up to the required thickness of airfoil sections was glued to each side of the profiles, the whole then being sanded to shape. Control surfaces were cut away, each fixed and control surface was then covered in plasticard, ribbed, tissue covered and finished exactly as described for the wings.

To give the model "life," all control surfaces were deflected a degree or two, the surfaces being fixed via short lengths of aluminum wire which were then disguised by the scale hinge shrouds. After painting and application of serial numbers etc (via LETRASET), the tail surfaces were assembled and fixed with wooden dowels, after which the various struts and control linkages together with their bell cranks were added. (See photo 7.) Bell cranks and control horns were cut by sharp scissors from thin sheet brass and cleaned up with ladies' finger nail emery boards.

ENGINES

Modelling the SINGAPORE was facilitated in that although there are four engines (two tractor and two pusher), they are all identical. A solid wood engine nacelle for one engine was carved (slightly undersized to allow for the thickness of the moulded plastic) in two halves, held together with double sided adhesive tape. The nacelle was then pried apart and the two halves in turn placed on a home-made vacuform machine; four mouldings being made from each (plus a number of spares) in 40 thou plasticard.

Joining the front and rear nacelles at the centre was made easier by cutting sections from the wooden pattern and using them as jointing pieces. This helped considerably in achieving perfect alignment. It was decided to open the cowlings on the two front (tractor) nacelles to display the Rolls Royce Kestrel engines, so various support bulkheads were inserted. Also, 3/16 inch diameter brass tubes were fixed in all four positions to accept and support the propeller shafts.

#7. Installed Tail Assembly. Alan confesses that the tail serial numbers (K3592) were applied with LETRASET dry transfers.

#8. Detail of Rolls-Royce KESTREL Engine Installation.

#9. Bow.

The two exposed engines were built up from scratch using various thicknesses of plasticard, slotted from the bottom so as to fit over the previously mounted brass tubes in the manner of a saddle. By this method the engines could be made, painted, and detail finished with ignition harnesses, etc. before being finally fitted into the nacelles. The representative engine bearers, from plastic rod, were fitted afterwards.

The most difficult job regarding the engines was the making of 24 identical, but handed, "rams-horn" exhaust stacks in sets of three. These were carved, glued, assembled, and faired from pieces of plastic rod, after which the slotted openings were cut. Each assembly was then painted and dry-brush weathered to represent the colouration of hot exhausts.

The two large radiators were each shaped from hardwood, wrapped with 5 thou plastic sheet, faired with MILLIPUT, ribbed, and finally covered in aluminum sheet (described elsewhere). Copper gauze and tubing were fitted front and rear in the manner of car radiators of the period. Oil coolers were made up from laminations of thin plasticard with suitable spacers inserted, the assemblies being retained by fine brass screws.

Finally, the propellers were cut in profile form from thin but rigid aluminum, taper twisted to their correct angles and faired with MILLIPUT body putty. Each propeller was then shaped and faired into its previously prepared spinner with body putty. After shaping, the complete props and spinners were painted and copper shim leading edges applied to the blades. The blue coloured tips to the spinners were found difficult to paint accurately in this scale, the solution finally being to dip them into a prepared pre-determined depth of paint in a tin lid!

The four propeller shafts, already affixed to the spinners, were now inserted into an outer brass tube and retained with a small nail head to allow them to revolve. At final assembly, these were then epoxied into the larger brass tubes already fitted to the nacelles. Thus, each propeller shaft/mounting consisted of three brass tubes, each a sliding fit into the other.

For the complete engine nacelle, radiator, oil cooler, engine, "rams-horn" exhausts, and propeller, see photo 8.

DETAILS

The float patterns and cockpit canopy were each carved from hardwood; 40 thou mouldings being made via the home-made vacuform machine in plasticard and glazing respectively. The canopy was then framed in thin aluminum strips with open hatches being incorporated at this stage. The floats were found to require being filled with epoxy resin to make them stable on their struts.

Identical gunners' Scarff machine gun rings (3 off) were made from brass shim. Six half discs of about two inches diameter were cut from brass using scissors, clamped in a vise together and filed to a uniform shape. Whilst still in the vise, a fine vee-shaped file was used to cut the teeth right across the six faces. After removing from the vise the inner radius was then cut and cleaned. Each resultant section was then folded and soldered to the gun ring together with its back support and "U" shaped gun mounting. For the gun rings, suitable clock wheels, minus their teeth and spokes, were used. Small discs were then epoxied into position and bungees fitted using fine elasticated thread. (See photo 9 for a complete assembly as described.)

Throughout the model all struts were fabricated from small diameter brass tube, faired with hardwood and shaped to airfoil section. They were then ribbed with LETRATAPE and covered with model tissue. Metal leading edges were then applied. Using tube as the basis for struts enables rods to be inserted into the wing strong points at an early state. Thus the struts can be cut to their correct lengths and epoxied over rods to make a much neater job on final assembly, remembering that the model already has its painted finish.

Bollards and mooring cleats were fabricated from suitable fine steel cheese headed screws filed down to below the level of the screw-driver slots. (See again photo 9.)

The beaching gear (photo 10) was fabricated from brass tube soldered together as shown. Buoyancy vessels were made from plastic tube and glass beads. The tail dolly (photo 11) was made up from hardwood with again buoyancy vessels from glass beads. Beaching gear for the model had to be substantial as the finished Singapore weighed in at around four pounds!

Bracing wires were various thicknesses of straight piano wire epoxied in to previously drilled holes at their anchor points. Streamlined "acorns" on the wire inter-sections were drilled and shaped sections of aluminium wire, first drilled and then shaped—not as difficult as it seems. Various methods of producing bracing wires, together with "acorns" for different aircraft types and scales, is described below, in the section RIGGING AND ASSEMBLY.

Port holes (scuttles) were in fact aluminium washers. These were made by stamping holes in thin sheet aluminium by a suitable office punch, roughly cut out individually, then collectively put on a suitable bolt, screwed down tightly with a nut and had their outer surfaces turned down on the lathe. These were then each epoxied into place after first fixing the glazing discs to the rear of each "washer." (See again photo 10.)

To date (1998). I have not used photoetched brass parts, though I may do so on some future projects. I mark and drill holes, as appropriate, before rough cutting out each brass element using fine fingernail scissors—finishing being performed with small files and sandpaper.

FINISH

The first SINGAPORE III, K3592, was, from photographic evidence, left in bare metal finish where appropriate. Subsequent boats were doped silver overall.

A large proportion of the model was therefore plated over and polished, these areas being the complete hull, engine nacelles, floats, flying and control surface leading edges, and all strut leading edges.

This technique evolved over the years (having first been tried by me when building a Northrop "Delta" in 1/24 scale circa 1983), utilizing aluminium sheet, as used on the real aircraft. Whilst many modellers have had superb results in using paint to represent bare metal, for me there is no substitute for the real thing.

The bulk of the sheet used is printers' offset-litho printing plates, which do not have to be new. The used plates from previous printing processes are equally useable, as any print is soon buffed off.

Where possible, the plating divisions on a model should be done panel by panel as on the real aircraft. Some cheating can be done by applying a large area, say over a wing surface, and dividing the area into panels by heavily scoring with a pointed scalpel and straight edge.

With most metal skinned aircraft, however, the majority of the surface area is double curvature (the wings usually excepted); the technique being as follows: panels are cut oversized but with at least one usable edge; the tension is taken out of the aluminium sheet by passing over a gas flame for a few seconds. This in effect anneals the metal, which then goes "floppy." A thin coating of Dunlop THIXOFIX (or similar) contact adhesive is then applied to both the rear of the aluminium sheet and to the area on the model being covered, using a fairly stiff chisel point paint brush. The metal is applied after a few seconds, the area being smoothed and formed from the centre outwards with the rear of an old spoon or similar instrument. The required panel outline is then scored with a scalpel and the surplus broken off.

After laying and trimming a plate, the surplus contact adhesive should be removed from the not yet covered model surface by means of a cloth soaked in acetone thinner to prevent an unsightly build-up of adhesive under the next panel to be applied.

Upon completion of all plating, the model should be cleaned and polished using ever finer grades of wire wool (down to grade 0000), followed by a final polish with a good quality metal polish. Various effects can be obtained with the wire wool by rubbing down the panels in one direction only with an adjoining panel being rubbed at 90 degrees to its neighbor.

After the polishing operation, rivet lines can be applied by means of various clock wheels set in simple handles, the positioning being established from knowledge of the rib and spar positions and with constant reference to any photographic evidence. It is a good idea to mark the positioning of such rivet lines by self-adhesive tape and being guided by flexible straight edges where ever possible. Any basic wood structure, such as wings, should be sheeted over with plasticard so as to give a uniform hardness base for impressing of the rivet lines. I have found that if such lines were marked onto aluminium directly over a wooden structure, the indentations would not be uniform where they fall on alternating hard and soft wood grain.

As an alternative to using offset-litho plates, these usually being of thickness in the range of 8-12 thou, pewter sheet can be used of a similar thickness. This is very easy to work as it is already of a soft nature and is conducive to double curvature work. The only problems are availability and cost!

It should be noted that whilst most panels on an aircraft are butt-joined to each other, some cases occur where lap-joining is required. This should be done with extreme care to prevent an unsightly step at the join. It is a good practice to feather the edge up to a previously fixed plate with a second coat of adhesive on the model before laying the lapped plate.

As a final thought, some may say it's a waste of effort to metal coat an aircraft that is ultimately going to be painted and/or camouflaged. This is not so, as very convincing effects of weathering can be obtained by wearing through the painted finish onto the bare metal with emery cloth or sand paper at obvious wear positions (cowling fastenings, cockpit access, leading edges, etc.)

#10. Beaching Gear.

Generally, my painted metal skinned models were hand brushed with Humbrol enamels, after which they were rubbed out with the finest grade glass paper or wire wool (0000 grade), in the direction of flight. This imparts a slightly oily sheen, as well as smoothing out any irregularities in the brushed surface. This rubbing down can be continued down to the metal for appropriate wear simulation.

On a painted model, the application of rivet lines should be carried out after painting, to prevent these delicate features from being obliterated.

Insignia were applied using the time-honoured method for roundels of painting the area of each roundel matte white upon which was drawn circles of red and blue using draughtsmans' bow compasses, the areas between being filled in by fine brush. The underwing serial (K3592) was drawn up on tracing paper and then pricked through at the two locations with a needle, then being ruled up with compass bows and drawing pen—again being filled in via fine brush.

Only very restrained degrees of weathering were applied to finish off the model, as the aircraft depicted was the unpainted prototype. Just a little exhaust staining around the engine cowlings, together with some minor oil streaks was all that was called for.

RIGGING AND ASSEMBLY

For accurate assembly of biplanes, and the SINGAPORE in particular, I use a box jig (or jigs). These were made from stout plasticard and were designed to go between each set of interplane struts. On these boxes were marked all strut positions, the top and bottom surfaces of which were cut out to fit the top and bottom wing airfoil surfaces. Incorporated in these boxes were, of course, the dihedral, stagger, and incidence allowances.

The wings were then installed with these jig boxes in place. After all glue joints had set, the boxes were then cut away with scalpel and scissors.

Needless to say, one of the most difficult aspects of building model biplanes is the application of rigging wires.

Before about 1916, aircraft generally had only stranded rigging wires, which can be depicted with round wire. Thereafter, most primary rigging was streamline drawn wire; so, for models of, say, 1/24th scale upwards, this aspect should be represented.

For my 1/36th scale SINGAPORE, I used various thicknesses of straight piano wire. Holes were drilled at the appropriate points in the wings, etc. (The metal plate anchor plates on the real aircraft were buried beneath the surface.) Lengths of wire were cut, using draughting dividers for point-to-point measurement, allowing an extra 1/4 inch or so on each end for insertion into the holes. When all were in place, their ends were fixed with epoxy. In this manner, no tension is imparted to the model structure, the wires remaining straight by virtue of their own stiffness. Indeed, if this method is employed for fairly long spans, only one end of each wire need be epoxied, the other being free to "float" within its hole. I believe that John Alcorn has something to say in this regard!

For previous biplane models to 1/24th scale, such as the Fairey SWORDFISH, thicker piano wire was used, but filed down to approximate an airfoil section. This was achieved by anchoring one end of the wire to the bench and pushing a file along, toward the opposite end. The wire was then turned over and this process was repeated. SWORDFISH flying and landing wires are all one inch wide on the real aircraft (I know: I've measured them!)

For the smaller scales, and indeed the SINGAPORE, the rigging wire turnbuckles were simulated by a few coats of "gun metal" coloured paint. For larger scales (my 1:18 scale ALBATROS, for example), short lengths of suitable size fine brass tubing were slid over the wires before installation.

"Acorns" at the intersection of the wires were each made for the SINGAPORE by cutting a short length of aluminium wire, and sharpening at the ends with a file. Two holes at the appropriate angles to each other were drilled through. The treated wire end was then snipped off and resulting stub rounded.

SUMMARY

Whilst I enjoyed the three years making my Singapore, as it combined my interest in ships and aircraft (I have a plank-on-frame wooden frigate of Nelson's era which I have been working on for 30 years!), I should point out to prospective modellers that building such a large scratch built project is very time consuming, and one can get bored with a single model under construction. My remedy is to tackle two or three projects at the same time and progress from one to another as the whim dictates.

#11. Fuselage Rear Area, Showing Beaching Dolly.

CHAPTER IV
How I Built My DeHavilland DH9A
by John Alcorn

ABOUT JOHN ALCORN

In the INTRODUCTION of SB!, I explained my modelling "roots," as did coauthors George Lee and Peter Cooke.

For this tome, again, in the spirit of "human interest," I have asked each HOW I BUILT MY... author to provide a capsule history of himself. So, here goes:

I emerged into the fresh, clean (pre-dust bowl) air of Tulsa, Oklahoma, on 29 February, 1932. This was the same night that the Lindbergh baby was kidnapped, and two days after Elizabeth Taylor's first *al fresco* appearance.

We moved to Houston, Texas, in 1935, my father becoming Chief Engineer for the Gulf Coast Division of the Pure Oil Company. I graduated from (Lamar) high school there in 1950, and from The Rice Institute (also in Houston) in 1955, with a B.S. degree in Mechanical Engineering. Having been NROTC, I spent the next two years aboard the USS *John R. Craig*, a Gearing class destroyer, out of San Diego.

I spent my entire professional career as a mechanical engineer at a series of physics research laboratories, or companies pandering thereto, retiring from CEBAF in Newport News, Virginia, on my 16th real birthday. For almost all of my career, I was involved in design and procurement/construction of large electromagnets—of the liquid helium cooled/NbTi superconducting variety during the last 26.

Francie and I were married (in Berkeley, California) in September 1959. We have two fine sons: Stewart (34, now living in Seattle); and Peter, 32, of San Francisco—both are married. I almost trapped Stewart into modelling.

Relaxing at the Club. The three pair of us, at the El Tovar, Grand Canyon, Thanksgiving period 1994. From right to left: elder son Stewart and Sue; younger son Peter and Kelly, Francie, and Y.T. Pete, Kelly, and I had bashed from the Rim to the River and back on this day, though we seem to be feeling no pain at this point. Incidentally, Sue's father, as Lt. Ralph Cary, flew 68 missions as a bombardier with the Martin B-26 equipped 323rd B.G., 8th and 9th A.F., between July '43 and August '44.

Despite having been bilked out of flying P-38s or B-17s during the Big One by my parent's procrastination, I have been an airplane enthusiast all of my life. Two early stimuli were those prewar StromBecKer kits (I still recall having rendered the China Clipper, Bell Airacuda, Curtiss A-18A, YB-17, and Boeing Stratoliner.) and evocative airplane paintings on the back of my Kellogs Corn Flakes boxes. As related in SB!, my first coherent memory of "scratch building" was in 1940, when I built a lead propeller equipped HAWK P-40. But, based upon archeological fragments in the garage, I had previously attempted a P-26A, P6E, and others.

Also related in SB! was the impact of seeing the "Me 109"(Werke Nr.1190, "Weiss 4" of 4/JG 26) brought down on 30 September 1940 and exhibited in Houston the following year during a Bundles for Britain drive.

I built solid models in great profusion throughout the War years and until 1950, when college impinged. Occasional production resumed after marriage, culminating in 1/24th scale SPITFIRE, HURRICANE, and Bf 109E "solids."

Then, in 1969, I met George Lee at the Stanford Linear Accelerator, where we both worked. By 1975 he had me scratchbuilding in plastic—an affliction from which I have yet to recover.

INTRODUCTION

Incredible (ridiculous) as it may seem: construction of my 1/24th scale De Havilland DH9A "NINAK" spanned nine years! Sure, during this period, I also rendered a complex pencil drawing, which took most of 1991; wrote most of and produced SCRATCH BUILT! during '90 and '91; completed a statistical study of the Battle of Britain, which consumed many hours during '94 and '95 (whose results were published in the September '96 *Aeroplane Monthly*); committed 1,500 or so Luftwaffe loss records of my study from 3x5 cards to disc file, by the time-honored hunt and peck method; and edited SCRATCH BUILT!-II. Oh, yes, until 29 February '96, I worked for a living; and then moved to the Seattle area. Nevertheless, during this period I kept a meticulous daily diary of the DH9A project, which reveals that the total time investment was approximately 6,400 hours!!!

I began making the wings on 21 October 1989: they were almost completed by the 1990 IPMS/USA Nationals in 1990. Upon my return, I began the fuselage structure.

Then, between 1 and 19 September '90, I was in England, for the two-fold purpose of attending the Battle of Britain 50th Anniversary activities and of photographing the interior of the RAF Museum's DH9A (No.F1010)—the only survivor of the type. Incidentally, I also visited Peter Cooke in Sonning-on-Thames and Group Captain James Pelly-Fry of No. 88 Squadron, 2 Group RAF fame, in Bristol. Oh, yes, and I almost bought it out in Devonshire, driving my rental car on the wrong (right) side of a country road, having become complacent on motorways and dual carriageways.

De Havilland DH9A. My 1/24th scale model depicts H3510, "L" of No. 8 Squadron RAF, based at Hinaidi, Iraq ("Mespot"), circa 1926. Ministry of Defence (MoD) photo #H101 was my guide and inspiration for this particular aircraft: a framed, glossy 11x15 inch print of this magnificent, evocative shot hung over my workbench for most of the project. I have long admired this handsome and purposeful-looking aircraft. While appearing only in the last two or three months of W.W.-I, it soldiered on through much of the next decade, both at home and "policing the Empire" in the Middle East, Egypt, and India, along with its workhorse stablemate, the Bristol F2B. Aside from the opportunity to depict their grungy, weatherbeaten appearance, part of the appeal of these "Empire" machines was the profusion of impedimentia with which they were festooned. Witness the extra radiator; auxiliary, top wing-mounted petrol tank; spare tire; picket stakes (strapped to the underwing skids); and underbelly stores basket. Additional interest to me was the Anglo-American connection provided by its LIBERTY 12 engine. (Michael Cole photo)

From then until year's end I prepared a detailed, multi-view interior structure/equipment drawing of the DH9A fuselage, based upon RAF Museum-supplied archival documents, my photos and those of Pete McDermott. These, recently traced in ink by Doug Carrick, are to appear in a forthcoming WINDSOCK DATAFILE on the DH9A, to supplement Doug's exterior general arrangement drawings.

"But, why the DH9A?", you might reasonably ask, and many have. Why not say the DH4, which was far more significant, at least during the Great War? Why lavish so much effort on an aircraft which barely made it into the War, only to soldier on for the next decade as a general-purpose workhorse in largely routine policing of the Empire and Protectorate Territories? In fact, I can't recall when, or exactly why I first became enamored of this aircraft. But, I have always thought it a handsome, purposeful, well-proportioned machine (no accounting for taste, as they say), and been fascinated by the great profusion of impedimentia with which it became encrusted during its service in the Middle East, India, and Egypt during the '20s. Then, too, its LIBERTY 12 engine provided an Anglo-American twist. Finally, the aluminum RAF paint schemes of the '20s and '30s have always appealed to me. But, the factor that pushed me over the edge in 1989 was the revelation that Doug Carrick had recently completed multi-view general arrangement drawings of the type, based upon the aforementioned archival material and thorough measurement of the RAF Museum's example. As for lavishing so much effort: in 1990, I never dreamed that I would still be hard at it eight years hence!

RESEARCH AND ARCHIVAL BASIS

As stated above, Doug Carrick's thoroughly researched general arrangement drawings formed the primary configuration basis for my model: conveniently, they were drawn to 1/24th scale. Second in importance was a photocopy of (RAF) AIR MINISTRY PUBLICATION 878: HANDBOOK ON THE DH 9A. AEROPLANE, obtained from the RAF Museum. These were supplemented by the HANDBOOK OF INSTALLATION OF LIBERTY ENGINE IN DE H. 9A and DE HAVILLAND AIRCRAFT CO. drawing No. 16241A: GENERAL ARRANGEMENT DH9A; SIDE ELEVATION dated 19 Dec. '22 (traced in Nov. '72 by Colin Owers), also from the RAF Museum. Finally, from this source I also obtained a

Another view of my NINAK. As related in the text, this project spanned nine years (1990-98) and took around 6,400 hours to construct! I completed it just in time for the 1998 IPMS/USA National Convention, held in Santa Clara, California, the first week of July. It was awarded Best Aircraft, Best Finish (a Testors award), and Best World War I Subject (Michael Fritz Memorial Award). In a shoot-out with the battleship USS *Texas*, by Derek Brown of Denver, it missed the George Lee Judges Grand Award by a vote of 54 to 51. Vickers and Lewis .303s against a 14 inch main battery—it just ain't fair. Besides, his wasn't even authentic—in the early '70s, I visited the *Texas* at the San Jacinto Battlefield site, and distinctly recall seeing a hot dog stand on the quarterdeck. (Michael Cole photo)

set of 12x16 inch prints of the BOOK OF ILLUSTRATIONS FOR THE DH9A AEROPLANES, dated October 1918. Then, from several sources (IWM, RAF Museum, Stuart Leslie, MoD), I gradually obtained an entire loose leaf notebook filled with fine 8x10 photo prints.

Pete McDermott of England kindly sent me an extensive set of color detail photos taken by him of the RAF Museum's F1010, taken as reference for his magnificent 1/8th scale RC model: these were an invaluable source throughout the project. Even so, I required more interior detail photos in order to adequately define the pilot's and gunner's compartments. These I took of F1010 in September 1990, with the generous assistance of the Museum staff.

Background reference on NINAK overseas operations, including numerous useful photos, was provided by PROFILE #248 and the book RAF OPERATIONS 1918-1938, both by Chaz Bowyer. The three part feature BY DAY AND BY NIGHT in *Aeroplane Monthly* (June-August '92), covering development and operations of the DH9A, was also of value in this respect.

During the course of the project, I occasionally had to seek further material on specific aspects and components. Details of the LIBERTY 12 engine were gleaned from a December 1918 *Aerial Age Weekly* report (obtained from the Stanford University Library); the 1919 JANES; WWI AERO No. 155 (via Jim Schubert), and from an actual example on display in Seattle's MUSEUM OF FLIGHT. AIR MINISTRY PUBLICATION 595: RIGGING NOTES of the DH9A AEROPLANE (courtesy of Alan Clark) provided some useful details. Harry Woodman came to the rescue when I had otherwise been unable to define the underwing Cooper Bomb Carriers (those on the RAF Museum's F1010 being incorrect for my subject). Finally, Doug Carrick and I corresponded voluminously regarding numerous detail configuration perplexes which emerged, especially during the early months (years!) of the project.

Having chosen to represent an aircraft in mid-20s overseas service, I selected H3510 of No. 8 Squadron, based in Iraq, for which my photo reference was Ministry of Defense (MoD) #H 101. A framed 10x14 inch print of this magnificent shot hung over my workbench throughout the project, as inspiration as well as reference. Such aircraft differed in many details from wartime examples such as the RAF Museum's F1010. Most obviously, aircraft in tropical service were equipped with a second radiator, projecting be-

Yet another view of the old NINAK. (Michael Cole photo)

Rib/Spar/Skin Wings-1: Here we see a rib being cut from a 20 thou plastic blank, using the brass template on a basswood cutting board; all pinned down to a balsa block. Pin holes (later enlarged to spar size) were predrilled into the rib blanks.

neath the engine compartment. By this time, the wartime wicker pilot's seat had given way to a metal bucket type, for accommodation of an Irvin parachute (developed and patented by an American named Irving!) Also, post war, the horizontal tail plane had been modified, and the landing gear was of a split-axle type. The purpose of a corkscrew looking affair lashed to the wing tip skids of most tropical NINAKs eluded me until one day, while idly browsing through Ray Rimell's RAF BETWEEN THE WARS, I chanced across a photo (#93) showing a tropical survival kit for aircraft in Middle East service: these things were picket stakes, to be screwed into the sandy ground for tying the aircraft down against desert winds. Other overseas impedimenta included an extra 28 imperial gallon petrol tank, slung from the starboard upper wing; a spare wheel, usually attached beneath the fuselage; and a large "stores basket," also beneath the fuselage, used for stowage of the crew's "kit" and such.

Rib/Spar/Skin Wings-2: Beside the previously pictured assemblage, we see a complete set of top wing ribs, assembled upon stub brass tube spars. This set is block-sanded, with several "shuffles," to produce fully uniform ribs. O.K., so there are only two holes in the brass template, yet three spar stubs through the rib package. I have no explanation.

I have dwelt upon this research in some detail in order to provide a feel for the amount of such effort generally required by scratchbuilders, particularly for the arcane subjects to which we tend to be attracted.

WINGS: RIB/BRASS SPAR/EMBOSSED SKIN METHOD

Since I began construction with the wings, this is where I will begin. They caused me by far the most grief: ultimately, I made three sets!: the first to 1/32nd scale, before conversion to 1/24th. (George Lee even urged me to jump ship again—to 1/16th scale!) In 1990, I constructed the first 1/24th scale set, using the rib, brass spar, and embossed polystyrene skin technique which I had learned from George. This method had served me well for the 1/16th scale Laird SUPER SOLUTION, built for the NASM in 1975. However, it is seen at its best today in George's awesome 1/32nd scale KEYSTONE B4A at the U.S. Air Force Museum, Wright-Patterson AFB. While I explained this technique thoroughly in SB!, I include it again here, so that MSB does not rely too heavily upon the former for completeness.

The wing structure closely follows that of the real thing. Basically, it consists of plasticard ribs mounted onto (usually) two brass tubing spars: it also includes leading (and usually, trailing) edge strips and tip pieces. The skin is flat plasticard, with the rib locations embossed on the inside surface.

Here we are afforded a glimpse into the NINAK crew's quarters: officer's country forward; ratings aft. Early on, I lavished much effort on the deep interior—most of which is scarcely visible to the observer. But, I had all of those photos which I had taken of the RAF Museum's F1010, so just couldn't contain myself. The Lewis gun, with its functional Norman Vane Sight (well, it does rotate if you blow on it), is my favorite part of the model. In the text, you'll read—if you get that far before falling asleep—that the fuselage roundel is seen here in its third incarnation! (Michael Cole photo)

RIBS: Let's consider the usual case, in which all, or most of, the ribs are identical. A template is required which can be used for cutting out all of the ribs from plasticard stock (typically 20 thou). The best template material is 10 thou brass sheet: it's tough to cut out with a knife, so we prefer to rough it out with shears and file down to exact shape. The template should be slightly smaller than the full airfoil shape, to account for thickness of the skin. However, some allowance must be made for collective block-sanding of the cut ribs (see below). So, make it about 5 thou undersize all around.

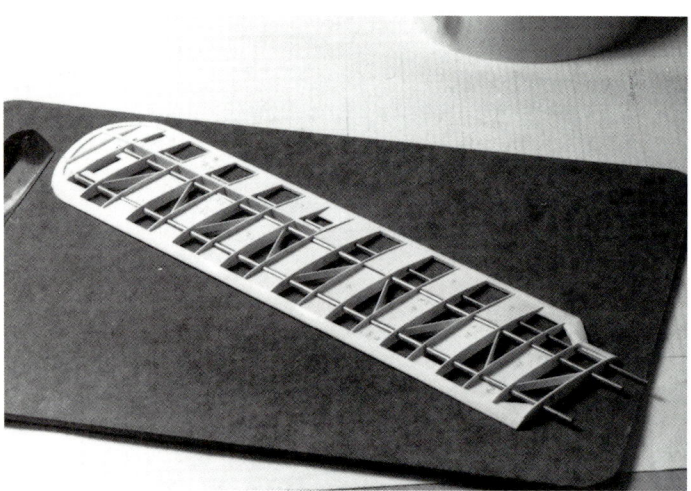

Rib/Spar/Skin Wings-3: Here we have a completed NINAK wing structure, replete with interrib shear panels and braces—probably an unnecessary precaution, as explained in the text. Now I remember: the third, smaller diameter aft spar was added primarily to stiffen the aileron.

Wing Skin Embossment-1. Rib locations are carefully marked in pencil on the underside of the plasticard skin blank. As shown here, the skin leading edge is pressed against a drafting triangle, which is clamped on a clipboard. Another triangle is located over the rib location tic-mark, with its right angle edge against that of the clamped triangle. The line is then drawn with a sharpened #2H drafting pencil. When all of the rib (and leading edge false rib) locations have been drawn, the same setup can be used to emboss the ribs. (Francie Alcorn photo)

Also, the chord should be undersize to allow for the trailing edge seam joining the upper and lower shells. In fact, the leading edge—and trailing edge, if appropriate—should be cut off to later accept the plastic strips. Select spar locations and drill a pin hole in the template at each.

Cut out the requisite number of rib blanks (plus a few extras) from 20 thou styrene sheet. Drill two holes in each rib blank, using the brass template as a guide. Then, one by one, pin the template down over the rib blank, which is backed by a basswood strip to serve as a "cutting board." This assemblage is mounted upon a thick balsa block which serves as a base and receptacle for the straight pins (see photo). The same two vertical "post-holes" in the balsa block should be used for all ribs.

Holding the template firmly down against the blank, cut out the rib with a No. 11 blade held vertically. After all of the ribs are cut out, drill out the spar holes using successively larger drills—the pin holes serve as the "center punch."

Feed all of the ribs onto one brass spar (or shorter tube section of the same diameter). Pack them tightly together and ream the other hole with the full size drill. Now, insert the second brass tube section. You now have a "solid" (actually, laminated) wing segment of length equal to the total rib thickness. It is probably damn tight, so it should hold together for the next step.

Block sand the rib pack: If you've cut them properly oversize, all should be sanded before you reach the final rib size and shape. The ribs should be removed from the brass tubes and shuffled two or three times during the block sanding process, to ensure uniformity.

LEADING AND TRAILING EDGES: A leading edge strip is always required. Trailing edge strips may not be added to certain thin wings, such as those with scalloped edges (wire stretched between ribs on the actual aircraft). Such strips are made from thick (40, even 60 thou) styrene strip, sometimes laminated to form "stepped" back edges. While rather a tedious process, both leading and trailing edge strips should be fully contoured in cross-section before wing assembly. This is best achieved by block sanding the strip, which is supported along its length by a table edge (or equivalent). For bulkier leading edge strips, this process can be preceded by careful "whittling" with a No. 11 blade.

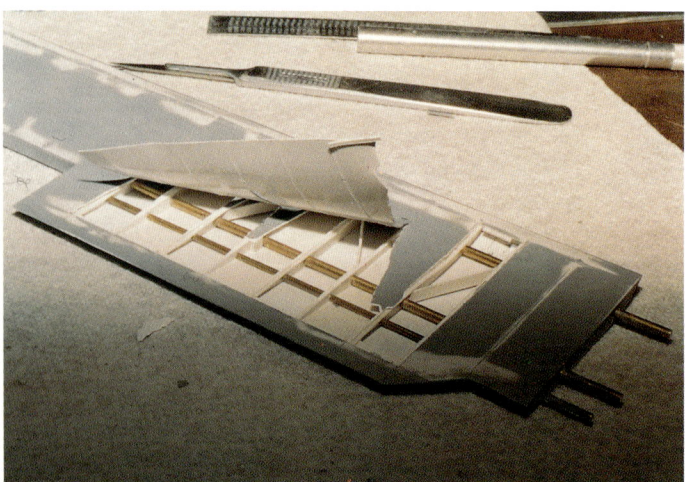

Rib/Spar/Skin Wings-4: This scene of carnage depicts the bitter end of my long, painful, and ultimately failed attempt to save my rib/spar/skin wings. I was beginning to de-skin them (again) when I realized that I must start anew, using the Ron Lowry wood core method—having recently seen his RE-8 at the 1996 IPMS/USA Nats. I wish to emphasize, however, that my failure on this model should not be construed as condemnation of this approach. These just got away from me, for reasons explained in the text. - *Abusus non tollit usum*

Wing Skin Embossment-2. Here a rib is being embossed. With one hand, the floating triangle is firmly held in place, care being taken to ensure that both it and the skin are against the edge of the clamped triangle. With the tool held perpendicular to the edge of the floating triangle, embossing is performed with one firm, smooth stroke. I learned that coating the pencil lines with (the edge of) a bar of dry bath soap allowed the embossing to proceed without danger of "hanging up" on the plastic surface. All strokes are facilitated by good lubrication. (Francie Alcorn photo)

SKIN: The rib embossing technique is discussed below, in the section WINGS: WOOD CORE/EMBOSSED SKIN METHOD.

STRUCTURE ASSEMBLY: I have found that it is best to assemble the wing structure directly on a print of the wing drawing. First, feed the ribs onto the two brass tube spars cut to the appropriate length. The ribs at the aileron locations must be cropped further, to receive trailing edge strips. After cropping, these ribs should be assembled upon two short brass tubes for block sanding of their trailing edges, to ensure perfect uniformity. Then feed them out on the actual wing spars. Very accurately mark the rib locations on the leading edge strips. Then, place the leading edge on the drawing and tape it down along its leading edge, so that during the assembly process, the wing structure can be rotated up ("hinged") for certain local gluing, and then laid back down with perfect registry.

Shear Panels: In the standard George Lee approach (see photo of his Keystone wing structure), the ribs are constrained longitudinally only by attachment to the leading and trailing edge strips: as the upper skin is applied, each rib can be moved slightly with tweezers until it slips into its embossment groove. I (Alcorn) found that this worked splendidly for my robust Laird Super Solution wings (see photos). Use of interrib shear panels is a "belt and suspenders" option for stiffening the structure and locking the ribs into position before skin attachment. In this case, the skin embossments must *exactly* match the rib locations beforehand: a non-trivial "quality control" operation. I used shear panels for the thin-ribbed wings of my NINAK (see photo). Prepare interrib "shear" panels (20 thou stock) whose width is cut precisely to the rib spacing less one rib thickness. As shown in the accompanying photo of the NINAK wing, interrib shear panels should be installed at every other bay, to later allow access to every rib for gluing on the upper skin. Note that three shear panel sections will be installed at each strengthened bay: leading edge, trailing edge, and inter spar.

Aileron Features: After the wing trailing edge strip at the aileron location has been installed, lightly glue in place a spacer strip to provide the proper wing to aileron gap when later removed. To it then lightly attach a third strip, which will become the aileron leading edge. Then, carefully shorten the rib rear portions which were previously cropped. The aileron structure is completed by installing these between the leading edge strip and the wing trailing edge, which *has not* been severed from the wing inboard region.

Wing Tip: For the tip structure of the NINAK, I added a 30 thou shaped piece, notched to receive the spar ends, as shown in the photo. It is MEK'd to the leading and trailing edge strips, as well as to the last true rib. "Fake" rib pieces are added to support the embossed top skin at the outermost rib location.

The completely assembled wing structure should be lightly and carefully block-sanded to ensure that the ribs are all flush with the leading/trailing edge strips. Some time during all this, add hard points for anchoring the interplane/cabane struts, etc.

The skin can be faired into the leading edge strip by providing a longitudinal step in the strip, or by overlapping the skin and later feathering it to the leading edge by block sanding.

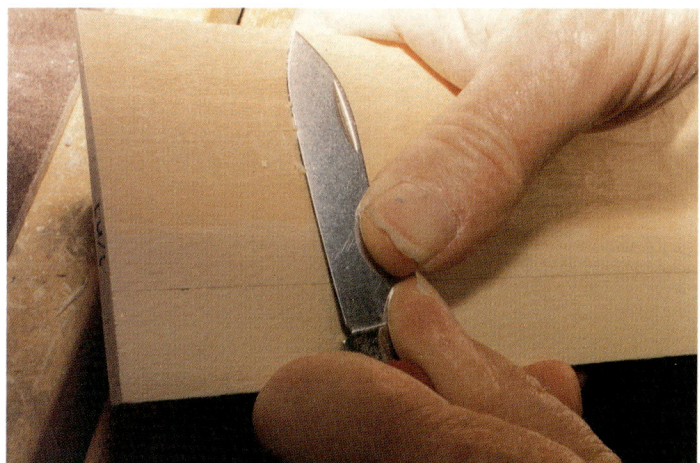

Wood Core Wings-1: Carving the basswood cores.

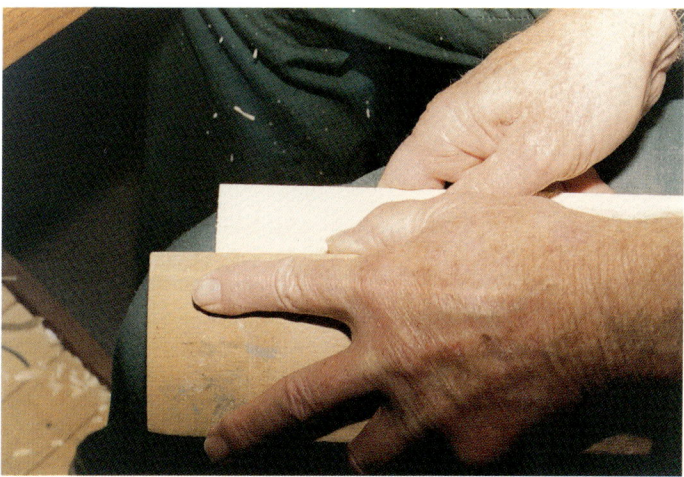

Wood Core Wings-2: Block sanding a basswood core.

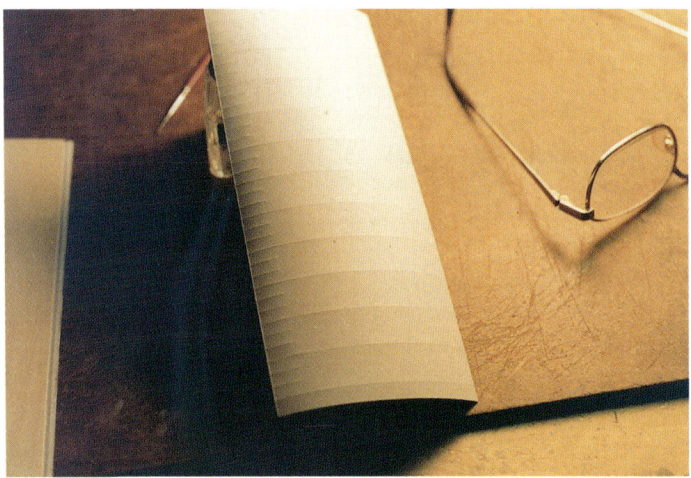

Wood Core Wings-3: Top skin of the test section, showing rib embossments.

Wood Core Wings-4: Core and skin of my test section. Prior to wing production, I made this section to verify, and refine, my technique, based upon Ron Lowry's explanation. At his suggestion, I added 5 thou thick (by 30 thou wide) plastic strips over each embossment, as shown: this caused each to stand well proud of the basswood core when attached. A lesson learned with the test section was that each 5 thou strip must be feathered fore and aft, so as not to leave an unsightly bump at its ends.

UPPER SKIN INSTALLATION: The upper skin is first glued to the wing root rib. Very careful fitting is required at this point to assure that the skin embossments are matched exactly with the rib/leading edge locations—and that the fore to aft alignment is perfect. Once this has been achieved, the skin can be brought down against the structure, and MEK'd into place from the underside, rib-by-rib. Sounds so simple, but there are pitfalls other than misalignment. One is warping of the wing due to stresses induced by the skin and effect of the MEK on the leading/trailing edge strips. So, wing straightness must be checked during skin application, and the wing taped down to a flat surface as it dries.

LOWER SKIN INSTALLATION: Installation of the wing underside skin presents a special challenge, particularly if the airfoil is cambered. The main difficulty, of course, is that the ribs are inaccessible for gluing, except by peeling back the skin, with the attendant risk of cracking or distortion.

Begin attachment at the inboard rib, alignment precautions being taken as for the upper skin. Progress outward one rib at a time, allowing five minutes or more between each for initial drying. Gently but firmly press against the prior rib with the thumb of your "holding" hand. Pull back the skin just enough to allow brush

Wood Core Wings-5: Core and top skin of the starboard lower wing. Note the plastic leading edge of the core, and previously attached underside skin extending beyond the core trailing edge. The wing inboard edge is capped with a plastic rib: this is so that no wood is exposed on the finished wing—even if it will not be visible. I wanted to completely seal the core, to prevent long-term dryout of both wood and contact cement.

Wood Core Wings-6: Here the critical maneuver of this technique is about to take place. Both mating surfaces have been liberally coated with contact cement—except along their leading edges. The leading edge of the core will be pressed against that of the skin, which will bear against a 1/2 inch thick basswood sheet. This is, in turn, restrained by two piles of barbell weights. Pencil tic marks on the core leading edge are registered with the juxtaposed skin rib embossments. Unfortunately, the flash obliterated the skin embossment/strip overlay features.

Wood Core Wings-7: The Moment of Truth! The skin is being brought down against the core. Once the contact cement begins grabbing, there's no turning back.

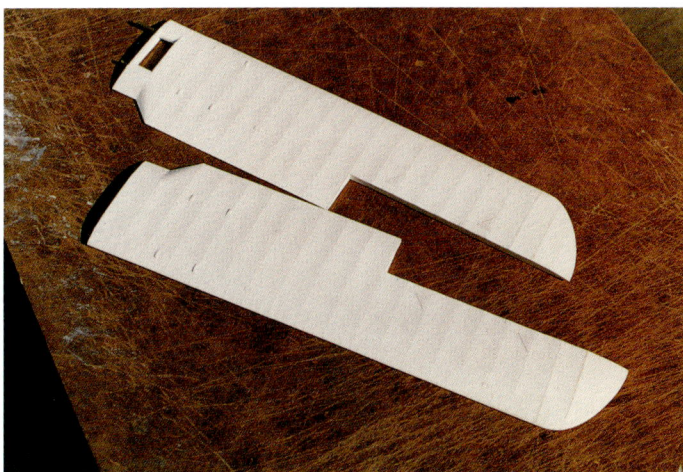

Wood Core Wings-8: The completed lower wings.

access to the next rib. The thoughtful reader will note that three hands are thus required for this operation. Should you be blessed with but two, the skin can be held back by a table edge, or some such projection.

For brushing the rib underside edges, Testors (or equivalent) Plastic Cement is recommended. While it contains MEK, it is less volatile, drying more slowly. Apply it copiously along the rib edge, taking care to neither touch the skin, or let a drop fall onto the skin elsewhere in the interrib cell.

Underside Billowing Representation: For the underwing skin, I embossed the outside surface in a vain attempt to represent the interrib billowing sometimes observed on vintage aircraft having strongly cambered wings. This proved disastrous: these interrib cells were more uneven than even those of the top surfaces. Here—after the fact—closer scrutiny of my photo references revealed that for the DH4, DH9, and DH9A, any such interrib billowing was so slight as to be ignored. So, eventually (1994), I tore off the underside skins, replacing them with unembossed sheet.

THE MOMENT OF TRUTH: By the time of my departure for the 1996 IPMS/USA Nationals in Virginia Beach, I had become thoroughly disenchanted with the wings: discouraged in fact over my inability to rectify the top surface deficiencies.

I was head judge of the SCRATCH BUILT AIRCRAFT categories, among which was Ron Lowry's lovely 1/24th scale RE-8 (which was awarded BEST AIRCRAFT and, very nearly the JUDGES GRAND AWARD). Commented upon favorably by all of us fellow scratch builders was his very neat and effective treatment of the wing upper surfaces: the rib locations were crisp, and the interrib catenaries were even and correctly curved. At this point, I knew that I must scrap my NINAK wings, and defer to his technique, whatever it was.

At this juncture, I must relate another revelation regarding Ron's RE-8, about which I still have not intellectually come to grips. Following the judging, while inquiring about his wing construction method, I casually asked how long the model had taken him to

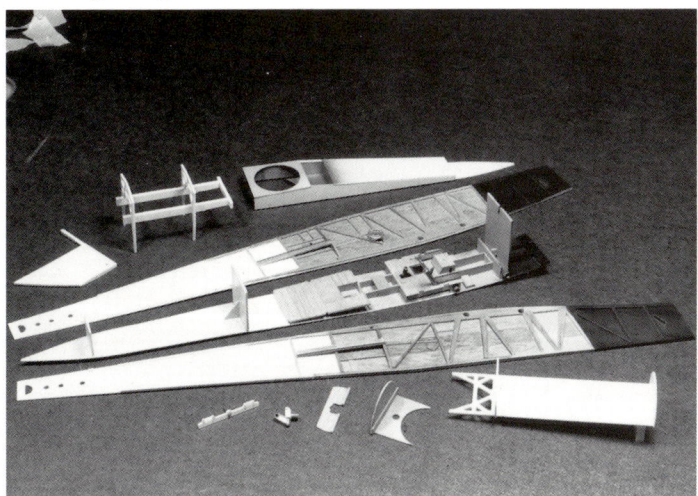

NINAK Fuselage Components-1: These are the basic "subassemblies" of the fuselage.

NINAK Fuselage Components-2: Here the port side panel has been temporarily mated to the bottom one, a process repeated countless times during fit-up.

build. "Oh, about three months" was his reply. Needless to say, I was utterly overwhelmed by this response, since I had already invested around 3,500 hours on my DH9A, which was two years (as it transpired) from completion. Bear in mind that his and my models are both to the same scale, and are both WWI vintage, two seat, single-engine biplanes of similar complexity. Later, while interrogating him by phone regarding further details of his wing construction, he volunteered that in fact, his total time investment had been about 350 hours. To this day, I can't imagine how he does it.

WINGS: WOOD CORE/EMBOSSED SKIN METHOD
The following description is of how I made my third and final set of DH9A wings, using the general technique outlined by Ron Lowry. Basically, this employs rib-embossed plasticard sheet ("skin") glued to a hardwood core. It is generically similar to that described by Harry Woodman in his (still useful) SCALE MODEL AIRCRAFT In Plastic Card, though with numerous refinements.

CORES: Step one (aside from careful planning, following multi-phone call consultation with Ron Lowry) was carving the wing panel cores, from basswood. I performed initial rough shaping to the airfoil section with a sharp knife (a VICTORINOX Swiss Army, in this case): final truing was done with large sanding blocks, the underside camber being obtained using a convex-curved one.

I added polystyrene strip to the leading and trailing edges, by the simple expedient of attaching with liquid plastic cement generously flowed into the wood/plastic joint, after which the two were pressed tightly together by hand for a few minutes, then left to thoroughly dry. Epoxy could, of course, have been used, but my method proved strong enough—and far less messy. Also, note from the photos that I added plastic elements to the tips and roots as deemed appropriate to ensure a plastic-to-plastic bond all around.

SKIN: The 20 thou plasticard "skin" was embossed at the rib locations in the same manner as for the George Lee rib/brass spar/embossed skin method. I used a Gestetner SP3 tool, having a 30 thou diameter ball end. I carefully laid out the rib locations on the sheet underside with pencil, using a right (90°) plastic triangle, with one edge guided by another set against the skin leading edge. Embossing was done with the marked skin lying on a manila file folder, which was in turn resting upon a smooth, flat table surface. Although I had previously used the two triangle method for guiding the embossing tool, I ultimately preferred holding a single triangle firmly in place, as I firmly and evenly ran the tool along its edge and over the pencil line. Previously, I had always experienced some difficulty with the embossing ball "hanging up" (unevenly dragging) on the sheet surface. This I solved by rubbing the edge of a dry facial soap bar over the penciled lines before embossing. This time, only the upper skins were embossed.

At Ron's suggestion, I added 10 x 30 thou plastic strips over each embossment, lightly liquid glued in place. This caused each embossment to stand well proud of the wood core, yielding the proper amount of interrib catenary. I learned that each such strip should be gently tapered in thickness at each end, so as not to leave a surface "hump" as the sheet came off the strips near the leading and trailing edges. After attachment of these "embossment raisers," the trailing edge of the skin was carefully feathered out with a sanding block, the skin edge being placed along the sharp edge of a table, or long wood block. Partial feathering of the leading edge of the skins is also necessary, in order to yield the desired "sharpness" without having to sand down the outside surface, beyond a slight finish rounding.

The skin edges which would later be juxtaposed to the plastic edges of the core were masked so as not to receive contact cement (see next section).

ATTACHMENT OF SKIN TO CORE: This is the crucial and most harrowing aspect of this technique, requiring careful planning, great care, practice, and no little luck. What makes it so crucial is the use of contact cement, since once the coated surfaces touch, there is no retreat, or even adjustment. Yet, on balance, contact cement is probably the best choice of adhesives, since it is strong, (hopefully) permanent, and—once mastered—instant, no subsequent movement becoming an asset (as with super glue).

Each surface is painted with contact cement; liberally and evenly, though not thickly. The bare wood core surface should be painted twice, since the first coat is mostly absorbed by the wood. The plastic edge portions of the core should be masked, so that no contact cement gets on them: likewise the opposing portions of the skin. The coated surfaces should then sit for 15-20 minutes, by which time they are no longer wet, yet still tacky.

The (plastic strip) leading edge of the core should be placed against a straight, vertical surface, preferably on a table top. As seen in the accompanying photo, for this bearing edge I used a 1/2" thick board, backed with barbell weights to keep it from slipping. The leading edge of the skin is then placed against that of the core, with the skin nearly vertical. Spanwise alignment is achieved by matching pencil tic marks on both core and skin underside. Chordwise alignment, so that the leading edges are registered along their entire length, is the challenging aspect. Part of the challenge is that the embossments distort and weaken the skin, which tends to pucker out at each. I tried several tricks, but ultimately had the best luck simply with my fingers, holding the skin against the core at six or eight points along its length (thumbs not being available for this purpose). Once the skin edge is firmly pressed down onto the core leading edge all along its length (and bearing against the retaining block vertical edge, which prevents embossment puckering), begin to bring the skin down against the core. The thumbs give some reflex curve to the skin trailing edge, preventing it from prematurely contacting the core. Once laying down of the skin against the core begins, it can be completed very quickly. However, I did not press the skin down tightly until I had flipped it and the core over and rolled the skin against the core on a flat table surface. I was concerned that the core may otherwise be slightly twisted: a condition which could not be corrected once the skin was firmly in place. Then, with the thumbs, press the skin down against the core, from front to back, and between each rib location.

I chose to attach the underside skin first, on the premise that this is easier and would provide added stiffness of the core for upper skin attachment. After attachment, the exposed top surface of the underside skin trailing edge (extending beyond the core) should be feathered by block sanding, to follow the core contour.

If—heaven forbid—a skin has been misapplied, it must simply be ripped off of the core immediately. While it will destroy the skin, the core surface can be wiped reasonably clean with contact cement thinner (which I never found) or lacquer thinner. Did I ever do this? Is the Pope Catholic?

TIPS AND ROOTS: I carved the tip and root features into the wood cores, adding some plastic elements, as evident in the accompanying photographs.

The tips posed a vexing problem for the skin, due to their double curved nature. I finally settled upon first attaching the constant airfoil (single curved) main portion of the top skin, as described above; and then adding the tip portion, previously severed from the rest of the skin at the outermost full chord rib location. This worked fine, except that it required later reconstruction of the bifurcated embossment. The relatively slight distortions of the underskin tip were accommodated without severance. The pictured root contours were achieved by slitting the skin part way forward at the second rib location. Note that, in this region, trailing edge plastic elements were added to the wood core.

SPAR PROJECTIONS: It was necessary to provide two brass spar stubs projecting from each outer wing panel root, for insertion into the next-larger-size tube receptacles embedded in the fuselage (lower wings) and upper wing center section. All this to simulate the wing spar extensions of the George Lee rib/brass spar/embossed skin technique.

This was "simply" a matter of very carefully drilling spanwise holes in each core root, into which a brass spar stub was epoxied. Having made no proper jigging fixture for this operation, I experienced considerable difficulty in drilling these holes straight, and at the precise locations (as Ronald Reagan's aides later confessed, "Mistakes were made.")

FINISHING: Once the two skins have been attached to the core well enough to be lived with (perfection is an elusive goal, especially for this process), liquid cement can be wicked into the leading and trailing edge interfaces. Along the latter, the edge must be pressed down hard against a flat surface, to ensure avoidance of waviness.

Once these joints have dried, final thinning, contouring, and straightening of the leading and trailing edges can be achieved by block sanding. I found that, despite my best efforts, I had to add a small EVERGREEN polystyrene strip along the leading edges in order to produce a sharp enough contour—otherwise, I would have had to sand off too much of the forward portion of the rib (and false rib) embossments. Fortunately, I was able to restore the proper chord depth by sanding off a proportionate amount of trailing edge (20 thou), sharpness being restored by further block sanding of the underside rear (which had no embossments).

Yet, some detail restoration of embossments still proved necessary. This was (tediously) accomplished by building up with polystyrene "paste," supplemented later with gray auto primer, then carefully sanded to blend with the intact embossments.

TOP WING CENTER SECTION: This component posed an especial problem, due primarily to the necessarily precise location and orientation (spanwise and dihedral) of the brass tube receptacles for the wing spar stubs. As it transpired, it was a nightmare, requiring several corrections to misdrilled holes, following epoxy (partial) filling. In fact, the first attempt was an abject failure!

Incidentally, this element had been somewhat easier using the rib/spar/skin technique, since the end holes were precisely defined by the prefabricated ribs. You might wonder: "Why didn't he just use the old one?" The sordid truth is that, in addition to all the other problems encountered with the rib/spar/skin wings, I made their airfoil too thick!—so that their center section didn't match that of the new wood core outer panels.

FUSELAGE

This process was also featured in SB!(-I), since the basic fuselage had been completed by the time it went to press. Again, I repeat the procedure, including photo illustrations, for the sake of completeness.

SLAB-SIDED PRIMARY STRUCTURE: I began by cutting out and trimming two fuselage side profiles, from the top longitudinal stringer down, in 30 thou plasticard sheet. I then added the simulated interior structure (longitudinal, vertical, and diagonal members) to the inside of each profile, as shown in the accompanying illustrations. The lower longitudinal stringer was set back from the profile bottom edge by 30 thou, the thickness of the fuselage underside.

The fuselage underside profile was then cut from 30 thou stock, 30 thou undersize along each edge, so that when mated with the sides, the overall fuselage width would be correct. Then the two bottom keel pieces were shaped and added: atop them were set the fully detailed floorboards of the pilot's and gunner's compartments.

NINAK Fuselage Components-3: The intent here is to reveal the simulated surface features of the side panels: plywood skin warpage; fabric panel wrinkling; and brass wire stubs to serve as lacing hooks.

Between the pilot's floorboard and the fuselage underside, the brass tube sockets for the lower wing spars were installed, projecting slightly, so as to later pass through mating 90 thou diameter holes cut in the side profiles. Precise location and alignment of these sockets was essential, needless to say. Proper dihedral was provided by cutting each brass tube element at its mid-point—not quite through, and bending at that point. Various plastic pieces were added to box in these sockets, after which epoxy was added for strength and rigidity. And, did it all work out as planned? Errr...sure, except that much later, during first assembly of the wings to the completed fuselage, I discovered that the sockets had been placed exactly 90 thou too far forward (i.e., one tube diameter)! Since by then there was no possibility of relocating the fuselage sockets, I was obliged to cut off the lower wing spar projections and add false spar projections, just forward of the existing spars and in through these ribs—requiring considerable surgery. Never mind that these wings were later scrapped.

But, you wonder: "How is it possible for an experienced modeller to make such a stupid mistake?" No trouble at all. (In fact, it had something to do with initial uncertainty over the amount of wing stagger, which had been resolved by the time of fuselage construction. But, old misunderstandings die hard.)

Then, as noted in the photos, three nonvisable (when completed) rectangular bulkheads were permanently attached to the fuselage bottom subassembly.

At this point, all of the fuselage side and bottom inner surfaces which would later be visible were painted. Since most represented varnished plywood, graining was (semi) dry-brushed with darker brown enamel (over the lacquer base color). Then, almost all other interior details were added, including rudder bars (fore and aft), control sticks (fore and aft), throttle controls, tail plane incidence wheel, etc. Though not evident in the photos, cable runs were added.

During fuselage construction, seemingly endless test fitting was performed, to minimize problems during final assembly. Nevertheless, they still occurred.

Prior to permanent attachment of the side panels to the bottom subassembly, I added features to the exterior surface. These included simulated moisture warpage of the plywood panels, wrinkling of the fabric panels, and representation of their lacing and grommets. My techniques for producing these features are described later in this chapter, under FINISHING: SURFACE FEATURES.

NINAK Fuselage Components-4: This detail of the floor areas shows the dual controls with which the type was fitted. Also, we see a small window in the pilot's floor—to see if the undercarriage was still there?

As noted in the accompanying photographs, there are two additional fuselage internal structural elements. One is the engine bearers and their associated transverse formers, which dimensionally stabilized the engine compartment, as well as later supporting the LIBERTY 12. The other is a long transverse shelf plus two partial bulkheads, which boxes in the upper fuselage between the engine compartment and cockpit. Note the carefully fretted piece projecting into the engine compartment: here I had begun detailing elements which would not be visible once the model was completed. Sanity returned before I fully detailed the engine itself, whose ultimate role was simply to support the exhaust manifolds and propeller.

UPPER FORWARD COAMING: This element, which extends from the radiator housing to the bulkhead just in front of the cockpit, capping the engine and petrol/oil tank bays, consumed around 170 hours during the course of the project.

Step one was carving the basswood form for vacuforming the coaming from 30 thou sheet stock. Its cross-section was constantly varying, from slab-sided with a triangular top at the front, to circular at the rear. Four bulkheads were added—a front, back, and two intermediates—for stiffness and accurate fit to adjoining elements. Contouring and trimming to mate with the then existing fuselage structure and radiator housing involved considerable trial and error, including detail refinement of the wood form and revacuforming.

The 22 small, plus one large, louvres took much of the time invested. I rough shaped each louvre from styrene stock, generating a concave surface on its underside with a half-round Swiss file. Each was attached over a precut and shaped hole in the coaming. Final outside shaping of each was performed after all had been attached, using Swiss files and sandpaper; the join seams having been filled with polystyrene paste, applied by brush and squeegeed in with the forefinger.

This coaming has many other penetrations, most of which required precise location and shape relative to the penetrating element. The odd shaped cabane strut cutouts, for example, totally constrained these elements (along with socket holes in the fuselage top decking and top wing center section), so that no external jig (fixture) was later required. Other penetrations requiring precise location included those for the engine carburetor air intakes; wind-driven petrol pumps; and cabane transverse, diagonal rigging wires.

All of the above, plus panel line scribing, nail pattern indentations, and post-painting addition of photoetched brass piano hinges, translated to a component of major challenge and complexity.

PILOT'S COCKPIT COAMING: The shell of this element was also vacuformed over a basswood form. The cutout for the pilot required careful shaping: after doing so, preshaped 10 thou stiffeners were added around the side and rear periphery, inside and out. Bulkheads were added ahead of the pilot (to later support the instrument panel) and between the pilot and gunner's compartment.

The final challenge was to shape the thickened pilot's coaming edge, in order to simulate the rather wrinkled leather padding. Once this was accomplished in a satisfying manner, 10 thou holes were drilled along the outer edge of the padding, through which fine nylon monofilament "lacing" was threaded after painting of the "leather." Another complex part. (In fact, I made two of these things, including the leather coaming and installation. I eventually realized that the first was too short!)

REAR DECKING: This "subassembly" was very easy. Top and side profiles were cut from 30 thou stock, and assembled with several rectangular bulkheads. The forward top piece has a one inch diameter opening for the gunner, which near the end of the project received the Scarff Ring assembly. The underside of the decking was fitted with an underwidth profile, which nested within the rear fuselage upper longerons at assembly. Also at assembly the forward portion of the decking sides were integrated with the rearward projections of the pilot's coaming.

FUSELAGE ASSEMBLY: Once the main fuselage bottom and side elements were completed, including interior painting and addition of most interior details, they were permanently joined together. Also installed at this point were the engine bearer unit; shelf/bulkhead element over the petrol/oil tank compartments; and rear decking. Then, the remaining cockpit and gunner's compartment fittings were added. This was followed by installation of the cockpit coaming, after it had been painted inside and fitted with the instrument panel. At this point, the fuselage was a fully boxed structure.

TAIL ELEMENTS

Basically, these are dead simple, using the George Lee method.

Each surface profile is cut out in 40 thou plasticard: rudder, fin, stabilizer, elevators. Polystyrene strip, say 20 x 60 thou, is applied along the hinge edge of each. Then, small plastic strips of the appropriate width and height are glued down at each rib location (use EVERGREEN precut strip). Each side is now block-sanded down to the cross-section (airfoil) contour, allowance being made for the skin thickness. For the rudder and elevators, the trailing edge should be "sharp," and 40-50 thou undersize in profile.

The opposing 15 thou skins are embossed at the rib locations in the now traditional manner. The profile should be cut slightly oversize (30 thou) along all edges, and the trailing edges of the fin and rudder skins feathered out on the inside, so that when glued in place they will be near sharp.

Liquid glue is liberally applied on the ribs of the core piece and the skin quickly set in place. After the opposing skin has been set in place, liquid glue is wicked into all edges, the trailing edges then being pressed down against a flat table surface.

This wonderfully simple technique should be entirely appropriate for the wings of many small (1/48th and 1/72nd scale) aircraft.

For the NINAK, I made the hinges for all of the movable control surfaces in the following manner. The fixed (forward) edge elements are "eye pins," filed from 10 thou brass strip (the hole being drilled, of course, with a pin vise). The mating elements on the forward edge of the movable surfaces are basically the same, but with a 20 thou brass wire stub superglued into the hole. The resulting hinges are fine—almost like the real ones—but at 20-30 minutes a piece for 50 pins, there went another three full working days of mind boggling tedia. Next time—if there is one—I'll have them photoetched.

PHOTOETCHED COMPONENTS

In retrospect, I can't imagine how I ever scratch built a model without custom-made photoetched parts. Certainly, I couldn't have rendered the NINAK without a great profusion of them. Ultimately, I had eight different sheets made, several sets of each. The cost? Non trivial. But then, I don't have to buy kits.

LEWIS GUN: For photoetching explanatory purposes, I will describe the sheet which I made/had made primarily for the 1/24th scale Lewis gun—since it features a method for producing certain three dimensional objects. Following much head scratching as to how best to make the body of the Lewis, I proceeded as follows: To 4 x scale, I drew four different lamina (two of each) of the housing

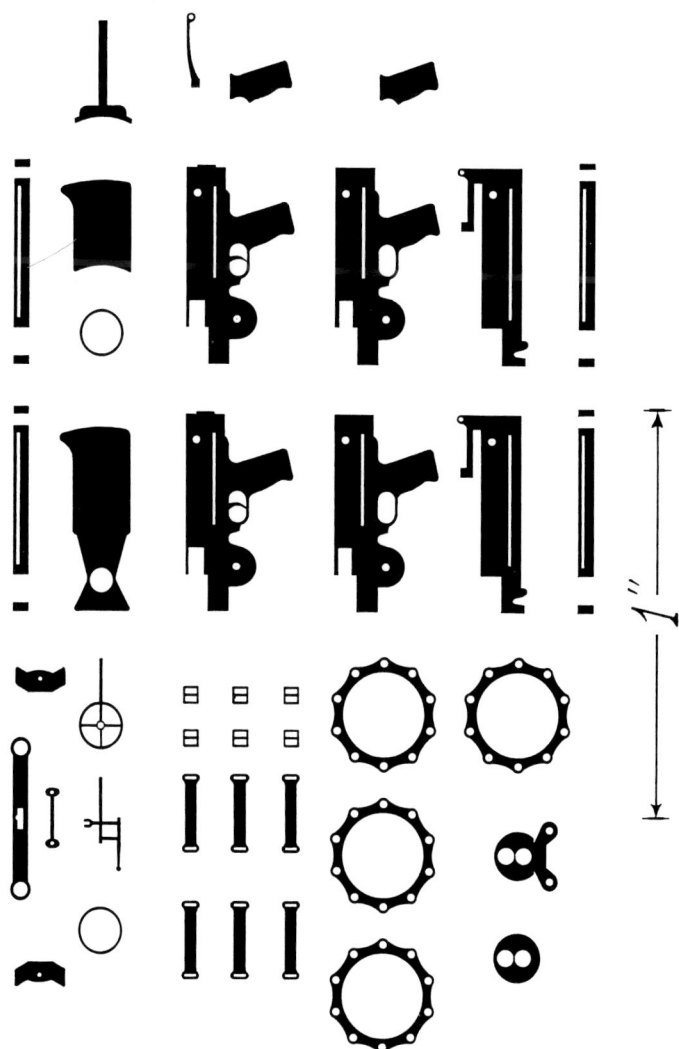

Photoetch elements for the Lewis Gun. Shown are the laminae, and other components of the housing; Norman Vane and ring sight pieces; plus attachments and buckles for the ammo drums. The four large "gaskets" are base flanges for the Liberty engine cylinders.

in side view, as shown in the accompanying figure, such that when assembled from centerplane outward, they would approximate its 3 dimensional shape. Pistol grip sideplates, top platform for the ammo can, Norman Vane sight and certain other bits were also drawn on the 9 x 12 inch Bristol Board, using India ink in a RAPIDOGRAPH pen (3X0, primarily). The big ring "gaskets" are for the Liberty engine. I sent this sheet off to FOTOCUT with appropriate instructions for material (brass), thickness (3 & 5 thou) and number of each. The returned 3 x 4 inch (actual design) sheets contained the exact pattern sent, but to 1/4 x scale and in brass, on a black rubber-like background. To achieve this, FOTOCUT had made a quarter size photo transparency of my "art work," as the shield for the etching process.

To begin making the housing, I first removed the laminae from the rubber backing by carefully picking each off with a #11 surgeon's blade—each is stuck pretty well and must not be bent during removal from the backing. Then—an important step—I set each on a double layer mat of kitchen toweling, in turn set upon a metal plate. With an eyedropper, I dribbled lacquer thinner over each lamina and soaked the folded end of a small toweling piece in the same solvent. Then, wearing a respirator and my trusty OPTIVISOR, I hunched over the assemblage and carefully wiped the hard (lacquer?) coating off of each lamina surface (both sides). With the light right, you can see the bare brass surfaces come clean of the coating—a must for subsequent use.

I began assembly of the housing by gluing the two inner laminae together (the ones with the trigger) using 5-minute epoxy. Fortunately, I had provided indexing holes in all but the outer laminae, through which I inserted 20 thou wire lengths. Once smushed together, with the pins in place, I began wiping off the excess epoxy—a messy, sticky job at best. Once the epoxy had begun to set up (crosslink), I withdrew the indexing wires and continued removal of the excess: mostly with bare fingers, wiped off after each pressing; and finally with lacquer thinner on a piece of toweling.

Then, one at a time, I added lamina to either side of this two-lamina core, including finally, the pistol grips. Once this basic housing was assembled, I carefully filed and sanded the edges so that the laminae were flush. The ammo drum base was then laminated (from the three components visible on the sheet, the top one of "T" shape) and glued in place atop the housing (and into the "slot" between the main portion and sight base of the outermost large housing laminae). Then, the two pieces at the front end of the housing were added: one with two support tabs, which must be bent 90°. Voila! A 3-dimensional Lewis gun housing, from two-dimensional brass photo etched laminae. While I'm probably not the first to have used this epoxy lamination technique, it was an independent "invention."

I made the barrel from 40 thou diameter brass tubing (HOBBY HANGER), tapered by "spin sanding" on a piece of 400 grit at the edge of my workbench: though time consuming and hard on the thumb and forefinger, it turned out fine. This was then inserted into the socket evident in the photoetch drawing and epoxied in place. The accompanying figure shows the completed Lewis gun before painting. Incidentally, the ammo drum (and spares in the gunner's compartment) was kindly resin cast, by Roy Southerland, from a master which I made from plastic, overlain with a photoetched spider to represent the radial stiffening ribs (see photo on p.81 of SB!.)

COWLING PIANO HINGES: These presented another challenge, handily met by photoetching. Numerous hinges, of three different sizes, allow opening and removal of the various metal and plywood panels on the upper forward cowling of the actual aircraft. Each hinge is a pair, with serrated, interlocking mating edges through which a wire is passed, and scalloped outer edges, with a hole pattern for attachment to the panel. Photoetching was the only hope for crisply providing these edge features, especially the interlocking serrations. In order to represent the (almost) cylindrical mating edges of an actual hinge, I settled for two-level photo etching, in which a second 2 thou layer is (somehow) superimposed on the

Lewis Gun. This all-brass 1/24th scale Lewis gun came out as well as any part of the model. As described in the text, the housing was laminated (with 5-minute epoxy) from a series of 5 thou photoetched profiles. The top ammo drum support, curved grip piece and front collar were also photoetched. The recoil tube and barrel are HOBBY HANGER tubing, the latter element having been tapered by (seemingly endless) spin-sanding. The "wood" grip was filed to shape from a length of brass tubing.

Scarff Ring. This was also made primarily from photoetched elements, and HOBBY HANGER tubing. The elevating arcs were rather challenging, both to draw with pen and ink (to 4x scale) and bend to shape. I invested considerable effort in designing, and constructing the base, so that the ring would rotate within the fixed portion. But, much later, when I sprayed it (with dark gray FLOQUIL), the paint got into the joint. Hence, it no longer rotates—what else did I expect?

basic shape, just along the projecting serrations. For the hinges, I provided two sets of pen and ink "artwork": one of the basic hinge elements; plus an overlay which was simply an array of dashed lines, precisely located to match the projecting serrations of the basic drawing. Three index marks (crosses in a circle) were provided on both sheets, to allow registration of one to the other. Despite my reservations, the hinges came out beautifully.

After cleaning with lacquer thinner to remove the film, I attached the hinge elements, one at a time, to the already painted coaming, using five-minute epoxy. With the hinge element held by tweezers, I applied the epoxy to one side using a 10 thou wire. After placing on the coaming (and perforce sliding about somewhat for precise positioning), I simply held it in place for a minute or so, after which I began removing excess epoxy—mostly by lightly pressing it with my forefinger, which was wiped off for another pressing, until no excess epoxy was visible. Sounds bogus, but it came out fine. Application of the mating hinge element was easier, since its position was determined by the interlocking, serrated edge of the one in place. After all of the hinges were in place, I sprayed overall with a final coat of aluminum lacquer.

RIGGING ATTACHMENT PIECES: There were many of those to be made, the most numerous—and complex—being the "spiders" on the wings, at the base of each interplane strut. Each leg is an anchor point for a rigging wire: each must be bent up to the appropriate angle. Fortunately, in a multi-sheet document entitled B*OOK OF ILLUSTRATIONS FOR THE deH.9A AEROPLANE* (Oct., 1918) I had a line perspective line drawing of each; not sufficient for precise two-dimensional layout, but far better than nothing but airplane photographs. O.K., so I didn't manage to get all of the angles just right.

SCARFF RING: This is another component which I simply could not have adequately rendered without photoetching, particularly the notched elevating arcs. The illustration on p. 82 of SB! shows the photoetched components, while the figure herein depicts the finished Scarff ring. For this, the most challenging aspect was bending the elevating arcs crisply and at just the right places. Yes, I squandered one set of photoetched arcs before I got it right. Which brings up a point: always order a few spare sheets, since mistakes are inevitably made and bitty parts tend to vanish into thin air off the end of tweezers.

PROPELLER HUB HARDWARE: This "ironmongery" consists of bolt pattern rings, plus a spider for support of the Hucks Starter Dog. Again, the photoetched components are shown on p. 82 of SB!, while the result is seen in the accompanying figure.

RADIATOR COOLING CONTROL SLATS: This was another head-scratcher, handily solved by photoetching. The frontal radiator of the NINAK has, directly in front of it, an array of shutters whose angles can be varied (by a control lever in the cockpit) to regulate the incoming airflow for cooling. Needless to say, in "Mespot" (Mesopotamia, renamed Iraq in the early '20s), the shut-

Wheel and Tire. The tire, including the central disc, was laminated fron 40 thou plasticard. Since I failed to develop an "automatic" method for achieving a uniform tyre cross-section (other than cutting the rings to successively smaller radial thicknesses), sanding to shape was a labor-intensive process: and, I had three such elements to make. Although DH9A wheels are spoked, my exemplar sported aluminium "wheel covers." Although I drew the 4x scale "artwork," the dry transfers for the PALMER CORD AERO TYRE markings were made for me by the kindly folk at ACCURATE MINIATURES. Thanks kindly folk!

ters were left open, and often removed, along with the formed aluminum radiator housing.

I drew up a 2 x size sheet which included the shutters themselves, plus the uprights on either side to which thin ends were attached, and the top and bottom base which resulted in a shutter support frame. Since the sheet was 5 thou thick, I epoxy laminated two (three?) shutter elements together for the appropriate scale thickness. Perhaps this gave me the later inspiration for laminating the Lewis gun housing.

Once the elements were trimmed, painted, and superglued together, a very satisfying and reasonably sturdy shutter/frame assembly was achieved.

COCKPIT: Numerous actuating levers and quadrants were photoetched: also the framing for the pilot's and gunner's windscreens. For most modelling, the interior spaces would be the primary recipients of photoetched components, as evidenced by the many aftermarket sets available for commercial kits.

OTHER COMPONENTS

I won't bore you with the descriptions of how I made all of the other NINAK components, but here are a few highlights.

PROPELLER: This was carved in wood, from a blank having the same number of (epoxied) lamina as the real thing. If simply varnished, it would have been pretty. Unfortunately, by the 20s these props seem to have been overpainted (presumably gray) and possibly fabric covered. So, you'll just have to take my word for the laminae, which are evident on my 1977 vintage RUMPLER C. IV model.

Stores Basket. This contraption hung beneath many NINAKs in "Empire" service, including H3510, primarily for the crew's desert survival kit, I suppose. They were hung from the bomb carrier rails, usually beneath the fuselage, but often under one wing. This is a reject, made before I realized that, since it hung from the bomb rails, it must be 21 inches wide. It was made from DETAIL ASSOCIATES brass strip, sharply bent, and superglued together over an *ad hoc* plastic form. 15 thou brass wire pins at its four corners fitted into very carefully measured and drilled holes in the PLASTISTRUCT rails.

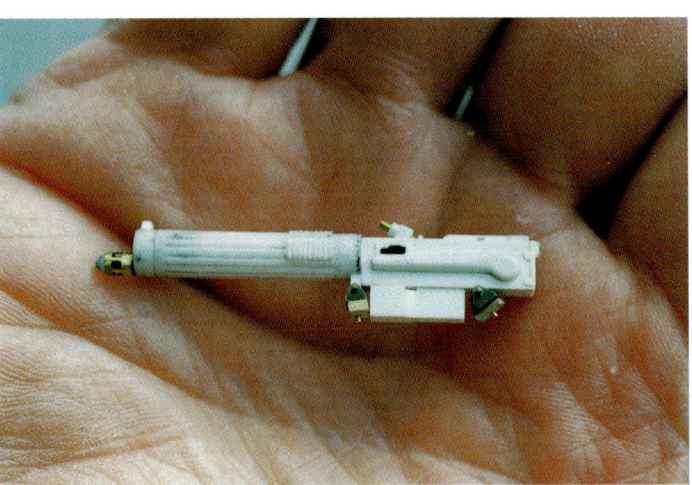

Vickers M/G. This affair was made mostly of plastic, the barrel housing from tube. All I remember is that the longitudinal corrugations, and transverse louvres were swines.

VICKERS GUN: This was a swine, mainly due to the corrugated barrel housing—mit louvres yet! I made this so long ago that I can't recall how I did the corrugations, but they came out O.K. This gun is mostly of styrene plastic, with a few photoetched parts (cocking levers, etc.)

WHEELS: I built these up from plastic sheet laminae. The central disc is two 40 thou laminae: the tires were built up on this with 30 x 20 thou rings—each being spin cut using a small bow compass with a sharp needle end (a blade end would have worked as well or better). Fortunately, I didn't have to deal with making spoked wheels, since H3510 has, apparently, aluminum wheel covers. These I vacuformed as a shallow cone. No, dammit, I didn't put a "bulged flat" on the tires, since I like to have them roll (doubtless eventually off the end of a table).

PILOT'S SEAT: Another feature which, mercifully, I didn't have to simulate was the wicker pilot's seat with which DH9As were initially equipped. My mid-20s AIR (MINISTRY) PUBLICATION 878 covering the DH9A says "The (pilot's) seat is of the standard Irving parachute type except that the front portion is cut away at the centre and the edge bent over to stiffen it and prevent damage (to the pilot?) caused when entering the cockpit." From these cutting and bending remarks, I assumed that the seat was metal, but, despite several inquiries, was never able to define this putative "standard Irving parachute type." So, I vacuformed a generic one which seemed reasonably appropriate for the era.

I added a leather seat cushion, on the premise that, at least in "Mespot" the pilot may not always have worn his Irvin. Judging by testimony in Chaz Bowyer's book *RAF Operations 1918-38*, it was probably better to go down in a blazing ship than bail out and be captured by Sheikh Mahmud's lot.

I roughed out the seat cushion in thick (100 thou) plastic. Then I marked and drilled a button pattern, and slowly scraped out a wrinkle (and edge seam) pattern using a N° 11 blade, with constant reference to photos of such cushions (the one in the RAF Museum's F1010, for example). Once the three-dimensional shape had been completed and sanded smooth, 30 thou diameter plastic rod was pushed into the holes, their rounded, slightly protruding ends representing the buttons.

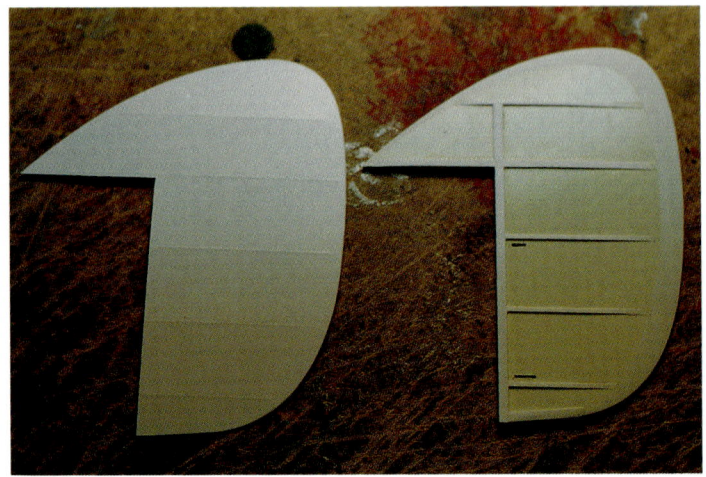

Rudder Components. O.K., so it's another lousy photo: but, it does illustrate the George Lee method for making such items. The central profile is 40 thou plasticard, with ribs and hinge spines glued on: then, it's block-sanded to cross-section (airfoil) shape on both sides, leaving a sharp trailing edge. The embossed skins are feathered along the inside surface of their trailing edges, to mate at installation, beyond the edge of the somewhat undersize core element.

A smaller, rectangular cushion was made for the gunner's bench, plus a cushioned headrest for the pilot. Once painted, with a darker brown hue in the folds, these cushions have a very satisfying appearance. While time-consuming, they had been fun to make.

STRUTS CABANE AND INTERPLANE: I made these from basswood strips (George Lee always used bamboo), since it is stiffer than polystyrene, and not subject to long-term creep. I drilled holes in the ends for steel pins (wire), for insertion into wing and fuselage holes.

LANDING GEAR: Aside from the wheels and (brass tube) axles, this consists of two "V" legs and a split axle/spreader bar. This, unfortunately rather complex, design was retrofitted to 20s vintage NINAKs. In both designs, the axle ends were flexibly supported with Bungee cord (simulated with fine nylon multifilament thread). I made the "V" legs from basswood, again for strength and rigidity.

COOPER BOMBS AND CARRIERS

General purpose/bombardment two-seaters of the period, such as the NINAK and Bristol F2B, typically could carry four "20 pound" Cooper bombs beneath each wing, mounted in a "Carrier" (*not* a "rack," admonishes Harry Woodman), which in turn was slung from a pair of rails, the ends of which were attached to what we would now call "hardpoints" at the fore and aft mainspars.

COOPER BOMB: For me, configuration of the Cooper bomb posed no problem: I have one! This I acquired from my first modelling pal, Alvis (now Jarmin) Lynch, in 1942. How he got it, I have no idea. Using it as my guide, I fashioned a 1/24th scale prototype from polystyrene stock; the "production articles" then being kindly cast in resin for me by one of our wizard local modellers, Ted Holowchuck.

Being thus...errr...armed with an original specimen, my prototype was scrupulously accurate, right? All too frequently ("ATF," as we say around home), it seems that my propensity for error equals my passion for authenticity. As I sat preparing Ted's resin cast elements for mating with their fins, I gave an occasional glance toward the original reposing nearby. At some point, I had occasion to make a further measurement of it, whereupon, to my abject dismay, I discovered that my 1/24th scale replicas were almost 1/10th inch too long, or 2 inches full-scale! How could I have made such a stupid mistake? No problem. Reconstructing the crime; based upon circumstantial evidence, I had evidently included the (assembled) two inch length of the collar between the body and tail section twice in my measurements. In the proverbial blue funk, I spent the next two days performing corrective surgery upon my lovely resin cast bombs (No, I didn't have the cheek to ask Ted to cast me eight more, from a revised master). This consisted of sawing 85 thou off of the bomb, just forward of the twice-measured collar, and then retapering the bomb body, before grafting back on the tail section (with a length of 62 thou diameter brass tubing inside, for strength and alignment). One more reason why it took me eight years to build the NINAK.

The bomb fins were photoetched in 5 thou brass, obtained several years ago. (Fortunately, I had drawn them right, with alternate fore and aft centerline slots for interlocking, 90 degree assembly.) They were inserted into saw-cut slots at the thin, tapering rear portion of the resin cast bomb—I had included longitudinal recesses, at right angles, in the prototype, to guide my later 6 thou sawblade.

Oh yes, I had also managed to mislocate the support lug feature on the bomb prototype—both axially and azimuthally!—so was obliged to file lug-ended pins from 12 thou brass for each bomb. Oh well, at least they are much stronger than the resin originals.

The arming propellers of the Cooper bomb are shaped like pinwheels, or 5-arm swastikas, with the blades at a pitch of about 45 degrees: a die-casting. Simulating these presented another challenge, again met by photoetching—and again botched on my first attempt! It seems that, for my initial photoetch "artwork," I had once again fallen to the trap of attempting to make the propeller hubs too close to the originals, no allowance being made for modelling practical-

Propeller. This was laminated from wood strips, epoxied together. But, in the end, I painted it overall, since the real ones were evidently fabric covered.

Pilot's Seat Cushion. This, the pilot's headrest, and gunner's seat were plastic chunks, scraped with a #11 blade to develop the wrinkled contours and edges. The "buttons" were plastic rod, stuffed into drilled holes.

ity. So, when I began to bend back the blades with my tweezers, the hub annulus was too thin to resist the twisting forces. So, once again, a hurried drawing revision, followed by more lucre in the FOTOCUT till.

When I thus finally had the configuration under control, I was then faced with the issue of correct colors for RAF Cooper bombs of the era: mine is a light green, doubtless a U.S. made item. Harry Woodman, in the article discussed below, stated that the body, in RAF service, was close to Methuen 4A8, which is Cadmium Yellow (Deep). Nevertheless, partly for scale effect, I mixed a color nearer to Methuen 4A6 (by lightening of FLOQUIL 110254 "CN YELLOW #12"). Then, with some difficulty, I managed to apply a 1/32nd wide band of red around the front of the bomb body, using CHAMP railroad decals (to indicate "HE," I believe). While they should also have had a (wider) band of light green further aft (denoting AMATOL), I could not come up with a convenient, practical, neat way of applying such a band on the tapered body portion.

THE CARRIER: When it came time to address the Cooper bomb racks—or "carriers," as Harry Woodman says that they should be called—I could glean very little configuration information from period photographs. After all, these items are almost always in shadow, and were rarely photographed *per se*. All I could tell was that those installed upon the RAF Museum's F1010 were of a different (later) type from those of my exemplar, H3510.

So, I wrote to the font of knowledge on such matters, Harry Woodman. He then very kindly sent me a facsimile of an article by him from some British publication (whose name I can't recall, and maybe never got), entitled THE 20 lb. COOPER BOMB AND CARRIER. There it all was: a multi-view line drawing, by him, of the Carrier Mk. 1, and Cooper bomb itself; a 1918 vintage perspective line drawing of the Carrier, accompanied by an "inboard profile" of a Cooper bomb; plus relevant text. I now had no excuse not to do it right—other than that the thing is beastly complicated. Another job for FOTOCUT. So, I drew up all of the bitty parts (to 4X scale) and sent it off. Later, armed with these elements, in 4 thou silver/nickel alloy, plus some 22 thou HOBBY HANGER tubing, I was able to produce reasonable representations without undo difficulty. Thanks again, Harry.

FINISHING: SURFACE FEATURES

FABRIC WRINKLING: The rear fuselage side panels of the NINAK were fabric, laced in place using boot type hooks and eyes. Most any fabric covered fuselage panels of slab-sided A/C revealed some wrinkling, especially those which were laced in place. This is evidenced primarily by radiating, slightly curved patterns, mostly from panel corners—visible in many photographs. The pattern selected should be sketched on the bare plastic with a pencil, and the shallow indentations scraped out, primarily with the edge of a #15 surgeons blade. Narrower contours, near the origin of certain wrinkles, are scraped out with a #11 blade, and finished with the folded edge of #400 or 600 grit sandpaper. As with all such effects, the important thing is to not overdue it.

PLYWOOD WARPING: The forward portion of the basic NINAK fuselage was plywood covered. Again, perusal of photographs of operational A/C reveals some moisture induced distortion—billowing, especially along the sides aft of the engine area. To see this effect, one must obtain good photos where the light is incident at a relatively shallow angle. Such effects, by the way, are common to DH4s and DH9s, as well as DH9As. This distortion, both inward and outward, due to moisture-induced expansion, can be represented mostly by indentions, although some buildup should be included. This smooth, gentle distortion occurs between fuselage structure elements to which the plywood was nailed. So, sketch the structure on the outside surface with a pencil: then gradually and lightly scrape away using a #15 blade, constantly referring to photos for guidance.

The nail patterns in the plywood are produced along the fuselage structure centerlines by drawing pencil lines, ticking the spacing locations (using the edge of a marked piece of paper, preferably POST IT) and indenting the holes with a scribing tool. (Most of the plywood paneling on a NINAK, or DH4 or DH9, was not fabric covered, so the nail locations show.)

SIDE PANEL LACING: For me, the greatest surface pattern challenge on the NINAK was representing the side panel lacing itself. First, I deeply scribed the panel edge, followed by application of 5x50 thou reinforcing "tape" around the periphery of the opening. Then, in lieu of 1/24th scale boot hooks, I inserted 10 thou wire stubs, drilled into holes spaced at staggered 80 thou intervals, along the panel and fixed border edges. All were installed into their holes, and superglued in place from the inside, before permanent assembly of the fuselage sides to the top & bottom elements. Then, I Swiss-filed down each row, so that the wire ends were all even. Later, after priming and preliminary aluminum painting of the fuselage, I added the "lacing": 6 thou diameter clear monofilament mylar line, applied in zig zag manner over the brass pins, and lightly superglued at each pin, to prevent "falling off." It was time consuming and tedious, but came out well.

Wing Rib Tape Simulation-1: Here one wing panel is being masked, with SCOTCH 3M #218 Fine Line tape (1/2 inch wide). The wing had already been painted, with aluminum automotive acrylic lacquer. The 80 thou wide rib tape locations have been carefully marked with pencil tics, 40 thou to either side of the embossment centerlines.

WING RIB & EDGE TAPE SIMULATION: Another major challenge was simulating the slightly raised tapes along the crest of the wing ribs, plus leading and trailing edges. Several options were considered, including application of thin tape or decal sheet. Ultimately, I rejected these over concern for long term stability (glue deterioration) and lack of compliance to the overrib double curves.

Upon the already painted wing, I masked the interrib cells with 3M #218 Fine Line Tape, leaving 80 thou stripes exposed, centered along the embossed crest. (Positioning was made to pencil ticks, from 40-40 thou marks on the edge of a small Post It.) I learned that to ensure a crisp line, edges of the tape should be pressed down onto the aluminum painted wing surface with the rounded end of a small paint brush. Full adhesion can be detected by the different appearance of the tape. Tape straightness was verified by a small (6") straight edge ruler, and the 80 thou unmasked width checked after application of both tapes. Several coats of relatively thick aluminum lacquer were applied along each tape location, with the airbrush held nearly perpendicular to the wing surface. Enough paint must be applied so that when the mask has been removed, a small but distinct lip exists all along each edge.

After removal of the mask, the wing should be left for a few hours, until the paint lips have fully dried. The first trimming step is to run the sharp edge of a small #600 sanding block down each edge of the tape, with the block edge perpendicular to the wing surface. This goes a long way towards ensuring that the final tape edge is smooth. Be careful though not to press too hard against the wing surface, lest the paint spall off in places. The bulk of the lip can then be broken or flaked off with a toothpick or end of a small wooden sanding block. Thereafter, the remaining lip fragments and edge can be cleaned up with strips of #1000 or #1500 sandpaper, curled around the end of the index finger. For a proper effect, the resulting tape edges must be smooth and evenly about 2-3 thou high.

Incidentally, the leading and trailing edge rib tapes were masked and painted after completion (clean-up) of the rib tapes.

While ultimately I was able to obtain satisfactory results with this method, it proved to be extremely tedious and time-consuming, especially clean-up of the masked and painted ribs. Also, the amount of paint build-up required to assure an adequate and consistent edge tended to "soften" the appearance of the embossed rib crest. So, in retrospect, I may have chosen the option of masking the wings as for the above method, but of simply applying a thin coat of aluminum paint of a slightly different hue. After all, even George Lee didn't bother with rib tape simulation!

FINISHING: BASIC PAINTING

PRIMER (BASE) COAT: As always, I used automotive lacquer for basic overall painting of the NINAK. The foundation, or base coats, were gray automotive primer which, despite reports to the contrary, can be applied directly to the bare high impact polystyrene sheet as long as it is not flooded on, which would degrade fine surface details in any case, such as panel scribing. Its sanding properties are wonderful: applied unthinned by brush to local imperfections, it is an ideal filler. I normally sand down the primer with #600 grit paper.

TOP COLOR COAT: For the NINAK, I used R-M Fine Bright Metallic (aluminum tinting color) for all external surfaces.

I have the following basic motives for using automotive acrylic lacquer:
• Since it dries quickly, the "down time" between coats and before subsequent finishing operations is minimized.
• After drying, the surface can easily be smoothed, if necessary, with sandpaper and polishes.
• Modelling enamels can be applied over the lacquer surface, and removed with impunity using mineral spirits, until the desired effect is obtained. This is an enormous advantage for creating weathering effects.
• I find lacquer less messy to clean up after spraying, doubtless due to its faster drying characteristics. For example, if you get some on your hand and work area, it is soon dry so presents no threat to the finished surfaces.
• Since I grew up using nitrocellulose model "dope," acrylic lacquer is very similar as regards application techniques.

A down side is the well known toxicity of lacquer thinner, whose base is toluene. This potential health hazard is easily overcome by

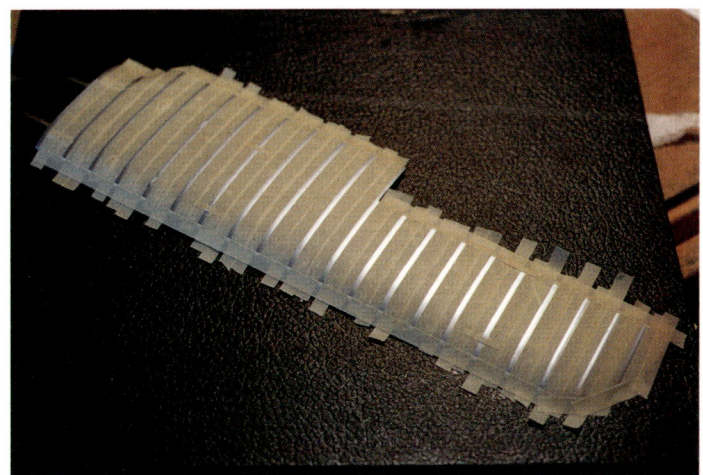

Wing Rib Tape Simulation-2: In this view, all of the rib tape locations are exposed, with masking in between. Also, the leading and trailing edge tape simulations are masked, so that paint will not be double thickness where these cross the rib tape buildup. Next, I will airbrush several coats of the aluminum lacquer along each exposed rib location—three passes at each rib, proceeding from root to tip; I will repeat this about three times for each wing surface—that's 8 or 9 coats for each rib! Then, after about one hour, the masking was removed, leaving...one bloody great mess! But, it looked much worse than it was in fact. Most of the mess was ragged paint edges, or even "skin" (flashing). With considerable effort, this all was removed and the edges cleaned smooth with a small sanding block, run along the edges: the sanding edge being perpendicular to the wing surface.
After the rib tapes were all cleaned up, a similar process was repeated for the leading and trailing edge tape simulations. Sound like a complex, tedious, time-consuming, mind-boggling nightmare? Good, you understand correctly. As discussed in the main text, I don't recommend this technique: I'd never do it again. Sure, it looked fine in the end, but I now believe that an equally satisfying rib tape simulation can be achieved simply by differential coloring, without the 3-dimensional madness.

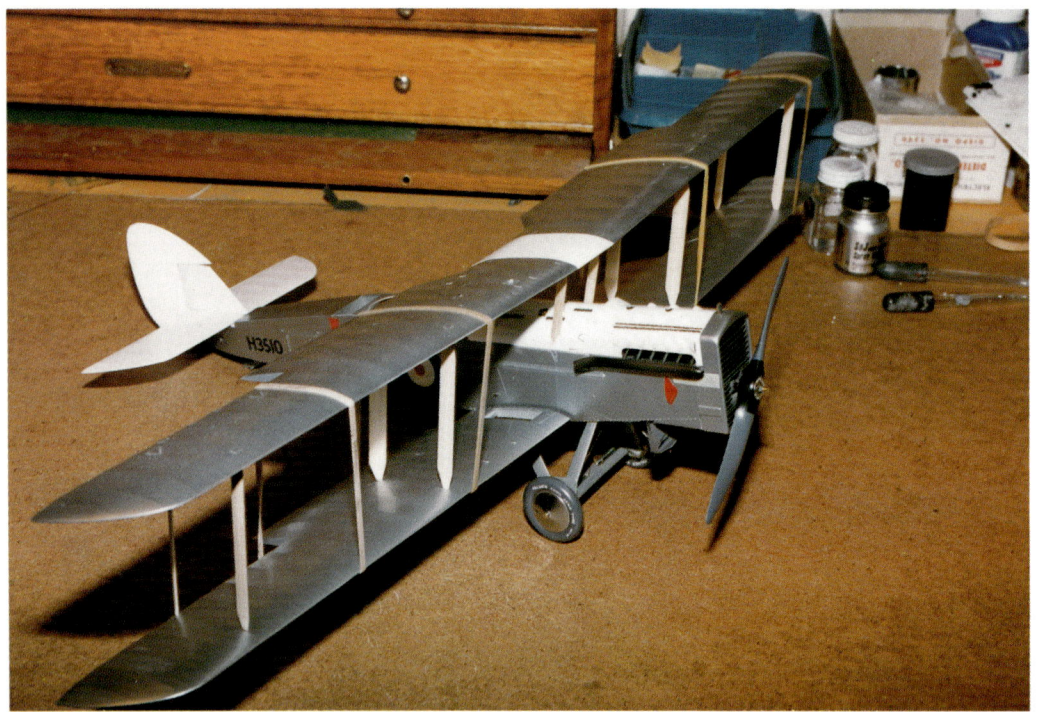

Preassembly. This shot depicts the first of numerous test preassemblies with the new, wood core wings, in late '96.

proper ventilation and the wearing of a respirator (which I only began using recently, after 50 years of lacquer thinner inhalation. I invoke this for explaining my many peccadilloes).

Another related problem is lack of availability in the future. The EPA Thought & Use Police are forcing it off the shelves as a threat to everything from the ozone layer to Darter Snails. So, I'm hoarding the stuff to see me through.

Another drawback, perhaps, is that most modeller users, including myself, mix our own hues from a relatively few basic tinting colours: yellow, orange, violet, and blue, plus black and white and, of course, aluminum. (Don't ask me why red isn't a basic tinting color, at least for the brands which I use.) Such mixing is a messy, wasteful, trial and error business.

INSIGNIA & LARGE MARKINGS: I masked and lacquer sprayed the British national insignia and large A/C letter "L"s. I used FRISK PRODUCTS USA, INC. matte frisket film. Circles for the roundels were cut from this using a very sharp GRIFHOLD blade, fitted into an "A" type, or bow compass. The secret to centering an outer periphery mask, which I learned from Peter Cooke, is to fit it in place around its disc, whose center compass hole has been carefully placed over a small mark on the wing or fuselage surface. Fitting the outer mask around the disc is surprisingly easy, even for large wing roundels: just start it at one point and work around in one direction. After the inner disc has been removed, mash down the mask edge with the blunt end of a wooden paint brush handle, or some such, to ensure firm and complete contact. Then, I thoroughly wipe the exposed region to be painted with a paper towel pad wetted with rubber cement thinner (heptane). Obviously, for a ring, such as the blue of a RAF roundel, I then add an appropriately smaller size frisket paper disc.

For such a roundel, I first spray a white disc, slightly smaller in diameter than the outer edge of the subsequent blue ring. Take care to lay down enough white to ensure full brightness (total opacity), but no more. After it has dried, the mask removed, and the white thoroughly wiped clean with rubber cement thinner, the outer edge must be deftly feathered out with #1000 sand paper, so it will not later be evident beneath the blue.

After masking and painting the blue, its edges must also be lightly sanded, so that no projecting lip remains on the completed surface. As with the white, clearly it is important to apply just enough paint for full opacity, to minimize edge lip build-up. For some reason, I always have more trouble with the red center than with the blue ring—both masking and edge build-up.

Since my model represents a heavily weathered subject, exposed to years of intense Middle East sun, I considerably lightened the blue and red of the insignia, and "L", on the top wing. For the fuselage sides, I faded the markings less: for the undersides of the lower wings, the colors were faded very little from basic for this period.

Incidentally, now that this project is over, I realize that I should have used FLOQUIL 110XXX series Railroad Colors, suitably mixed, for painting these markings. This is because they have more finely ground pigment than automotive lacquers, so that full opacity is achieved with less paint buildup.

NATURAL METAL SIMULATION: While NINAKs in mid 20s service were basically painted aluminum overall, certain metal components were left unpainted, at least on the example which I represented. These included the over-engine cowl, radiator housing, and wheel covers. After much trial and error with the various metallizers available to the hobbyist, I settled on FLOQUIL 110100

She never looked prettier! Here the forward fuselage is shown just prior to application of thin gray lacquer overspray, which I did with some trepidation. But, I felt that the indicated appearance was more appropriate for Hornchurch than Hinaidi.

"OLD SILVER" over a finely sanded base of aluminum lacquer. While the tinting powder is somewhat finer than that of my basic R-M Fine Bright Metallic, the final surface was not significantly more metallic looking. While SNJ superfine powder rubbed over a smooth lacquer surface looked very metallic, I could find no clear overspray which did not destroy its high sheen and brightness. Though perhaps overcautious, I was afraid to leave the powder uncoated, feeling that it would eventually oxidize to very dull aluminum. In any event, this was all rather academic for my rather heavily weathered model.

WEATHERING: While the DH9A's in home squadrons during the 20s were evidently kept in regulation "spit & polish" condition, those deployed to overseas units, especially Iraq and India, were soon far from immaculate: H3510 of No 8 Sqdn, the subject of my model, being no exception. Fabric, especially on the wings, was worn, grimy, and patched, while the fuselage underside and plywood coaming between engine and pilot's windscreen showed evidence of staining and general discoloration from engine compartment fumes. Yet, from photos, I see little evidence of exhaust staining along-side the fuselage, no doubt due to the outward flaring of the exhaust manifolds. Dust and or mud is often in evidence along the fuselage underside aft.

As for the wings, I have a few 8 x 10 glossy photo prints of "Empire" A/C which clearly reveal serious discoloration (darkening), along the leading edges especially; yet less so on the rib tapes. I eventually concluded that this was probably grime/abrasion, which would affect the single-layer fabric more than the glued-on rib tapes. (Yet another possibility was that it was PC10 showing through beneath the aluminum overcoat, which had been almost worn away by sand and dust abrasion.)

For the general grimy appearance noted above, I applied relatively dark gray lacquer, greatly thinned. On several painful occasions, I overdid it the first time, necessitating a sand off, and reapplication of light aluminum top coat before trying again. Each time, I remorsefully said, "John, you idiota, why didn't you use enamel for the gray overspray, which you could easily have wiped off until you had it right?" But, each time, like Charlie Brown (un) kicking the football which Lucy had just whisked away, I again used lacquer. The rationale was that I could then apply any localized weathering with enamel over the basic grayed down finish. Ultimately this proved correct. For example, I was able to brush on/wipe a wash of dark gray enamel over the cowl piano hinges and other hardware to yield a reasonably satisfying grungy effect, after the elements had been wiped down with a mineral spirit dampened bit of toweling. Also, I could represent spill staining, dirty paw prints, and boot scuffing with wet/dry brush application.

TOP COAT: Finally, I lightly oversprayed the main components, before final assembly, with very thinned down TESTORS Dullcoat

THE DREADED RIGGING

RIGGABILITY: Either you're born with it, or you weren't. I weren't. Sure, I rigged my two Wedell-Williams#44 models successfully, using flat monofilament nylon fishing line. No problem then, and better yet, it's still taut on both. But, they were dead simple models in that respect. And, I rigged my 1/32nd scale Rumpler C.IV in 1977 using nylon thread, with little difficulty, as I recall. (But then, I did have George as my technical advisor.) I suppose that it

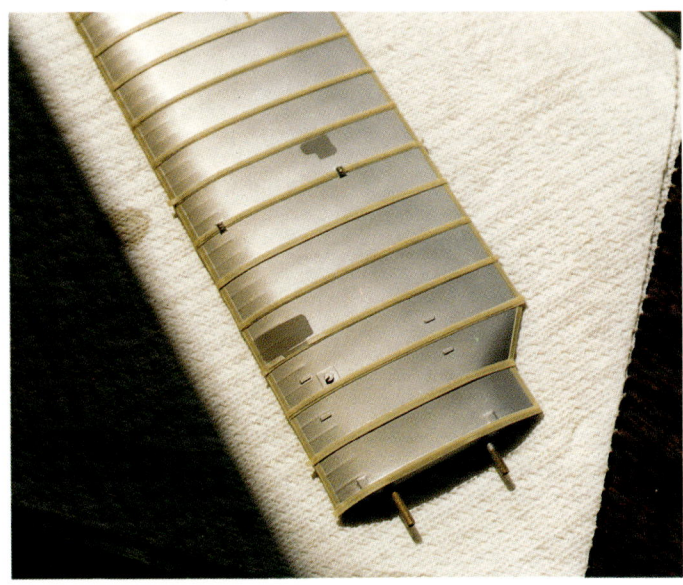

Wing Masking For Weathering. Here the starboard upper wing has had its rib and edge tape simulations masked (with SCOTCH #218 Fine Line Tape) for spraying a light coat of very thinned out gray lacquer weathering. Later, with the tape removed, I applied a final, even lighter weather overspray to the entire surface. All this because, in a few photos of NINAKs in mid-20s "Empire" service, I could clearly discern that—for reasons still unclear to me—the rib and edge tapes of the wings were considerably less darkened (weathered) than the single-layer fabric in between. It did have the effect of further emphasizing the tape areas; and, in retrospect, may have been enough, without the very laborious paint buildup process described earlier.

would still be intact if the top wing hadn't eventually warped, and the cretin movers hadn't knocked it off in 1988—despite my best packing efforts.

But, most of the big kids tend to use steel, at least for larger models: i.e., 1/32nd scale and larger. George Lee did for his epic Keystone B4A; Alan Clark did for his Short SINGAPORE III; and, well, look at the rigged examples in ON MINIATURE WINGS—Tom Dietz' book on NASM models.

In late March '98, I called Ron Lowry, inquiring as to the status of his 1/24th scale Gloster GAMECOCK—the subject of his HOW I BUILT MY... chapter herein. He said "Oh, everything is made now. I'm about to begin painting." To which I replied: "But, then you are still faced with assembly, including the dreaded rigging," knowing that he also uses wire. "Oh, that's no problem," he said. Some people have Riggability.

RIGGING MATERIALS: Rigging ship models is an art (craft) form that goes back centuries—indeed, millenia, recalling those in the Pharoah's tombs. Traditionally, they have used twine and cotton thread: more recently, nylon thread or monofilament.

Monofilament Nylon Thread: This material, in gray, or "smokey," is ideal for rigging small scale airplane models (1/48th and smaller) and secondary (control line) rigging of larger ones. Its great advantages, of course, are flexibility, elasticity, lack of "furriness," and durability. Models using this material can be truly rigged: that is, their lines are installed (and maintained) under tension.

Piano (Music) Wire: This is a high tensile stress, hard-drawn, round steel wire, which is popular for airplane rigging due to its great stiffness. Thus, it can be inserted into drilled "sockets" at either end by bending. When released, if it is the proper length and the holes drilled deep enough and at the proper angles, it will spring into place straight. It need not even be (super) glued in place, but, if done so, helps to support the elements to which it is anchored. Alan Clark and Ron Lowry sometimes file piano wire flat, to represent streamline flying and landing wires: see their HOW I BUILT MY... chapters. Piano wire rusts, so should be sanded clean with 1500 grit paper and then sprayed with clear lacquer or enamel.

Stainless Steel Cable: As evidenced by many models in ON MINIATURE WINGS, this material has been (is) frequently used to represent cable of the original. However, cable does not scale well: the fewer filaments of scale material producing a textured (lumpy) appearance much in evidence in certain model photos.

Stainless Steel Orthodontic Wire: George Lee used this material for the flying and landing wires of his 1/32nd scale Keystone, to represent the streamline wire of the original. In this case, he used 8x22 thou 3M/UNITEK material, conveniently supplied by his dentist son. While this wire is very convincing in appearance when installed correctly, there are two challenges and one caution. First is the challenge of termination (anchoring) in a strong and realistic-appearing manner. The second is availability. The caution is simply that it should be pulled through 100 or 1500 grit paper before installing to subdue the bright finish, and provide "tooth" for gray painting, if desired. George terminated his Keystone wires by filing down and notching the ends, which were then served with fine copper wire, whose loose "pigtail" end was passed through holes at the appropriate wing or fuselage locations: a sketch of this is included in SB!. I used another method, described below.

Availability presents a serious problem. First, it can only be ordered through a dentist/orthodontist—for reasons unknown to me. Perhaps because babies may swallow it: or, parents might attempt to perform orthodontics themselves on their teenagers, to save on dental expenses. (It couldn't be any more difficult than rigging a model with the stuff!)

Far more serious is the fact that the relatively high aspect ratio cross-sections required to simulate landing and flying wires are no longer in production; the orthodontists having evidently gone over to low aspect ratio (nearly square) material. However, at least in Winter 1997/98, 3M still had some remaining stock of the discontinued shapes. Incidentally, they supply round stainless steel wire in various diameters, down at least to 7 thou.

FLYING AND LANDING WIRE ELEMENTS: I chose to use orthodontic wire: specifically 3M/UNITEK "PERMACHROME"; their (discontinued) catalogue number 241-228 (12x28 thou) for the inner bay; and #241-820 for the outer—the latter remaining from George's supply.

Anchor Points: For these, on the wings, at the ends of each interplane strut, I simulated the actual multiprong plates by 5 thou photoetched elements: first from brass, but ultimately from beryllium copper, as explained later. Fortunately, as an approximate guide to the shape of these plates, I had a sheet of drawings from the aforementioned BOOK OF ILLUSTRATIONS FOR THE DH9A AEROPLANES. Similarly, I prepared pen and ink drawings for and obtained photoetched attachment elements for the fuselage and top wing center section. Eventually, just prior to superglue and pin installation of these elements, their prongs were bent up at approximately the correct angles for receiving the rigging wire ends.

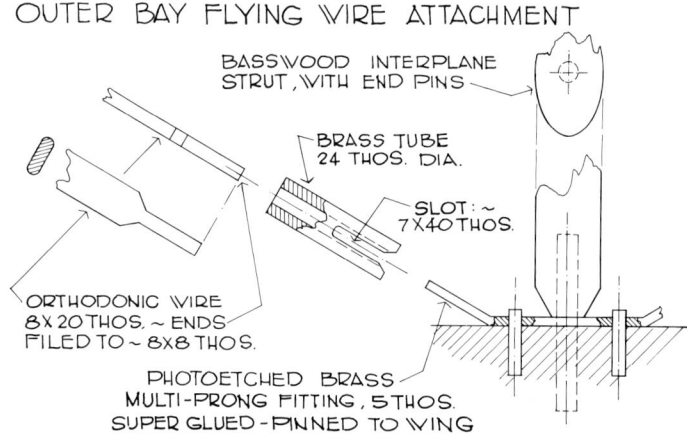

Flying and Landing Wire Rigging. Refer to the text explanation of this method for making and installing these elements, using orthodontic wire.

Wire Termination: This presented an especial challenge, eventually solved in the following manner:

I filed each end of each orthodontic flying and landing wire down to a short length which was basically square: i.e., 12x12 thou for the inner bay wires and 8x8 thou for the outer. I then made end fittings from HOBBY HANGER brass tubing: 32 thou diameter (by 100thou long) for the inner bay wires; and 24 thou diameter (by 80 thou long) for the outer. The critical, and most tedious, task here was the sawing of a slot into one end of each brass tube fitting, for later insertion into the photoetched attachment points. A particular problem here was finding a saw blade whose teeth were fine and whose thickness was no more than 5-7 thou (X-Acto type hobby saws are 10 thou thick, with teeth too coarse for this delicate job). Mercifully, this was solved by a benefactor during one of the IPMS/USA Nationals (who must remain anonymous, to shield him from a barrage of requests for such blades, which he would be unable to supply). Actual sawing of these slots at first seemed impossible to achieve, adequately centered in the short tube piece. However, I soon became quite proficient at it, through great repetition rather than innate skill. With the uncut length of brass tube clamped into a small Starrett pin vise held in my right (clamp) hand (I am left-handed), I pulled the saw across the tubing end with my left hand, two fingers braced against the right; rotating the vise slightly, if necessary, to center the initial cut. Once started, it was fairly easy to saw it straight down the tube, for about 40 thou.

WING INSTALLATION; GENERAL: Surprisingly perhaps, I did not employ a jig (fixture) for rigging; wing positions being almost entirely predetermined by placement of the wing tubing sockets in the fuselage and top wing center section. This latter element was held quite firmly in place by the cabane struts, which were themselves constrained by the snug cutouts in the forward fuselage upper coaming. In other words, the role of jig was borne through very careful—and tedious—placement of the wing tubing sockets and by installation of the top wing center section. Nevertheless, as later explained, a fixture would have saved me much grief when installing the wires—not so much for alignment as for rigidity.

TOP WING CENTER SECTION INSTALLATION: I invested a great deal of effort in placement of the wing tubing extension sockets into this element: this aspect was discussed previously, in WINGS.

Location and orientation of the top wing center section was fully defined by the length of the cabane struts; by their drilled, wire extension sockets into the fuselage top longerons; and by the snugly fitting cutouts in the fuselage forward, upper coaming. Producing the latter features was a tedious cut and try process, including periodic slabbing on of plastic "slivers," when too much had been cut away.

Final truing of the coaming cutouts and length of the cabane struts was performed during repeated test fitting of coaming, struts, and wing center section to the fuselage: the top and bottom wings being inserted into their tubing sockets, with interplane struts set in place. This oft-repeated preassembly was then set upon a very flat surface (a marble table in our living room), onto which Doug

THE DREADED RIGGING. Ever see a Matthew Brady of Pickett's charge; a good, clear shot of the Tommies heading towards Thiepval Ridge into the maw of the German Mincing Machine on 1 July 1916; of Lt. Cdr. Wade McClusky's SBD-3 leading VB-6 down towards the Akagi, Kaga, and Soryu; of mortal, desparate, hand-to-hand combat inside the Tractor Factory at Stalingrad; or of U.S. Marines wading neck deep in the bullet roiled surf off Betio Island of Tarawa Atoll? Such moments are rarely captured on film. So it is with the darkest hours of modelling.

Carrick's plan view drawing print was laid. The preassembled model was set atop Doug's plan view, the rear fuselage being propped up so that it was nearly horizontal. Exact positioning of the model over the drawing was achieved using large, plastic drafting (draughting) right triangles. Wing perpendicularity to the fuselage was checked using both the triangles and "calibrated eyeball." Front view horizontality of the wings was measured perpendicular to the table using my trusty 6" steel rule. Because final horizontality is what matters, the main wheels were in place for these measurements.

LANDING AND FLYING WIRE INSTALLATION: I began with the front landing wires of the inner bay. For each, I snipped off a piece of 12x28 thou orthodontic wire, filed down one end, made and installed its brass tube end fitting, and test fit it for length by slipping the completed end over one anchor plate prong. Several such test fits, followed by successively shorter snips of the unfinished end were required, until the latter just cleared the opposite anchor plate. I then shaped this end of the wire, made and installed its brass tube end fitting. Needless to say, I had to install each end fitting, with superglue, such that its sawn slot was parallel with the flat sides of the wire. I then "painted" each end fitting with "BRASS BLACK" chemical, and, with the wire assembly laid on my workbench, sanded the wire itself with 1500 grit paper (lengthwise), to reduce the shine of the bright stainless steel. (I had considered gray-painting each wire prior to installation; but, aside from the added work, realized that the poorly adhering paint would probably chip off during tweezer installation.) After pinching both slots almost shut, I slid the lower (outer) one onto its attachment fitting at the base of the forward, inner interplane strut. I then turned the model upside-down, on a large, thick piece of foam rubber, to slip the other end over the attachment prong on the top wing center section underside (at the top of the forward cabane strut). After assuring myself that all was well as regards the wire assembly length and orientation of the attachment prongs, I superglued the upper, inner wire end fitting to the prong. I then rotated the model right side up to perform superglue attachment of the lower, outer end. But, lacking a third hand, or assistant, I now faced the challenge of securing the wire in the "just taut" condition. If the wire termination slot had been pinched tightly enough prior to insertion, it would grip the attachment prong well enough by friction, once pulled taut with tweezers. If so, I then applied superglue, with a length of 8 thou diameter brass wire. The "tynes" of the 32 thou brass tube end fittings of the inner bay wires were strong enough to maintain adequate tension, if well pinched. This was less certain for the 24 thou fittings of the outer bay wires.

For the inner bay landing wires, adequate tautness could be further assured by slightly flexing (raising the tip of) the lower wing during superglue attachment. Of course, I did not have this luxury during attachment of the inner bay flying wires, the wing now being restrained by the landing wires.

Note that repeated inversion of the model was required for this approach, since I was not dexterous enough to confidently place and superglue the wire upper ends to the attachment fittings on the underside of the top wing, with the model upright. This is one reason I chose not to use a rigging fixture. But, since my wood core wings are relatively heavy, the repeated gravity reversals threw considerable strain upon the wires supporting this weight. This strain was especially severe for the first wires being installed.

So, needless to say, the beginning of my rigging ordeal occurred when certain wires loosened from this process. Sometimes, a superglue attachment would simply let go, others the attachment fitting would break loose from the wing or fuselage. But, for some, I could see no such obvious cause for the looseness. The crisis, of course, was that each time this occurred, I was obliged to remove the loosened (i.e. no longer taut, and visibly bowed) wire entirely, by somehow breaking apart the superglue attachments, in order to saw clean the end fitting slots, and reattach the anchor plates, if they had broken loose. (Note that an anchor plate at the base of a strut could not be removed, but simply reglued while pressing down on it with tweezers.) Breaking the superglue joints entailed tugging on and rotating the wire with tweezers; with resultant stresses to both model and modeller. Often, this tugging and straining caused adjacent wires to loosen; that is, to become slightly curved. - *Aegrescit medendo.* At this point, my worst fears over the dreaded rigging were beginning to be realized.

Eventually, however, after 3 or 4 days of angst and toil, I managed to rig both inner bays, including the "X" (incidence) wires between the fore and aft interplane struts (using piano wire). I then installed the (8x22thou) landing wires of the outer bays, in similar fashion.

The First Great Rigging Crisis: At this point, I realized that, lacking a third hand—and brain region to guide it—I needed professoinal modelling assistance to superglue the lower, inboard ends of the outer bay flying wires, while I held them taut with tweezers. (Recall that the tynes of the 24 thou wire end fittings were not strong enough to maintain much tautness through friction alone.) So, I made an appointment with Jim Schubert, one of the premier modellers in the Seattle area, and by now a good friend. After supper, I drove over to his home in Bellevue, about 15 miles away. The NINAK had been placed in a sturdy box, resting upon a thick sponge rubber pad—the box sitting alongside me, strapped down with the seat belt.

Upon arrival at Jim's, I removed the model from the box and placed it upon their kitchen counter top, for perusal by Jim, his wife, and myself, before we set to work. I then looked at the rigging. Almost all of the wires had loosened: that is, appeared slightly curved! I was thunderstruck—"lightning struck" would have been a more apt expression. Following the initial shock, I began to wonder: "How could this have occurred?" Our retirement chariot, a 1994 Cadillac sedan, gives a very gentle ride and has soft seats: the model was further cushioned by the aforementioned foam rubber pad; and we encountered no bumps of consequence en route. Even as an (ex) mechanical engineer, I could offer no explanation for acceleration loads of a magnitude to wreak such havoc. So, without further social intercourse, I despondently plopped it back in the box and drove home.

The Second Great Rigging Crisis: During the following long, tedious, angst-filled day, I managed to remove all of the wires. Then, I removed the wings, which I had not glued into their tubing sockets, and all of the photoetched attachment (anchor) fittings which had pulled loose. Fortunately, I managed to save most of the rigging wires, whose termination fitting slots I then sawed clean of remaining superglue. I cleaned and reset the removed attachment fittings, reinstalled the wings and began rerigging.

About two days into the (re)rigging process, and after suffering a few more loosened wires from constant model handling and inversion, the awful truth began to dawn, to wit: A fundamental flaw of my rigging method was that the photoetched attachment fittings were too flimsy—"wimpy" in the modern jargon. At this point, I again removed all of the superglued rigging wires, plus *all* of the attachment fittings. I then revised the pen and ink "artwork" for the fittings, by thickening each: that is, by widening the longitudinal body, especially where it is pierced by the hole for the pin extension of the interplane strut. Once again, in my zeal to make the fittings as much to scale as possible, I had made no allowance for modelling limitations. While doing this, I realized that it may take considerable time to get the revised photoetched parts back from FOTOCUT: quite aside from the mailing time, Fred Hultberg was not exactly sitting around idly, awaiting more work from me (despite the fact that I *felt* as though I had been supporting him for the past few years!) I called to alert him of the job and to request "rush" service: but, no answer, which increased my anxiety: "What if he has gone off to Fiji or Boora Boora for a months R&R?" Incredibly, however, I then managed to find a photoetch shop 1 1/2 miles from my house—who had the parts in my hand by noon of the following day!!! Not only that, while I had asked for brass, they apologized for having to substitute 5 thou beryllium copper—far better for my purpose, due to its much higher yield stress, resulting in a far springier material.

The Third Rigging: That afternoon, I began to install the new, far stronger attachment "plates." A week later, I had completed the third mainplane primary rigging. Yet, despite the new, much stronger attachments, I was still experiencing occasional wire loosening, evidently due primarily to the stresses from constant inversion of the model.

INVERSION STRONGBACK: By this time, even I realized that frequent inversion of the model during rigging (and afterwards) remained a serious problem. This I belatedly solved by the simple (in retrospect) expedient of making a rigid balsa wood splint, or strongback, placed over the top wing to prevent it from flexing during inversion. Referring to the accompanying photos, the basic element is two full-chord and span balsa sheets, set at the precise dihedral of the top wing, with a "mainspar" backing. Fore and aft edges were added, to restrain it from sliding off the wing; plus end brackets to prevent longitudinal motion. I now invert with impunity, using this device in the manner shown.

TRANSPORT FIXTURE: The First Rigging Crisis was doubtless, in retrospect, a blessing in disguise. Suppose that I hadn't discovered this vulnerability to motion until after the model had been completed: in particular, until its 800 mile journey to the 1998 IPMS/USA Nationals in Santa Clara at the end of June?

While I remain at a loss to fully explain how such a gentle, short car ride to Jim's in February could have wrought such havoc,

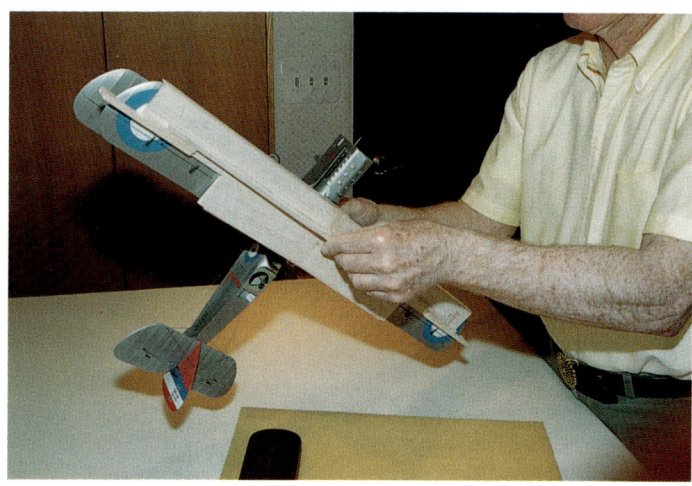

Inversion Strongback-2. (Jim Schubert photos)

it is clear that, in addition to stronger attachments, this heavy, fully wire rigged model must be totally restrained against the inevitable acceleration loads encountered during even the most benign transportation.

The transport fixture which I made, with model in place, is shown in the accompanying photo. Its base is 1/2 inch thick by 18 3/4 x 20 1/2 inch particle board, which just fits into its shipping box—the sturdy container for our new POWER MAC G-3 (with which these words were typed by me, using the time-honored hunt and peck method). Two centerline supports are provided: one to snugly cradle the landing gear spreader bar; the other for the fuselage rear. Far out on their spans, the lower wings rest upon carefully fitted balsa pylons: both these and the centerline supports are padded with felt. A "goalpost" in front restrains the model from lateral motion by bearing against the radiator housing sides.

Upward motion, from negative "g" forces, is prevented by the means indicated in the accompanying photo. I extended the front and back fuselage supports, the back one to receive a "gate," held down against the rear fuselage decking by insertion in slots, and a wedge. With the Strongback set on the top wing, a long balsa strip was slid over it to fit into cutouts in the front and rear centerline "towers," so that it has a slight bow—exerting a slight downward force on the Strongback.

In retrospect, this transport fixture—the gravity portion, at any rate—should have been used during rigging of the wings: not so much for alignment as to prevent distortion during installation—and occasional removal and resetting—of the rigging wires.

STABILIZER WIRES: The NINAK stabilizer was rigged with eight sets of paired wires: the four (two on each side) forward pairs were fixed, uppers to the fin, and lowers to the fuselage bottom longerons. The centerline termini of the rear pairs were attached to a vertically travelling post in the fin/fuselage, to allow stabilizer incidence adjustment from the cockpit. The wire pairing was a safety precaution, in the event of fraying or battle damage.

I chose to use 7 thou diameter steel piano wire, fitted at each end with a short length of 22 thou brass tubing, slotted at its end for anchoring to the photoetched brass fittings attached to the fin, fuse-

Inversion Strongback-1: These two photos depict use of this device, made (of balsa) to cradle the top wing along its entire length, precisely at its upright dihedral angle. Using this, the model can be inverted, and set on a foam rubber pad without the weight of the wooden wings subjecting the rigging attachments to excessive stresses from the 2g reversal. This simple fixture finally allowed me to complete the rigging, and to perform subsequent model-inverted operations without putting the rigging at risk.

lage, and stabilizer. Incidentally, the most tedious aspect of each end fitting was not sawing the 6 thou wide slot, but reaming its bore to accept the 7 thou wire. Despite the fact that the I.D. of the HOBBY HANGER BT022 tube is nominally 10 thou, it was, in fact, sometimes smaller: far worse was that, with slot sawing and opposite end cutoff, the bore tended to become clogged with brass debris. I broke many a #90 (0.0087" dia.) drill doing this—at $5.78 a pop!

Prefitting each wire was another tedious chore. I would first attach one brass tubing end fitting to a slightly overlength wire. This I then slipped onto one photoetched fitting on the model: two or three such test fits, followed by wire snipping, were required for the opposite end of the wire to just clear the opposite fitting. It was then necessary to attach the second wire fitting so that its slot was coplanar with the first; so that the wire came just up to the end of the tubing slot; and so the fitting was reasonably straight relative to the wire. This was accomplished by inserting a scrap piece of 5 thou brass sheet stock into the slot of the installed fitting; and mounting the loose fitting onto a similar piece of brass sheet—the slots being tweezer-pinched enough to hold the brass scraps. With both elements lying on the workbench, the loose fitting was slipped onto the wire and pushed enough to ensure that the wire bore against the scrap edge within the loose fitting. The two pieces of brass scrap sheet ensure that the slots at both ends are coplanar, and also that the loose fitting is reasonably straight in this plane. Perpendicular straightness is simply "eyeballed." Superglue was applied and—*voila!*— a loose end piece is loose no more. Then—if I remembered—I pulled on both of the end fittings to make certain that they were attached tightly to the wire (not always the case, for reasons unclear to me). The end fittings were then "painted" with BRASS BLACK acid solution, after which the wire was sanded with 1500 grit and then airbrushed with clear lacquer.

Then came actual installation. Each pair, of course, had to be well aligned for parallelism and attached with equal tautness. As I proceeded from one pair to the next, I began encountering a chain of events which very nearly drove me over the edge; as my long-suffering wife can verify. Previously installed pairs would lose their tautness, for reasons which I was absolutely unable to explain. This frustrating—indeed, maddening—process continued for two dreadful weeks, as I went back, removed, and reset wire pairs: some as many as four or five times!

During the depths of my despair, I called my old structural engineer wizard and ex-work colleague, Lew Creedon (late of Southampton, a co-worker for 13 years at General Atomics, now retired in Port Townsend, Washington). The subject of differential thermal expansion kept arising in our conversation: the fact that the coefficient for plastic is greater than for steel.

So, shortly thereafter, I began installing the wires early in the morning, when the room—and therefore the model—was quite cool (around 60° F). Although this was by no means the entire solution, it clearly began reducing the frequency of post-installation loosenings. Another factor, of course, was simply that each time I wrenched off one superglued pair, the stresses and strains therefrom took their toll upon others. After all, the stabilizer is not a rigid element, nor is it rigidly attached to the fuselage and fin—except, eventually by the rigging wires. Gradually, I began gaining upon it, until by 10 April, following 14 days of unremitting struggle, I had it done.

The Third Great Rigging Crisis: But, that wasn't the end of it. The following incident occurred over two months after completion of the model, and six weeks after return from the 1998 IPMS/USA Nationals. I relate it as yet another caution regarding wire rigging.

For this book, I yet lacked photographs of the completed model within its transport fixture, and of the model's underside. Since Jim Schubert is a good photographer with good equipment, I made an appointment with him for a session at my house on 19 August. We photographed outdoors, in direct sunlight. (Yes, despite its reputation to the contrary, this phenomenon does occasionally occur in Seattle.) The ambient temperature was in the low 70s.

The model was in sunlight for around half an hour: although it had become slightly warm to the touch, I was not overly concerned. However, upon post-session, indoors inspection, I saw, to my horror and despair, that *all* of the elevator standing rigging (16 wires) was trashed! Clearly, in retrospect, the stabilizer had expanded from solar radiation enough to overtension the wires—or, more correctly, their attachments. So, once again, all must be removed, cleaned up, and reinstalled—a dreadful, onerous chore (not accomplished as of this writing, late August).

Also—and perhaps even worse from the standpoint of replacement—was the fact that the control line "cables" to the elevators had become loose. I am simply unable to explain why the brief exposure to sunlight would have caused this. After all, this fishing line is elastic, and, in any case, should have tightened back up when it cooled.

CONTROL LINE CABLES: For the "cables" which actuate the rudder and elevators, I had planned to use 6-7 thou monofilament fishing (or sewing) line. However, when the time came, I was unable to find any to this size having an acceptable color. Clear, or even "smokey" didn't look right: I wanted opaque gray, or even "silver." My modelling buddies said:"No problem, just paint it," but I was unable to do so to my satisfaction. Eventually, I came across some opaque gray, 6 thou monofilament fishing line called "FIRELINE," marketed by Berkley. Although its material was not stated on the package, I was told that it is "Spectre," similar to Kevlar. Though not quite as uniform in cross-section as monofilament nylon, and somewhat stiffer, it served my purpose.

For termination under moderate tension, I used the method employed by Bob Rice and others, wherein the line is passed through a hole in the anchor fitting (control horns, in this case) and back through a small brass tube collar on the line. Even though the line is smooth, friction of the returned end through the tube—when pushed up to the loop—is sufficient to maintain tension, when pulled ("cinched") with tweezers. This cinching had to be performed incrementally for the lines attached to either end of the rudder and elevator horns to end up with the correct tension and "set" of the control surface. This achieved, a drop of superglue was applied to each collar. Snipping the emerging tag end ("pigtail") of the line from the collar proved tedious. I managed to cut them off using a sharp #11 surgeon's blade: incredibly, for me, I managed to avoid the obvious pitfall of also severing the installed line.

In the past, for such elastic lines, I have prestretched the lengths before installation, by suspending a 1 1/4 pound barbell weight from them for several days. Although I forgot to take this precaution this time, so far they have remained adequately taut. (But, see "The Third Great Rigging Crisis" above.)

Rigging of the model to this point took me from 11 February to 22 April 1998: six dreadful, tedious weeks.

DRAG WIRES: These were cables actually, on the full-size DH9A. These elements run from a fitting at the forward, lower end of the fuselage (just behind the radiator housing) to the anchor fittings at the top and bottom of the forward, inner interplane struts. Eschewing scale cable for the aforementioned reasons of appearance, I used 9 thou piano wire, with forked ends of 22 thou brass tubing. Conventional turnbuckle bodies were represented by a short length of more 22 thou tubing just behind the terminal fitting. These were among the last items installed on the model, due to their extreme vulnerability. The Dreaded Rigging fought back to the bitter end—even one of these wires had to be reset three times before remaining adequately taut.

MY WING RIGGING METHOD - AN ASSESSMENT: I was led—indeed, driven—to selection of the rigging method described above primarily by the desire to simulate appearance of the actual subject as well as possible. This included reasonably convincing portrayal of the streamline flying and landing wires, including their terminations; and the attachment (anchor) plates. For example, at this scale, the wires could not simply have been anchored into holes drilled in the wings and fuselage, even if fitted with tubing lengths near their ends to represent the terminations.

Also, wire is the rigging material of choice for many scratch builders, especially for larger models. The motives are evidently both appearance and long-term durability: that is, once set in place correctly, the wires *should not* eventually loosen—a potential danger with organic thread, and possibly even nylon. Further, since wire rigging is set into place under minimal, or no tension, forces are not transmitted to a (largely) plastic model structure, which may eventually cause strain induced creep distortion.

However, my method is dreadfully tedious and time-consuming. The worst aspects in this regard are sawing of the fine slots into the wire termination fittings, and precise pre-fitting of each wire in order to obtain the correct length.

Worse yet is the lack of compliance inherent with wire rigging, at least when both ends are anchored. I recognized this problem

A final glimpse of the old NINAK. (Michael Cole photo)

Chapter IV: How I Built My DeHavilland DH9A

Transport Fixture. This device has allowed me to transport the model in our car with relative impunity—well, at least to Santa Clara, California, and back (1,600 miles). The thick base just fits within a sturdy box, coming to rest upon a thick foam rubber pad. Within the car, the box rests upon, and is snugly constrained by many pillows. The car is air-conditioned, and we never park it in the sun, or even warm shade while en route. His Serene Highness, The Nizam of Hyderabad, never rode in greater comfort. But, this outdoor photo session caused The Third Great Rigging Crisis (see text). (Jim Schubert photo)

early in the project and so pondered for a long time over possible means of providing some termination elasticity: sadly, we lost George before I had discussed it with him. (However, he had the same difficulty with his Keystone, as evidenced from photos.) This characteristic manifests itself first in the difficulty of setting the wires with just enough tension so that they remain taut—or, at least, visually straight, following installation of subsequent wires and ambient temperature variations.

Second, and ultimately more threatening, is the fact that, lacking compliance, the rigging is highly vulnerable to handling or transport induced stresses. The wire itself is, of course, very strong. Also, the superglue joints of the wire to its brass tube terminations, and of the terminations to the anchor fittings are quite strong, if the mating surfaces are clean and if the superglue wicks between them properly. The weak link in the chain is attachment of the photoetched anchor fitting to the surface of the wing or fuselage. Since the load path is not straight, a tensile, tearing force is exerted upon the superglue joining the fitting to the mating surface. Not only is the glue far less effective in this mode, but adhesion of finish paint to the plastic is even less so. Therefore, scraping of the paint from this immediate area is a help, since one obtains a metal to plastic superglue joint. Further strength can be obtained by pinning the fitting to the surface just beyond the prong which is to receive a wire termination: by this means, the superglue, if it wicks into the pin socket, acts in shear, which is quite strong. And, the pin is almost along the load path. Nevertheless, lack of compliance (elasticity) translates to lack of shock (load) absorption—like driving along in your car with no suspension springs or Munro Load Levellers ("King uh thu Road").

Third is wire rigging's vulnerability to temperature-induced stresses, due to differential thermal contraction between steel and styrene plastic. See "The Third Great Rigging Crisis" above.

Scale working turnbuckles would be an obvious solution to the problem of length adjustment during, and following wire installation. However, I am unaware of such devices suitable for a 1/24th scale airplane: that is, having a body whose outer diameter is around 25 thou. This is not to say that such a device is impossible to make, given (mechanical) watchmaker technology: just beyond modelling budgets, for few-of-a-kind custom orders. In any case, NINAK primary rigging did not employ conventional turnbuckles: instead, the termination fitting consisted of a short tube, threaded at one end to receive the threaded streamline wire end; and forked at the other, to slip over (and bolt to) the prong of the anchor plate. The termination at one end of a wire had left hand threads; the one at the other, right hand threads. So, you adjusted the length of a rigging wire by rotating it, perforce through 360 degrees, in order for the wire cross-section to be oriented properly to the slipstream.

CONCLUSION

I have often been asked "How can you spend so much time on one model without losing interest in it?" Good question, whose short answer is "I'm a plodder." While true, the complete answer is somewhat more complex. First, when I began the DH9A project back in '90, I never dreamed that it would take eight years to complete. (Had I known, would I have begun it?) But, in addition to sheer bloody mindedness, I was sustained throughout by regarding each major task or component as a "stand alone" project. The wings are a classic example: each set made was a project of its own; completion of the final set, at least, providing a great sense of achievement, in part due to its newly learned technique. Finally, though, it's like gambling, I suppose: having invested so much time and effort into it at any given point, there was simply no emotional possibility of just giving it up.

Another commonly expressed sentiment is "I couldn't (wouldn't) spend so much time on one subject. I want to model so many of my favorite aircraft." I share this sentiment, but "Yer pays yer money and tykes yer choice." I've always carried a "must (scratch) build" list around in my head. The subjects varied from year to year, but the short list has long included the P-38H, Ju88A-4, Bf109E, A5M-4, DH-4, W-W#57, Halberstadt Cl.II and Boston III. I'm now down to perhaps one—after completion of George Lee's O3U-3 float plane.

The accompanying table shows the approximate time investment on various aspects of the NINAK project, extracted from my detailed day-by-day diary. Not fully evident here is rework time, i.e. correction of my many mistakes, the most notable of which was discard of the first set of 1/24th scale wings. I estimate that around 20% of the total time was spent in rework. But, I was in good company: George Lee often spoke of the scratchbuilding rhythm as "two steps forward, one step back."

Part of the explanation for this is the demanding nature of scratchbuilding, in which one's powers of innovation are often taxed to the max. Each "step beyond" entails an element of danger that the technique experiment will fail. For this project, a classic example was my effort to simulate the taping over ribs and edges of wing and tail elements. As discussed above, my chosen method of masking and painting to produce slightly raised features was tedious in the extreme and resulted in much rework before finally achieving a satisfactory "look."

But, there is another factor: as a person who spends years on a scratch-built model, by the time I am ready to perform a given task, I've half forgotten how I did it the last time! This is no joke and is especially evident to me with painting. After all, to date (that is since 1972, when I began my A-20A) I have built only six models. Prior to this, I air brushed two large solid models (a Hurricane and Bf109E) after having been introduced to the technique by George. That makes a total of eight air brush finish jobs in 28 years. (And no kits in between.) Anyhow, you see my point.

DH9A CONSTRUCTION LOG: TIME INVESTMENT

The tabulation below of hours invested by major component/activity was extracted from my detailed construction log, compiled in three 6x9 inch ring binder steno pads.

1. INTERIOR DRAWING		260	
2. FIRST WINGS (RIB/SPAR/SKIN TYPE)			
A. CONSTRUCTION	450		
B. REWORK ATTEMPT	150		
		600	
3. FINAL WINGS (WOOD CORE/ SKIN TYPE)			
A. BASIC CONSTRUCTION	320		
B. AILERONS	207		
		527	
4. FUSELAGE			
A. FALSE START (rejected)	40		
B. BASIC STRUCTURE	506		
C. ENGINE UPPER COAMING	166		
D. PILOT'S COAMING	156		
E. SEAT, CUSHIONS, HEADREST	134		
F. INTERIOR	316		
G. INSTRUMENT PANEL	140		
H. RADIATORS	140		
I. ASSEMBLY	40		
		1638	
5. TAIL		151	
6. UNDERCARRIAGE		395	
7. ARMAMENT			
A. LEWIS GUN	140		
B. VICKERS M/G	157		
C. SCARFF RING	100		
D. BOMBS/CARRIERS/RAILS	188		
		585	
8. PHOTOETCH/MARKING "ARTWORK" -except Lewis Gun & Bomb Carriers		234	
9. PROPELLER		60	
10. ENGINE (INCLUDING EXHAUSTS)		172	
11. MODEL ASSEMBLY		154	
12. PAINTING			
A. FUSELAGE	84		
B. TAIL	155		
C. WINGS (including rib tapes)	276		
D. MARKINGS (including rework)	178		
E. WEATHERING (including rework)	226		
		919	
13. RIGGING			
A. WING, FIRST ATTEMPT	50		
B. WING, RERIG	26		
C. WING, FINAL	69		
D. STABILIZER	96		
E. ELEVATOR CONTROL	7		
F. RUDDER CONTROL	20		
G. DRAG WIRES	29		
H. MISC'L.	51		
		348	
14. MISCELLANEOUS			
A. TAILSKID	28		
B. WINDSCREEN	16		
C. CABANE STRUTS	36		
D. PETROL PUMPS	36		
E. INTERPLANE STRUTS	46		
F. ALDIS SIGHT	16		
G. RATIONS CAN	13		
H. UNDERWING SKIDS	16		
I. STORES BASKET (two made)	23		
J. PITOT TUBE	20		
K. TRANSPORT FIXTURE	21		
L. MISC'L.	74		
		345	
PROJECT TOTAL HOURS		6388	
POST-COMPLETION REPAIRS (December 1998) Control wire rigging, plus resetting of stabilizer and drag wires.		40	

CHAPTER V
How I Built My Gloster Gamecock
by Ron Lowry

ABOUT RON LOWRY

Ron has been interested in aviation since boyhood and still remembers the first time he saw an old biplane skywriting "Coca Cola" high above his head when he was about four years old. At age seven he began to whittle model planes from balsa wood. In December 1985, Ron retired from Bell Canada, after more then thirty years of service, to pursue his model building and aviation artwork fulltime.

At age fifty-five Ron took flying lessons and earned his Private Pilot's Licence; "because I was sick and tired of people asking me...'and do you fly? Now I can answer 'yes' to that question." Ron presently shares half-ownership of a Cessna 150.

Ron is a fine yet prolific scratch builder, with many modelling awards to his credit. He has models on display in the National Aviation Museum in Ottawa, Ontario, as well as in the National Air and Space Museum in Washington, D.C.

INTRODUCTION

To me the appearance of the GAMECOCK personifies the two British traits of stubbornness and perserverance. With a little imagination the stance of the GAMECOCK even resembles that of a wide-legged English Bulldog. This pugnacious-looking fighter biplane fits well in the Golden Age of Aviation. It just oozes with colour and character, providing the scratchbuilder with plenty of challenge and a healthy dose of satisfaction upon the model's completion.

Years of experience have taught me to start a model by first giving considerable thought as to which method of construction will serve me best. Thinking this through to the end must be firmly established in my mind. By having a clear mental picture and facing any possible problems in advance, so to speak, helps me to save time, energy, and frustration throughout the actual process of construction.

I used a scale drawing of the GAMECOCK I found in an old issue of "PLANES" Magazine, Vol.l, No.3, drawn by Alfred Granger, a very skilled draftsman. (These drawings are reproduced in the fine book "ON SILVER WINGS: RAF Biplane Fighters Between The Wars," by Alec Lumsden and Owen Thetford.-ed.)

WINGS AND TAIL

I find basswood or hard balsa to be the most suitable for carving a model's wing and tail cores. For the skin, I used 20 thou plasticard. The now familiar wood core and plastic skin method of wing and tailplane construction has proven itself to me, over and over again, as a reliable means of providing strength, a solid bed for struts and a firm support if ailerons need to be cut away. Also, the core-and-skin method permits the leading edge to be built without having to fold or bend the styrene. My methods of construction are straightforward, with no need for a vacuforming machine or costly power tools. I'm a modeler who still finds the X-Acto type blade a mighty tool. I also aim for simplicity over complexity.

For the GAMECOCK, I selected strips of hard balsa, which comes in 36 inch lengths and is available in any good hobby store. For the upper wing I used a strip l/4" thick by 3" wide: for the lower wing I used a 3/16" thick by 3" wide piece.

Tracing from the scale drawing, I made paper templates of the wings and tail elements. I then pencilled the outline of the templates on the measured strips of balsa, whose shapes were cut out, but slightly smaller, using a sharp knife.

The cut out shapes were now ready for carving the airfoil cross-sections. With X-Acto type No.26 "whittler's" blade in hand, I began to carve lengthwise along each balsa core, keeping a watchful eye on my work, as it is vital to create the correct taper to the trailing edges. Still carving length-wise along the cores, careful attention was also given to proper rounding of each leading edge.

The next step was to taper the wing-tips. I find it of the utmost importance to begin tapering towards the wing-tip a slight bit sooner than what is actually shown on a scale drawing. My reason for doing this is that when the skin is later applied, the correct shape of the wing-tip will take place smoothly, without the dismay of seeing the skin pucker and wrinkle.

The next phase of construction pertains to the upper wing panels only. I hollowed out two troughs, each measuring 2-1/2" long by 3/32" wide by 3/32" deep on the underside of each upper wing half to accomodate brass tubing, whose purpose was to add further strength, as well as obtain the correct dihedral.

I cut two 5" lengths of brass tubing and bent each just enough to provide the correct dihedral. Then I butt and glued the wing-halves together. But before this glue had time to set, I quickly epoxied the brass tubes into the prepared troughs. Thus, I was able to achieve the correct dihedral with little effort. Finally, I sanded the upper wing-core smooth.

WOULD YOU BUY A USED CESSNA 150 FROM THIS MAN?

GLOSTER GAMECOCK-1: Great subject; fine model; lovely photograph. This is Ron Lowry's 1/24th scale rendition of the RAF No.23 Squadron GAMECOCK I flown by Squadron Leader Raymond Collishaw of W.W.-I fame, circa 1927. It is difficult to imagine a subject more evocative of the "ON SILVER WINGS" era than this dramatically colored little biplane. -Ron Lowry photo

GLOSTER GAMECOCK-2: This 3/4 rear view reveals other aspects of both subject and model which emphasize its remarkable character. -Ron Lowry photo

Chapter V: How I Built My Gloster Gamecock

GLOSTER GAMECOCK-3: Yet another revealing perspective of Ron's delightful model. Ron took these "portrait" photos himself, using his MINOLTA X-370N 35 mm eamera. -Ron Lowry photo

To skin the upper wing, I first made a paper template of its shape and traced its outline, twice, onto a sheet of 20 thou styrene. I now penciled on all wing rib lines, with the aid of a steel rule. Still using this rule, I embossed the rib lines with the tip of a ball-point pen, extending each line beyond the wing outline to allow for the later curve of the airfoil. Then, I cut out the two wing skins, leaving a 1/4" margin all around. This excess allows ease of handling when gluing the skins to the core.

I find it easier to attach the wing's underside skin first. I brushed contact cement evenly over the top of the skin and the under surface of the core, which were then set aside for a few minutes to give the cement time to cure.

Fitting the glue-coated shapes together is a one chance only challenge of alignment, requiring a steady hand and a pinch of patience. When two contact cemented pieces touch....that's it....they're stuck, and a strong bond has occurred! So care and patience are mandatory.

Now the 1/4" excess margin of styrene can be trimmed away. The remaining narrow plastic outline of the wing shape should still be visible, due to the wooden core being slightly smaller, as mentioned earlier.

Next, I beveled the trailing edge of the skin flush with the core upper surface, using a small block of wood wrapped with sandpaper. This provides a sharp trailing edge for later attachment of the upper skin.

Now I cut 80 thou off the wood core leading edge and replaced it with a strip of 80 thou styrene. This strip was glued to the lower lip of the wing skin and the now flattened edge of the core, using Insta-Cure + (a brand of superglue). It was then beveled to follow the contour of core top airfoil. I could now contact cement the upper skin to the core.

Next, I sealed the remaining styrene joints all along the leading and trailing edges and the wing-tips, using Insta-Cure +. Light sanding was now needed to round the leading edge, completing the upper wing.

I followed this same method of construction to build the lower wing and tail elements.

FUSELAGE

I began the fuselage by making a profile paper template from the drawings, but omitting the cockpit and engine areas. The outline of this shape was then drawn on a sheet of 60 thou plasticard and cut out, to form the centerline keel.

Next, I cut out the bulkheads from 60 thou plasticard. One bulkhead would become the engine fire-wall, and three others, which were cut in half vertically, and glued on each side of the keel: at the front of the cockpit, behind the cockpit, and in front of the stabilizer.

Using 60 thou styrene I cut out the cockpit floor and glued it in place. Then, I cut away a 60 thou strip from the bottom of the for-

GLOSTER GAMECOCK-4: This shot reveals fuselage construction details, as described in the text.

ward keel and replaced it with a separate section of 60 thou styrene measuring 2-1/4" long by 1-1/4" wide. This section would provide a stable platform to anchor the lower wing later. It would also become a solid foundation to support the undercarriage. Then I cut out a slot, 1-3/8" long, at the rear of the keel to accomodate the stabilizer.

Then, using blocks of balsa, I filled in the spaces between the bulkheads, excluding the "office," of course. This assembly was then carved and sanded to conform with the correct shape of the fuselage.

Now I had to address the area some modelers seem to never get out of....the cockpit interior. This consisted of building a simulated wooden framework with its wire bracing. For a likeness of the framework I used "Evergreen" strips, and to make the wire bracing I simply used the thinnest piano wire available and just left it in its natural state.

The next step was to make six small bulkheads of 30 thou styrene and cut out a concavity from each. These were then glued, one to each of the vertical posts of the framework, to later hold the machine-gun barrels.

Now, in one fell swoop, the cockpit floor, the framework, and small bulkheads were painted a medium brown and stained with a Burnt Sienna rash, lightly streaked to simulate wood grain.

Then, I brought out my scrap box and began to equip the cockpit, starting with the pilot seat and moving along to the control stick and rudder pedals, followed by the machine-gun breaches, complete with cocking handles. Next, I made the engine throttle controls and the stabilizer adjustment mechanism peculiar to the GAMECOCK. Then came the radio and oxygen controls, followed by two oxygen bottles, placed on the floor behind the pilot seat. Just above these bottles I installed a small shelf on which to set the radio and a map case.

To make the instrument panel, I used the old, familiar "sandwich" method. However, to create more authentic looking bezels I

Consolidated P2Y-3. This model represents a boat from VP 7, Flag Unit USS *Wright*, 1937.

sliced thin rings from different sizes of aluminum tubing to match the varied sizes of instruments.

Now I could skin the forward portion of the fuselage. I cut shapes of 20 thou styrene to represent the metal panels on the GAMECOCK, and glued them in place using Insta-Cure +. This also meant I had to maneuver around the inside of the six small bulkheads attached to the vertical posts of the framework. The easiest way I could think of was to cut two narrow lengths of 20 thou styrene and gently bend each to fit along, willingly, into the concavities. The fast drying properties of the Insta-Cure + allowed this task to be accomplished with a minimum of time and effort.

The rear portion of the GAMECOCK's fuselage consists of a fabric-covered framework. To create a visual likeness, I used 20 thou styrene and cut out the shapes for the top deck, the underbelly, and the port and starboard sides.

Then, by taking the shapes, one at a time, I carefully but firmly pressed each against their corresponding area to help them take on their desired form. I hoped this trick would alleviate possible problems when it came time to fit and glue.

Now I penciled on the length-wise ribbing lines and embossed them in the same manner as for the wings. I then glued on the upper deck and underbelly skins. I had been a little concerned over fitting and gluing the two side skins because of the compound curves on each side of the GAMECOCK's fuselage. But having taken the time earlier to pre-shape the styrene, both skins fit well and conformed to the compound curves accurately and with relative ease. A minimum of trimming and sanding was needed where the styrene sections came together and were glued.

I did not need to skin the remaining tail-end of the keel, but I did need to widen it. This was easily achieved by laminating two lengths of 60 thou styrene to fit on each side. Each laminated section was provided with a measured slot, to match that already cut out of the keel, to later receive the stabilizer. Once glued in place I only had to trim and sand the laminations to their finished shape.

Now I could concentrate on detailing the outer surface of the fuselage, beginning with a few doors. I cut out and glued two small panels of 10 thou styrene to represent the machine-gun access doors, one to each side of the fuselage. Then I cut away the measured area that, in a few minutes, would become the pilot access door. To make this door operable, allowing it to be opened or closed, I supplied it with a hinge.

To make a hinge is really quite basic. For a facsimile of a regular looking hinge I cut brass tubing, of the smallest diameter, into six 1/8" sections. These were then glued, alternately, one to the door, one to the door-sill, one to the door, and so on. I used Insta Cure +, but any superglue will hold this rudimentary hinge in place. I then inserted a 3/4" pin of thin piano wire through the six sections of tubing to secure the hinge to the door. Friction alone holds the

Boulton & Paul DEFIANT I. This 1/24th scale model represents an aircraft of No. 409 "Nighthawk" Squadron, RCAF. In addition to first in its scratch built category, Ron's DEFIANT won BEST CANADIAN SUBJECT at the 1997 IPMS/USA Nationals, in Columbus, Ohio. -Ron Lowry photo

Armstrong Whitworth SISKIN III A. This 1/24th scale model, built by Ron Lowry, represents A/C No. 306 of No. 1 Sqdn. RCAF, 1938. It won Judge's Best, Best Canadian Subject and Best Aircraft at the 1992 IPMS/Canada Nationals. -Ron Lowry photo

"pin" in place at both ends. The pilot's door can now be opened or closed at will, many times. I made a similar hinge for the door of the radio compartment.

My next phase of detailing the outer surface of the fuselage was to apply the "stitching" to the "fabric." Using sheet styrene to simulate an aircraft's fabric-lacing, or stitching, is not difficult. As the starboard side of the GAMECOCK required stitching, I cut out a wider than necessary length of 10 thou strip styrene and, using steel rule, I scored a line directly down the centre, from end to end. Then I trimmed away the excess margin, leaving the strip to now measure 1/16" in width. I glued 1/32" Evergreen strips diagonally over the top of the indentation side of the scored line. Any excess of these strips was trimmed away. I now glued this "stitched" section to the fuselage in accordance with the scale drawing.

A zig-zag pattern of stitching surrounds the prepared slot at the tail-end of the keel. To imitate this design I cut out a measured, U-shaped, length of 10 thou styrene. I then penciled on the zig-zag pattern and cut it out to the required 1/16" width. I completed the stitching by adding tiny strips of stretched sprue to provide the centre line to the design.

Now I could build the lower wing attachment. However, it should be noted that although I constructed the lower wing in the same manner as the upper, I did epoxy two, 2" lengths of 3/32" brass tubing into the prepared troughs of each wing-half at their root, providing a sheath to now accept the wing attachment. To begin the lower wing attachment, I cut away just enough of the fuselage skin to accomodate each of the lower wing-roots. This bit of surgery intentionally revealed the floor of the forward fuselage.

Now I could glue and box-in two, 6" lengths of 1/16" brass tubing. These tubes would slide into the larger sized brass tubing provided at the lower wing roots. Dihedral was accomplished by slightly bending the two inches of tubing protruding from the fuselage floor.

THE ENGINE

The GAMECOCK was powered by the Bristol Jupiter VI radial engine, of superb performance for its time. The aircraft's highly aerobatic capabilities were greatly facilitated by the unfailing reliability of the Jupiter VI. The GAMECOCK served from the mid-1920's to the early-1930's and, together with the pleasant "humming" sound of the Jupiter VI, was the star performer at the famed R.A.F. annual Hendon Airshow.

Williams Bros. manufactured a 1/24th scale kit of a basic radial engine. Luckily, I purchased one several years ago for some future project. My GAMECOCK has now become that project. Unfortunately, I understand this particular engine kit is no longer available.

To the assembled basic engine kit, I added to the cylinder heads the necessary valve springs, rocker arms, spark plugs, and connecting wires, using scrap styrene and left over pieces of wire. For the push rods I used thin piano wire, cut to size.

The Jupiter's exhaust was ejected into a circular collector ring mounted in front of the engine crankcase. I simply cut out a measured ring-shape from 100 thou styrene and glued it to the engine block. At the back of the engine block I placed another fire-wall, but this time of 40 thou styrene, 1/32" smaller in circumference. To provide the engine with the intake and exhaust pipes I used 2mm

Lockheed P-38L #1. This fine 1/24th scale model of the LIGHTNING is now in the collection of Paul Ludwig, of Seattle, Washington. It depicts "Taffy," an aircraft flown by Walter Zurney of the 82nd Fighter Group, 15th Air Force, Italy, 1945. (Paul Ludwig photo)

Lockheed P-38L #2. Another view of "Taffy." (Paul Ludwig photo)

84 The Master Scratch Builders: Tips & Techniques from the Master Aircraft Modelers

wire solder, because it is so flexible and easy to manipulate. The engine was then painted black.

To make the aluminum plates for fitting between the cylinders, I used 20 thou styrene and glued them to the exhaust collector ring and the fire-wall behind the engine. I then drilled a 1/16" hole, from the crankcase through to the fire-wall, for fitting the 1-1/2" long propeller shaft of 1/16" brass tubing.

UNDERCARRIAGE

I use brass tubing throughout model construction where ever possible, in order to provide strength. As a good friend and scratchbuilder of exquisite model aircraft, the late Dan Dossert of Syracuse, N.Y., once said to me, "Ron, ya gotta build 'em strong." I have tried to follow Dan's good advice ever since.

In order to build a sturdy undercarriage, I compressed brass tubing to the desired thinness using long-nosed pliers. Then I dressed any imperfections with a file. As with most biplanes of the era, the GAMECOCK's undercarriage was a V-type with a single axle. Therefore, the ends of the four undercarriage struts were compressed until flattened. A 1/16" hole was then drilled into both ends of each strut. Now the axle could pass through the holes at the V-join, as well as where the struts would be joined to the fuselage floor.

Next, I glued and boxed in two measured lengths of brass tubing across the fuselage floor. The ends of these tubes would then be fit into the holes provided at the ends of the undercarriage struts, with careful attention given to the correct alignment.

WHEELS

For the tires of my model I used round plastic curtain-rod rings of the correct size, found in a fabric and sewing accessories store. The wheels, though, were carved from 100 thou styrene and glued in the tires.

I wanted to detail the wheels by suggesting spokes underneath the taut fabric.

Before explaining the method I used to achieve this feature, I will digress for a moment to emphasize the importance of starting a model by first thinking the method of construction through to the end. My wheel-cover construction happens to present a good example to show I do practise what I preach. In this case I did not want any unpleasant surprises down the road, nor did I want to waste time by having to correct, or worse still, re-do. In reality a wheel-cover is a single item. Yet I chose to build the wheel-covers using several pieces of styrene. To start, I cut out two discs for each side of both wheels from 20 thou styrene, but just slightly larger than the wheels themselves. Then I drilled a 1/16" hole in the centre of each disc to enable the undercarriage axle to pass through. Now I glued narrow strips of 20 thou styrene to the outer edges of the discs, each facing towards the centre to, once again, resemble the appearance of stitching.

Brewster F2A-1. This 1/24th scale model, also from the Paul Ludwig collection, depicts a BUFFALO of the USS *SARATOGA*-based VF-3, in 1940, flown by Lt. "Jimmy" Thatch. This was the only U.S. Navy squadron to receive -1s; most (43) having been diverted to the Finns as the Model 239, who made good use of them against the Soviets. (Paul Ludwig photo)

Then I carved a small conical shaped mold from basswood. I glued pieces of stretched sprue onto the mold to represent the wheel-spokes. I used the standard male-and-female method to form the wheel-covers with 20 thou styrene. I also drilled a 1/16" hole into each wheel-cover so the tips of the axle could fit through. As the wheels and wheel-covers are to be painted in different colours, I have just avoided the need of having to mask these small parts.

PROPELLER

I traced the front and side profiles of the propeller blades and hub from the scale drawing. I penciled these outlines on a piece of elmwood 4-1/2" X 3/4" X 1/4". Then I drilled the usual 1/16 hole dead-centre in what would become the hub, for inserting the propeller shaft later. Using an X-Acto type No.11 blade, I began to carve and shave the wood to its proper shape, being particularly careful to attain the correct taper and twist of the blades. A certain degree of carving experience and dexterity is a bonus for shaping the hub. The unit was then sanded smooth. I carved the spinner from scrap plastic.

WING STRUTS

In an attempt to correct the GAMECOCK's persistent and dreaded wing flutter, the engineers of the Gloster factory festooned the wings with no less than twenty struts.

Ten of these supported the upper wing centre section. With this number of struts condensed in one location, I decided that a wing assembly jig would be impractical. Instead, I took the option of accurately measuring and pinning this group of struts into precisely placed access holes drilled into the upper wing and forward fuselage. I again relied on the strength of compressed brass tubing to make these ten struts, except that I inserted and glued thin piano wire into the tubes, allowing the ends of the wire to extend for later pinning and gluing purposes.

For the outer main struts I used 40 thou styrene, gluing a pin of piano wire into the ends for later fitting purposes. My reason for using styrene for these struts was due to its flexibility, allowing easier fitting into the holes provided in both wings. I reverted to the compressed brass tubing and piano wire method to make the remaining outer auxiliary V-struts.

It's interesting to note all that was really needed to cure the GAMECOCK's wing flutter was a one degree washout of the outer upper and lower wings. It is even more interesting to note that this solution to rid the GAMECOCK of its dreaded wing flutter had been omitted from the Air Ministry Rigging Instruction Manual. Once this important information had been discovered the four outer V-struts were removed. And I had to go and build the twenty strut version!

Douglas AD-6 SKYRAIDER. This 1/24th scale model represents an aircraft of VA-145, operating from the USS *HORNET* (CV-12) in 1957, piloted by Lt.Jg. Paul Ludwig. (Paul Ludwig photo)

RAF RE-8. Here is Ron Lowry's 1/24th scale depiction of a "Harry Tate" from No.52 Squadron, RFC, l917/early 19l8. Fine model of a less than fine machine. The poor old RE-8 represented 1915/16 technology in a 1917/18 environment: as such, it was Albatros bait during "Bloody April" 1917, and unfortunately soldiered on into 1918, when the depredations of D.Vas, Dr.Is and D.VIIs took the lives of so many young Britons, who may have survived in RR Eagle-powered DH-4s or Falcon-powered F2Bs. His model represents the personal mount of Lt. Percival E. Biggar, who much later designed the amphibious DUKW of W.W.-II fame. -Ron Lowry photo

TRIAL ASSEMBLY AND FINAL CONSTRUCTION

The moment of truth had arrived; the trial assembly of all model parts. The moment always brings with it a twinge of apprehension. But the time spent on precise measuring, particularly at attachment points, had paid off. The model went together commendably. Even setting the upper wing down onto all twenty struts went well. I was lucky.

To complete the construction I cut away the movable controls and covered the now visible wooden cores with 10 thou styrene shaped to fit. I used piano wire cut to size to make the pins for re-attaching the ailerons, elevators, and rudder, with careful attention given to the correct alignment.

I used scrap styrene to make the partially exposed wing fuel tanks, the lower tail fin, and the framing for a SIG plastic windshield. Brass tubing was used to make the tail skid, gun barrels, flare holders, an external lower wing generator, and exhaust pipes.

PAINTING THE MODEL

The most colourful of all the RAF GAMECOCK squadrons was No. 23. The line of red and blue squares along the sides of the fuselage and across the top of the upper wing made an everlasting impression on anyone who saw these vivid markings.

The Commanding Officer was Squadron Leader Raymond "Collie" Collishaw, a top scoring W.W.-I ace, with 62 victories to his credit. It was the colourful livery of Collishaw's GAMECOCK that I wanted to portray on my model.

The model parts just seemed to lend themselves to being painted disassembled, This was fine with me, as it meant I only had to mask the squadron markings.

First I airbrushed the parts with Dupont Hi-Speed 30-S Gray Primer. Then I used standard wet and dry method of sanding until the surfaces were free of blemishes and became satiny smooth.

Collishaw's aircraft was painted silver. I airbrushed the model using R-M 1978 Volvo silver automobile lacquer. It was also my good friend, Dan Dossert, who initiated me, more years ago than I care to remember, to use auto lacquers for painting model aircraft.

As has already been mentioned, I had to mask the red and blue squadron markings. I was fortunate to find a local automotive parts shop where a supply of auto lacquers were still available. I used GM red and a Toyota medium blue which offered a hue of ultramarine that matched the colour of my RAF paint chip. I cut out the roundels from frisket paper using a compass with an attached blade. I airbrushed them using the GM red, the Toyota medium blue, and a GM white.

For a good match of the light gray cockpit coaming, I used the Dupont 30-S Gray Primer.

I gave the propeller several coats of varnish and then painted the blades a cream colour to give the impression of the doped fabric covers. I airbrushed dark silver to the leading edge of the blades to represent the protective metal cap. The boss remains in its varnished wood state.

The tires were painted a dark gray with white Letraset used to provide the manufacturer's name. The tires were then given an overspray of light gray to simulate wear. The fabric wheel covers are painted white with red conical centres.

It will be remembered that the engine had already been painted black, leaving the back firewall and between the cylinder plates to be painted. I airbrushed the 1978 Volvo silver lacquer over the entire engine. By doing this I was able to regulate the amount of silver paint desired until the engine took on the appearance of being metal. At the same time the lacquer reached the firewall and between the cylinder plates, providing the illusion of aluminum.

The horizontal tail plane was painted with the Toyota medium blue lacquer. The rudder stripes were another bit of masking I had to do, and these were painted the usual red, white, and blue using the auto lacquers.

If my research findings are correct, 23 Squadron reversed its blue, white, and red stripes to the now familiar red, white, and blue long before the official 1930 date.

For a subtle weathering effect I hand brushed the model parts with a wash of Burnt Umber and a hint of black using oil based artist paints mixed with turpentine and linseed oil.

The only decals I used were for the aircraft's serial numbers, found in my file of "yet to use" markings.

Now I drilled holes in the wing and tail surfaces at the attachment points for the wire rigging.

FINAL ASSEMBLY AND WIRE RIGGING

The final assembly was carried out with a minimum of effort, requiring a drop or two of Insta-Cure + to glue the already snug fit of model parts at joins and attachment points.

Once the major parts were fit and glued, I began to rig the wings with piano wire, filed until flattened to represent the Royal Aircraft Factory flying wires.

The GAMECOCK did not have any visible turnbuckles, enabling the rigging wires to carefully fit into the drilled holes fairly swiftly. A drop of Insta-Cure + in each hole held the wires firmly in place.

My next step was to mount the engine. First I made two lugs from scrap styrene and glued them to the fuselage firewall. Two holes were then drilled into the engine firewall to accomodate the lugs. The engine was then mounted and glued in place.

To make running lights for the tail and upper wing I used scrap styrene for the teardrop shaped casings and MV Products for the coloured lens. Short pieces of piano wire became the shafts for fitting the lights into the surface of the upper wing. A small piece of flat brass became a supporting base for attaching the tail light to the rudder.

I used monofilament thread stretched taut for radio antenna and the eyes of sewing needles for the attachment posts.

CLOSING THOUGHTS

Many years have come and gone while waiting for the opportunity to bring Alfred Granger's scale drawing to life in the form of a model. Now I've done it, and I'm encouraged by the result: particularly as the model won a Gold Award at the '98 World Expo held in Toronto, Ontario, this July.

I have always admired the GAMECOCK as a colourful aircraft of the Golden Age of Aviation. It has been recorded that Flying Officer Richard "Batchy" Atcherley became a legend in his own lunch-time for his astonishing demonstration of Gamecock aerobatics during the mid-day interval at the RAF Hendon display on the 3rd July 1926. The GAMECOCK's last public appearance was perhaps the most historic of all. One of the two pilots featured in a duel aerobatic display was none other than Pilot Officer Douglas Bader.

To take photographs of the GAMECOCK and other models, I used a Minolta X-370N with a 35mm to 70mm telephoto lens attached. The camera was set at F.22 with a 2 second time exposure in a room flooded with summer light.

I estimate the time spent on building the GAMECOCK was 405 hours.

Brandenburg D.1. This model represents a mount of the famous Austrian ace Josef Kiss of FLIK 24. Designed by Ernst Heinkel, the "Starstrutter" was not one of his better efforts.

CHAPTER VI
How I Built Grumman My TBF-1C Avenger
by Arlo Scroeder

INTRODUCTION

It was inevitable that my most ambitious modelling project would be the Grumman TBF-1 AVENGER. This, because I made two cruises with VT-10 during W.W.-II, as a TBF turret gunner; first aboard the *Enterprise* (CV-6), then on the *Intrepid* (CV-11).

Actually, I have scratch built three TBFs! The first, to 1/32 scale, was entered in the 1977 IPMS/USA National Convention in San Francisco, where it was awarded First Place in the Aircraft Scratch Built, Large Scale category. The second, also to 1/32nd scale, was built for President George Bush—naturally representing his VT 51 aircraft. The third, and the subject of this chapter, was to 1/16th scale for the NASM's Sea/Air Gallery. Needless to say, these honors have been sources of great satisfaction to me.

Incidentally, another source of satisfaction was the fact that the recent 1/48th scale ACCURATE MINIATURES TBF-1C featured markings of "my" plane when we were credited with sinking the Japanese cruiser YAHAGI, on 7 April 1945.

For the NASM's model, I chose TBF-1C, BU AER NO. 47826, "T-41" of VT-10; the aircraft of Lt. Cdr. William I. Martin, who commanded this unit aboard the U.S.S. *Enterprise* from January to June 1944.

The model took me 2,600 hours—two retirement years—to construct.

EDITOR'S NOTE: Following his discharge from the service—and graduation from high school (he had joined the navy in August 1942, at age 17!), Arlo spent 33 years on the flight line at Boeing Wichita. This experience explains his fascination with aircraft functional detail, and the technician/machinist skills he brings to bear upon replication of those aspects.

When I asked Arlo if he would provide a chapter for MSB on his 1/16th scale TBF-1C, he said: "Just use the feature which appeared in the January 1991 IPMS/USA MODELERS' JOURNAL,"

This photo of Arlo dramatizes the size of his *magnum opus*.

and sent me a copy. While some additions and editorial changes have been made, that's what I did. It appears here with the kind permission of David Van Almen, IPMS/USA Journal Editor/Publisher, then and now.

DOCUMENTATION/PREPARATION

Fortunately for me, the TBF has been widely photographed and documented in various publications: my file on the Avenger is bulging! I had the foresight, while still in the Navy, to latch onto portions of the TBF pilot's manual which contained station line drawings and cockpit photos with many other details. This allowed me to prepare full sized drawings for this project simply by establishing the scale of the handbook drawings, and relying upon the station line dimensions. After I was well into building the model, Squadron/Signal came out with their TBM/TBF IN ACTION book, which contains very accurate 1/72 scale drawings of the variants. Had this been available to me at the onset, a great deal of time and effort would have been eliminated. Prior to this publication, the only drawings were by Willis Nye which appeared in "Model Airplane News." While these drawings did provide a great deal of good information, they also oontained some glaring inaccuracies, particularly in the fuselage profile, and cross section in the cockpit area—which failed to allow for the wing center section! Probably my best source for details was the fact I had access to a real TBM-3, parked next to my home for one week. I had arranged to have it here on the airstrip where I live for our first ever Torpedo Ten reunion. This allowed me to take numerous close-up pictures and document many details I would need. Subsequent to this, I obtained a copy of the TBM-3 Erection & Maintenance manual, plus the original pilot's handbook on both the TBF-1C, TBM-3 and Aircrewman's Gunnery manual, which provided turret details—that I didn't recall from 50 years ago!

WRIGHT R-2600-8 ENGINE CONSTRUCTION

First I made dimensioned sketches, from various books, photos, a Navy engine training manual, and a TBM maintenance manual. I then made master patterns made for cylinders, crankcase, & nose section. The cylinder masters were made by stamping out cooling fin wafers from .005" sheet aluminum and barrel wafers from .020" sheet aluminum. These wafers were then stacked on a 1/8" bolt and trued up on a lathe. The vertical cooling fins, valve, and rocker box housings were made from .005" sheet aluminum and .l90"ABS plastic, with .020" brass tubing for intake and exhaust ports. Two master cylinders are required, one for each row, since the rear row of cylinders is mounted in reverse of the forward row. Rear row cylinders have exhaust and intake ports on the same side as pushrods. The master pattern for the main crankcase section was made from 1 1/2" diameter polyester rod, .032" ABS sheet plastic and .30 brass tubing for cylinder locaters. The forward nose section master pat-

Grumman TBF-1C. This 1/16th scale model depicts TBF-1C, BU AER No. 47826, "T-41" of VT-lO; the aircraft of Lt. Cdr. William I. Martin, who commanded this unit aboard the USS *Enterprise* (CV-6) during the first half of 1944. Arlo was a turret gunner with VT-lO during this cruise. - NASM/Eric Long photo

Grumman TBF-1C. Arlo reports that this model took him 2,600 hours—two retirement years—to construct. It is now in the NASM's Sea/Air Gallery. - NASM/Eric Long photo

Grumman TBF-1C Cockpit Detail. This shot emphasizes Arlo's meticulous attention to detail on this labor of love. Of note is the fact that the halves of the AVENGER's forward cockpit canopy could be opened independently. - NASM/Eric Long photo

tern was turned on a lathe and included simulated mounting bolts & nuts around the outer periphery.

The next step was making molds from the master patterns. For the cylinder molds, sheet plastic boxes 2"x1 3/4"x 3/4" with slightly out-board canted sides were made. The master pattern was positioned in the box with the cylinder protruding half way through the bottom, which has a cutout to match the profile of the cylinder at its vertical cross section. Nesting structure to support the cylinder in this position is added to the bottom of the box. A plunger plate that fits the mid point of the mold box, with handle attached, is used to force the mold material around the cylinder. This plunger plate has a series of holes in it to allow air to escape as pressure is applied. Mold material is forced through these holes, and after cure hold the mold to the plunger which then may become an integral part of the mold. With the master pattern in place in the box, the box is filled with mold material with a spatula and the plunger is forced down into the box. Mold material is forced around the cylinder and oozes out through the cooling fins at the bottom of the box. After cure all excess is trimmed away, the box and plunger are separated, the master pattern is removed, and you have a mold. A mold is required for each of the two master cylinders.

I used "IMPREGUM POLYETHER IMPRESSION MATERIAL TYPE I," which I obtained from a local dental supply house. It's rather expensive and sets up in about two minutes. For later efforts I switched to CASTOLITE CASTOMOLD SR-B flexible silicone rubber material. I found this to be just as satisfactory and costs considerably less. Both products do a good job of picking up detail. Even though the spacing between the cooling fins is .020, and fin thickness is 5 thou, they reproduced up to 20 cylinders from one mold.

To make the castings, I used Polyester fiberglas resin, which has about the viscosity of maple syrup. After pouring the resin into the mold, I held a running open chuck drill against the mold handle to act as a shaker, to work any air bubbles out of the resin, which sets up in about 5 minutes. It's quite brittle, and care must be taken so as not to break off any of the cooling fins. After completing the casting of both cylinder halves, they must be sanded to their midpoint and glued together. I have since also made a PRATT & WHITNEY R-l340 for my Boeing F4B-2, in 1/16 scale. In that effort I made a one piece cylinder mold in a 35mm film container. By removing the mold from the film can and splitting one side with an Xacto knife, the cylinder was easily removed from the mold. The mold was reinserted into the film can for subsequent castings. This method eliminates the matching up of the two cylinder halves and reduces the number of molds required.

The procedure for making the crankcase molds is similar to the above. Two main crankcase parts are required, one for each row of cylinders. After painting and mounting the 14 cylinders, I proceeded with detailing the engine. The push rod housings were made of aluminum tubing. Spark plugs, ignition harness, and prop governor were fabricated and added. Building an engine from scratch is quite a project in itself: I'll not go into further detail here.

FUSELAGE AND WING CENTER SECTION

FUSELAGE VACUFORM PATTERNS: Since there are no compound curves between the windshield (station 0) and the midpoint of the turret (station 146), I decided patterns would be required only for the forward and aft sections of the fuselage. These patterns were carved from balsa wood blocks in right and left halves. Starting with a photocopy of these section profiles with vertical station lines, these patterns were glued to the rough block and cut to profile shape with a band saw. Utilizing body station templates of every third station, the blocks were carved and sanded to correct shape. After final sanding, superglue was rubbed onto the balsa and then resanded. This process was repeated twice and resulted in a very rugged pattern.

Sections were then vacuformed from 9"x17" sheets of .025"ABS plastic. I use a vacuform rig built into the top of my work bench, a Sears ShopVac for vacuum source, and a paint stripper heat gun for heating the plastic. Considering that not every form-

TBF-1 Reference Material. Note the 1/16th scale drawings, prepared by Arlo himself. Scratch built models often require scratch built drawings.

Fuselage Structure/Wing Center Section Assembly.

ing run produces a satisfactory part, it takes a lot of plastic to build a model of this size. That's why I buy the plastic in 4'x8' sheets.

After obtaining good fuselage half shells, I proceeded with the aft section. Solid bulkheads were cut from .025" ABS plastic sheet for each station between the tailcone and aft the end of the turret. These bulkheads had rough circular holes cut in them to allow later final trimming to inside shape. These essentially full section bulkheads provided rigidity during glueing and assembly and were then glued into the right half fuselage shell. Vertical fin, rear spar, and internal structure to support horizontal stabilizer and tail wheel assembly attach points were added, as were the retractable tailhook and mechanism. Upper and lower centerline joint splice plates were also added. The left outer shell was not added until after this rear section was attached to the wing center section to develop the forward fuselage section. After this had been done, it was removed and the left side shell was glued in place. The vertical fin was then added along with insertion of brass tubing for the horizontal stabilizer attach points. Balsa form blocks for the lower aft tunnel windows were made, and these clear parts were formed from 1/32" plexiglas. These, along with the four side windows, were glued in place. The entire rear section was sanded, along with the clear parts, to final smoothness, and the windows were polished to their final original clarity.

To prevent having to handle the large sections of a model this size, I chose to do as much of the detail work in the smaller sections as possible. The tail assembly was then added. The complete aft fuselage section was mounted like a rotisserie between two stanchions with brass tubing running through the centerline. The stanchions were glued directly to a work board so the fuselage could rotate 360° around its centerline axis. A slidable stylus holder was fabricated from brass tubing which was clamped to the work board. The stylus arm had a small chuck attached to it which held the point of a large sewing needle. This arrangement allowed me to accurately scribe the eleven station panel lines by rotating the section around its axis at each station line. The inside of the bulkhead formers were trimmed to final shape, floor panels and other visible details added, and interior green paint applied essentially completing this section, and held for final attachment to the center section.

WING CENTER SECTION: This is the heart of the model since it contains the wing fold hinge plates, landing gear, and associated linkage hard points. The section is built up of sandwiched brass rectangular tubing and canted .060" brass wing fold hinge plates and various thicknesses of ABS plastic sheet. Airfoil NACA 23015 section was plotted and layed out and ribs were cut out of .125" and .025" ABS plastic sheet. The axis of the wing fold hinge pin is canted both outward and aft. Its positioning is extremely sensitive in that any misplacement in either direction would not allow the wing to stow correctly to the horizontal stabilizer or would hit the ground line during the folding cycle. A dummy aft fuselage section and horizontal stabilizers were made and temporarily fitted to the wing center section to prove the location of the wing hinge plates and the geometry of the folding axis. A similar exercise was gone through to locate and prove the proper location of the landing gear attach and pivot points. Once these critical hard points were set, the main part of the center section was skinned. The aft fuselage section was then attached to the center section. The firewall bulkhead, cockpit floor, turnover bulkhead, along with basic structure to the upper mid fuselage section, was added.

The bomb bay section and doors were made as a separate assembly. Bomb door hinges were made from .004" brass sheet to fashion a continuous piano hinge. This was accomplished by bending segments of the sheet brass around .016" piano wire and soldering. First attempts at making these hinges ended in failure because the solder flowed around the piano wire and locked everything up tight. This problem was solved by coating the wire with "Pam" non-stick cooking spray, and the task was finally accomplished. Bomb bay and door framing, along with bomb shackle vertical supports and cross members, were made from various sizes of square and rectangular brass tubing. External skin, formers, and perforated internal liners were made from ABS plastic sheet. If you think the SBD Dauntless dive flaps have a lot of holes in them, you should count the holes in these bomb bay door inner skins! The forward and aft door actuators and associated linkages were made from .060"

Fuselage/Wing Center Section Assembly. Here the engine and turret are being test fitted.

brass sheet. The geometry on this mechanism is also quite a nightmare. The bomb bay was configured to hold 12 100# bombs, so 12 bomb shackles were made using fine wire and .010" aluminum sheet. After assembling and painting the various components, this section was joined to the center section and aft fuselage as an assembly.

COCKPIT AREA: Prior to closing in the fuselage side panels above the wing center section, much of the cockpit detail was added. The area between the pilot's turnover bulkhead and the turret contained all the autopilot servos and associated linkage, along with radio and radar black boxes, Oxygen bottle, hydraulic reservoir, and associated plumbing. The pilot's cockpit consumed a great deal of the effort in building the model. This included rudder pedals with brake master cylinders, left and right consoles, etc. Every switch knob, control, and piece of equipment shown in cockpit photos was replicated. Switches on the right electrical console were made by utilizing hypodermic needles threaded with wire to simulate toggle switches.

I use black ABS plastic sheet for any cockpit panels or black boxes. This allows scribing panel lines and other markings which are brush painted with white paint then wiped clean and sanded after the paint dries, leaving panel lines and markings nicely highlighted. The instrument panel was made by mounting 1/4" instrument faces, obtained from the radio control model supply section of a local hobby shop, to a panel shaped sheet of black ABS plastic. These were faced with thin clear plastic sheet sandwiched between the outer panel of black plastic sheet with matching holes for the instrument faces. After most of the interior details were added, formers were made up and installed with the fuselage side skins. This included sliding canopy hatch tracks made from square brass tubing.

ENGINE AREA: I next concentrated on the area forward of the firewall. Scale engine mounts were made from 3/32" brass tubing and the engine was mounted. Although this detail cannot be seen, it's an interesting way to mount the engine. Exterior closeout of the area between the windshield and the firewall was accomplished by cutting these segments from the forward vacuformed sections. The remaining portion of these forms made up the nose cowl. The nose cowl was fabricated off the model as a separate assembly and required some additional vacuformed parts for the cowl flap and side oil cooler transition contours. Panel lines were scribed, and .04" diameter holes were drilled on all removable panel peripheries for Dzus fastener locations. Stretched sprue was then pulled into all these holes, cut flush and sanded on the outside and roughly trimmed on the inside of the cowl. After final painting, these were slightly pushed out from the inside, thereby highlighting their location.

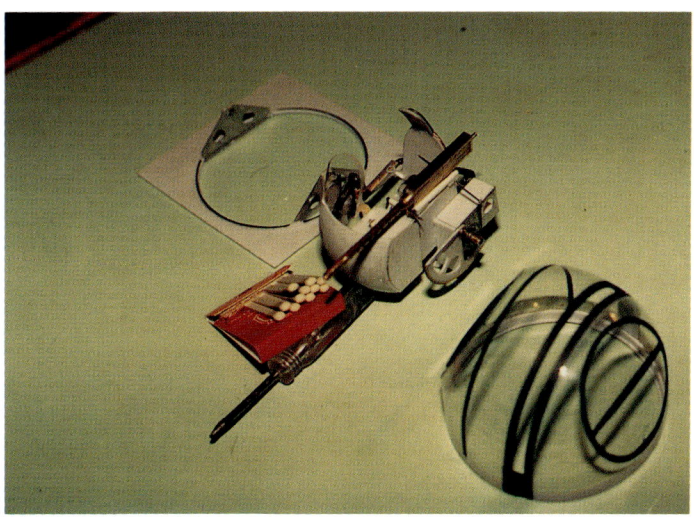

Turret Components.

LANDING GEAR
The Erection and Maintenance manual was loaded with drawings and details of the main landing gear, which were easily scaled. I used brass exclusively for all components, which function just like the real thing, including unlock and retraction sequence. The inner strut cylinder and axle assembly was chrome plated to accurately display the polished surface of the exposed strut. The scissor links were hand cut and filed to shape, as were the side and drag braces. The downlock latch mechanism was especially intricate and required close tolerances in order for it to function properly. The struts are spring loaded and extend as the model weight is removed. Pivot attach point location in the wing center section was critical in that the wheels must be "toed" in when retracted to properly nest in the wheel well.

The wheels were a big problem. I thought I had it made when I located some flying model wheels with the proper rubber tread, but they measured 2.25" in diameter, while the model required 2.06" diameter. By utilizing the rubber tires of these hobby wheels and cutting out a cross section segment and regluing, I now had a good pattern to make a mold for casting new wheels of the proper size. The wheel hub with all its spokes and cooling ribs required considerable time in making a master pattern. Once the master patterns and molds were made, the casting process, again with polyester resin, was no problem.

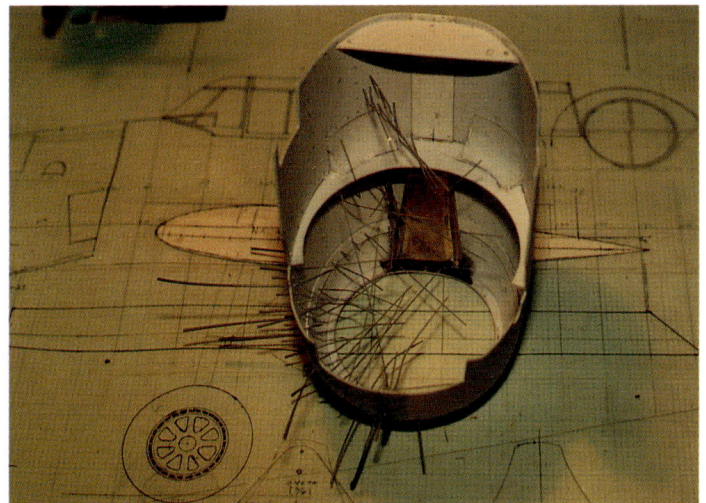

Cowling. The porcupine needles are, in fact, lengths of sprue passed through 40 thou holes and cropped, to represent Dzus fittings.

OUTER WING PANELS

Having established the correct wing fold axis earlier, construction on these sections proceeded similar to normal vacuform kit assembly. Construction started with a full length aluminum spar, made from .040" aluminum sheet, along with the formerly made brass hinge fitting for the inboard end. Leading edges are .025" ABS plastic, vacuformed over balsa patterns. The exterior skin aft of the front spar was flat .025" ABS sheet. The internal structure of the wing panels included a .125" plastic rear spar for closeout of aileron and wing flap bays, and provided attach structure for the spring loaded, operable flaps. Between the spars, 4 ribs made of .125" ABS were located. The voids between spars and ribs were filled with polyurethane sheet foam.

The inboard end portions of the outer wing skin were edged with .005" aluminum sheet to provide an accurate and neat seal with the wing in the extended position. The exposed portions of the inboard end of the outer wing panel, and the outboard end of the center section with the wings folded, include all the numerous details shown in photographs and the maintenance manual. The wing lock pins and hydraulic actuator are functional and are mechanically operated with the small stowable handle extension. Normal method for locking the wing was by hydraulic pressure, but Grumman wisely added the mechanical feature. For the leading edge slots I used sheet brass to better control the integrity of the thin section of the slot trailing edge. Wing tips were vacuformed entirely from clear plexiglas sheet and covered a tip light bulb of the proper color. Wing stowage cable compartments with brass hinged covers were included in the tip assembly. The flaps were made from .005" aluminum skin and .015" ABS ribs and .125" square brass tube front spar. A spring loaded cylinder protrudes into the wing, which provides tension to hold the flaps in the retracted position. The center wing section flap segment is driven by the outboard flap through an interlock fitting. The triangular door on the lower wing surface in the area of the wing fold pivot point is hinged and spring loaded to close out the opening with the wing in the extended position. A full span (40 inches) dihedral locating jig was made of .080" aluminum to insure correct dihedral during attachment of outer wing to the outer wing fold hinge plate.

CONTROL SURFACES

The horizontal stabilizers were made from a layup of two .125" ABS plastic sheets. Brass tubing, sized to slide into that previously imbedded in the vertical fin, were built into each horizontal stabilizer. Brass hinge fittings were made from .060" sheet for rudder and elevators to duplicate those shown in the maintenance manual drawings.

The rudder, elevators, and ailerons were vacuformed over form patterns made from 1/4" sheet styrene. Chart tape was layed out on these forms to simulate ribs. Ten thou ABS plastic sheet was used in the vacuforming. Assembly involved buildup of .125" plastic spars and 1/16" brass tubing to receive piano wire hinge pins. The voids between outer skins were filled with slow curing epoxy glue. Control tabs were made separately, and tab acuator rods were made from 1/32" tubing split at the end and spread slightly and filed to form a clevised rod end. Hookup bolts were made from brass nails with head ends filed to hex shape to simulate bolts.

GREENHOUSE

I began by carving a balsa wood pattern to the shape of the entire greenhouse area. After sealing with superglue as mentioned earlier, a plaster female mold was made. From this plaster mold a polyester casting was made. This final polyester form was carefully hand filed to insure good surfaces in the flat areas, wet sanded and polished to a perfectly smooth surface. Forming of the greenhouse was accomplished using .028" plexiglas sheet. I prefer plexiglas over other types of acrylic or acetate sheet. It is more difficult to form because it takes more heat to soften, but once formed it is clearer and less prone to "see thru" distortion. The form was stretched out in the cockpit area to allow for material loss when making cuts to separate windshield and sliding section. After trimming and fit to fuselage, inside framing was painted interior green before installation. Exterior framing was painted after installation. The sliding canopy tracks were made by bending .005" aluminum sheet into channels.

TURRET

Through the use of information in the Erection and Maintenance and Aircrewman's gunnery manuals, all the details to make an exact replica were available to me. Every detail seen in any of this information was duplicated. Again, vacuforming was utilized in making the armor shield and gunner's seat. The main 2" tubing structure to which everything is attached was duplicated by using 1/8" copper wire soldered into the basic startup structure. The turret has many very small detail parts, such as maplight, gunsight, pistol grip control handle, gun charging linkage, and emergency crank handles. The .50 cal. machine gun was made entirely from brass, with holes drilled in the barrel jacket. The turret was made to rotate in both elevation and azimuth. The elevation driven quadrant is visible with the gun elevated and has gear teeth in a 200" arc. These gear teeth were duplicated by filing both sides of a no. 8 screw flat to a thickness of .040". This was then split lengthwise,

Tailwheel Detail.

bent to the correct arc, and soldered to the brass quadrant: thus the screw threads became gear teeth. The clear glassed area for the turret was done in the same manner as the greenhouse over a polyester form. The escape hatch, sliding window, and jettison handle were duplicated prior to final installation of the glass dome. The turret project was especially interesting for me since I spent about 500 hours sitting in one.

PROPELLER

Another problem in scratchbuilding in this scale is that you have to make everything. The spares box is of no use. Again, master patterns were made of the Hamilton Standard hydromatic propeller hub and one blade. Molds and polyester castings were made. During casting of the hub, a section of 3/16 tubing was inserted as a propeller shaft. The next size tubing had been molded into the engine forward case to receive the propeller shaft. I like to have the prop free to spin and be removable, but I don't like to have it falling off the airplane when the nose is pointed down. To prevent this, I made the prop shaft about 1/2" longer than the tubing in the engine and cut cross slots in the end and slightly spread and bowed the cut segments. This allows the propeller to be easily removed. It won't fall out, and it's free to spin. The blades were painted flat black, and the hub was painted silver with an over coat of silver Rub 'n Buf.

IN CONCLUSION

Some might wonder: Why go to the trouble of making landing gear retractable, wings foldable, bomb bay doors and flaps operable? My reasoning is that unless these mechanical operations function correctly, the model may not be an accurate representation of the real thing. It also allows more versatility in the display of the model. (Besides, Arlo, you like to do such things.-ed.)

Wing Root/Landing Gear Detail. As a dedicated and accomplished mechanisms person, Arlo provided folding wings and retractable gear.

Since construction of this model to the NASM's 1/16th scale, I have remained with it for subsequent projects. Remember those "Cleveland" SF 3/4"=1' (1/16) scale kits? When you get one of these larger models in your hands you feel you've really got ahold of something. It might be thought that these larger models are easier to detail. Not necessarily so. There's nothing more highly detailed than a full sized aircraft. So, the larger the model, the more detailing is expected, and therefore required.

Incidentally, my current project is a 1/16th scale Curtiss SOC-3, naturally on floats.

CHAPTER VII
How I Built My Mitsubishi G4M "Betty"
by Bill Bosworth

EDITOR'S NOTE

As most of us know, Bill Bosworth is a founder of ACCURATE MINIATURES. As such, he is something of a folk hero to us airplane modellers; right up there with Ray Rimell, of ALBATROS PUBLICATIONS fame. Imagine a person with the affrontery, and guts, to go head to head with the likes of Hasegawa, Tamiya, and Monogram, and not only survive, but set the pace as regards model quality, subject authenticity, and subject choice—with just a few dedicated, talented people in an old warehouse.

To me, the ingredients that made it work, aside from those cited above, are the love and knowledge of vintage airplanes exhibited by the principals, plus Bill's modelling skills and Clark Macomber's production experience from his years at other modelling companies. The photos of Bill's models in this chapter are ample evidence of that ingredient.

Bill Bosworth himself.

INTRODUCTION

When John asked me to contribute a chapter to this book I was once again both honored and somewhat overwhelmed. His request was quite simple: "How I built the Betty." (More appropriate would be "Why I built the Betty." That would have been a very short chapter entitled "Temporary Insanity.")

With a little time and thought some seriousness returned and I put some effort into actually thinking of not just this project but a whole lot of other things that brought me to this kind of modelling. Much credit or blame must go to John and our much missed friend George Lee. These two guys were single-handedly responsible for dragging me away from the world of FROG and Airfix and into a world of real challenge. If the sight of John's magnificent A-20A at the 1974 IPMS convention wasn't enough to inspire, then you probably needed to take up a new hobby. The willingness of these two gentlemen to share the "secrets" of scratch building was and is an example of the type of individuals they were and are, and also represents the special bond that exists between our sometimes fragmented and esoteric hobby. I went home from that convention inspired and determined to learn as much as possible about this scratch building business.

Reams have been written about the techniques that various builders/authors have discovered over the years. But to me the real value in a book like this is not so much in the lessons that can be learned, but from the pure inspiration that other model work provides. Whether the subject is a personal favorite or some new technique is explained, if a reader walks away from these pages ready to try something new, this "technique" book has served its purpose. Back in the days of that A-20 there were no how-to books and very few modelling magazines to help the modeler through the maze of plastic modelling. Progress and change are wonderful things.

This section will offer a simple explanation of how the Betty was done and will explain a few additional discoveries that I have picked up over the years that go along with technique.

RESEARCH

So where do you start? It's my strong feeling that the most beautiful scratch project is just another model unless the builder has devoted substantial effort into researching the subject. The one thing about our hobby that still stymies me is the willingness of many builders to accept models that simply lack accuracy. I am not talking about some psychotic cumpulsion to achieve perfection—an impossibility in any case. But, since our hobby is really about replicating the real thing, it seems to me that we should strive for as much authenticity as possible. This goal is not always an easy reach. My personal acceptance level is something I call the 85 Percentile. If you can complete a project and feel comfortable that it meets 85% of the real thing in its accuracy and execution, you'll probably be as close as most humans can get. Getting to that 85% can be a challenge in itself. I've always enjoyed the research portion of a

Mitsubishi G4M2e Betty/Okha. The largest of the Japanese bombers, the Betty flew the entire war with very few changes to the basic design. This version represents a plane modified to carry the Yokoshura "Okha" suicide bomb. The bomb bay was slightly modified to accommodate the missile. This plane is from the 722 Training Group, on February 15, 1945. (Dan Ormsby photo)

Mitsubishi G4M2e. At 1/32nd scale, Bill's "Betty" is a large model, spanning almost 31 inches. The actual G4M had a wingspan of 25 meters, or 82 feet: by W.W.-II standards, that was a large twin! (Dan Ormsby photo)

"Betty" Cockpit details.

Scratch builders have to do their own digging. Quite often this will go a long way toward determining the subject. If you can't find reliable information, how are you going to build it? You may also find a particular aspect of the subject that you want to build to be pushing the limits of your capabilities. Sometimes a well drawn set of plans will be enough to inspire a scratch builder to proceed. I personally couldn't resist the siren song of a set of Hs129 plans in a Czech monograph. Heck, I've actually built some German subjects just because the Waldron rudder pedal set looked so cool. Just be sure you can back up your effort with information that you feel you can trust. And how do you know you can trust that information? You don't. The most beautifully drawn set of drawings from the "expert in the field" can in reality be a mess. Not all three views are created equal! Wherever possible, rely on photographs to confirm your drawings. Photos don't lie. Well, most of the time they don't. They can sometimes confuse, often contradict, and most of the time provide solid evidence that you're on the right track. Any project should allow plenty of time to just stare at the photographic evidence that you will need to gather. It's just amazing how much "new" you will find in a photo when you think you've "seen it all." As you get deeper into the scratch building process, you will find yourself spending more and more time in the study of the photos.

project as much as the actual building. It can be said that finding information is almost a hobby unto itself. Turning that two dimensional information into three dimensions is both a challenge and a reward. The chapter in this book on how to go about gathering information will help explain the research process in greater detail.

I feel that picking the subject is the easiest part any hobbyist has to make. For a scratch builder it's the same. Some builders have that special project that may involve years of research and construction, while others (like me) have a list that is just too long for one lifetime. Either way, once the subject is chosen, things become very different. The kit builder has essentially all the research work done for them by what we trust is a competent manufacturer.

WHY THE "BETTY"?

The Betty project is a pretty good example of just how this process can work.

About twenty some years ago, I scratch built a 1:32 scale Ohka. There was plenty of trustworthy information to do it right. I had no sooner finished it when a good friend started asking when I was going to build the "mother ship." I won't repeat the answer. But like a lot of "in the future" projects, the seed was planted. I started gathering information. And to this day there still isn't very much reliable information on this subject. Drawings, photos, books, anything that pertained to the plane became another item to put in the file. The gathering process went on over the next fifteen years or so. I never did obtain a nice, neat turnkey package of reliable information, but the cumulative effect of all this collecting made me feel

"Betty" Fuselage halves. Nice oak floors, too!

Heinkel He 111H-2. This aircraft represents a Battle of Britain bomber from KG53 on September 15, 1940. This is the plane in the often seen plan view photo taken over the Isle of Dogs on what is now known as Battle of Britain Day. The aircraft was damaged by fighters and later crashed in Belgium with two NCO's injured. (Dan Ormsby photo)

confident enough to think that the end result would be somewhere in that magic 85 Percentile. It is amazing just how much you can piece together from a bunch of disparate photos. Even those countless wrecked plane pictures revealed valuable new information. With a large envelope of pictures, drawings, etc., it was time to start.

Years of searching for the "perfect" set of Betty drawings ended up producing nothing that I felt was close to trustworthy. This caused me to fall back to a system that has been helpful in the past. Make your own drawings based on the parts of the plans that you feel you can trust as being fairly authentic. Assembling and confirming all those miriad details through the cross checking of the photos will take you a long way toward that magic 85 percentile. This is hardly the easiest or fastest method, but I feel that it can and does work when you can't find a nice, neat turnkey source. It's a little like assembling a giant jig saw puzzle. You've just got to find all the pieces and assemble them into this composite drawing.

CONSTRUCTION

The basic techniques in the construction were the tried and true vacuform methods that modelers have been using since, well, since those A-20 days.

Using the basic information contained on the drawings, and constantly consulting those countless photos, allowed me to begin carving the basic fuselage, wings, tail surfaces, and engine nacelles in basswood and maple. I feel that these two woods are the best for the kind of work that we do. There are very dense (and expensive) plastic materials that may also be used to make your molds, but personally I don't see a whole lot of advantages in them for our purposes. Remember to make the molds on any project to allow for the thickness of the plastic that you are planning to mold the pieces in, i.e.: If you plan to use 40 thou plastic, carve the molds 40 thou undersize from the outer dimensions. Remember that once the plastic is heated and stretched over the molds it will thin out slightly. This new thickness will vary depending on the depth of the draw. On most simple shapes the plastic will drop to about 30 thou thick. To allow for this change in thickness the builder will have to decide just how much modification, if any, they want to incorporate into the molds. This becomes an exercise in judgement. Remember, the whole model building thing is an art form as well as mechanical process. Trust your "eye." It will tell you things that the best set of plans will often miss.

A trustworthy set of drawings will allow you to cut templates for the various cross sections of the many components. I mount a copy machine duplicate (40 thou undersize) onto thin paper card stock and carefully cut out the contours. It is very important to consult these frequently. Hold the carved pieces at arms length every so often to make sure that you capture that elusive "look." Too often a model captures every element of the real thing and misses the subtle character of the big one. This is one of those not-so-little things that is very difficult to explain but is very important to the finished model. Unfortunately, not everything can be quantified. If it both measures right *and looks* right, it probably will be right when you're finished.

The biggest departure for me in building this plane involved the substitution of entire sections of the opaque plastic fuselage moldings in clear plastic. These clear parts were molded on the

Henschel Hs 129B-3/wa. The Harry Rheems of ground attack aircraft. A few of this well known aircraft were modified to carry the awesome Bk 75 75mm cannon. These "buchsenoffner" (can openers) operated with two ground support units on the eastern front in 1944. It was not favored by the pilots for very obvious reasons. (Dan Ormsby photo)

Dornier Do 217E-5. Entering service in March 1941 (with KG40), the BMW 801-engined Do 217 was an entirely new design, despite its generic resemblance to the Do 17Z and Do 215. Despite its good performance, only 1,366 bomber versions were built, the Luftwaffe having settled upon the Ju 88 as its standard type. Bill's 1/32nd scale model, built about 20 years ago, represents a machine of KG 100, carrying a Henschel Hs 293 guided missle beneath its starboard wing. (Dan Ormsby photo)

Nakajima B5N2 Kate. This particular aircraft, from the carrier *Akagi*, took part in the Pearl Harbor attack as well as the Battle of the Coral Sea. It was eventually lost with the *Akagi* at Midway on June 5, 1942. Finished in the Midway color scheme, it carries an 18 inch aerial torpedo. (Dan Ormsby photo)

same molds as the opaque plastic and were formed in co-polyester plastic. I have found this to be the best clear heat formable plastic. This substitution was done to make the many windows in the plane easier to replicate. The daunting task of individually fitting all those curved windows was something that I just didn't want to face. By molding the opaque and clear in the same thickness (40 thou), it was possible to blend the clear areas into the opaque plastic fuselage sections with a minimum of problems. Now all that was required to finish the windows was to mask off the clear panels and finish the frames around them.

Blending of the clear plastic to the opaque sections was straightforward and used conventional painting, putty, and finishing techniques. I prefer to use a primer with a heavy concentration of filler. This is not just an excellent way to see the surface flaws, but also can be used to build a very thin skin layer that helps to frame the windows. I use Plasticoat automotive gray primer and have been very pleased with the results. It is lacquer based but "plastic-compatible" since it dries quickly.

As with all projects, you need to construct from the inside out: don't "build yourself into a corner." A cardinal rule for me with all projects is "don't rush!" I spend large amounts of time just staring blankly at the various pieces as they are finished, just thinking through the assembly process. Remember, these projects don't come with instruction sheets, and one of the most challenging aspects can be figuring out just how you're going to get it all together. "Thinking it through" is time well spent. You'll find that all those kits you've built over the years can translate into scratch building quite naturally. Scratch building is often not much more than an extention of kit building. This statement sounds like an over-simplification to many folks and doesn't mean that the process is "easy." It just isn't the daunting challenge that scares many people away. Just use your common sense and the experience of others to guide you. This is where all those "how to" articles and books come in handy.

Once the project is underway, I like to keep myself "honest" by constructing as many components and small details as possible; then putting them aside for later installation. I find this has a twofold benefit. It really makes you double check all the pieces you are making for dimensional accuracy (it will be nice if they actually fit!), and it helps you keep interest in the project when it invariably bogs down in that ("I don't think I'll ever get this thing finished") mode. Sometimes building a piece of armament is a lot more fun than tackling that pesky wing root. Obviously, you'll need to test fit as much as possible before you get too far along. There's also that visceral pleasure of seeing it all come together in the form of all those little pieces. For the Betty, my favorite pieces were the armament and the flight deck. These subassemblies were a joy to build. Research played a big role in this enjoyment. Nothing beats good drawings and photos of a fifty year old Japanese cannon to make it easier. I'm not a stickler for keeping everything in plastic. If brass works, use it. Too many modelers are so used to working with plastic that they overlook materials that might be more appropriate. It's also true that scrounging the parts box can save time and effort. Sometimes you may actually turn up a piece that is better that anything you are capable of building. I don't use the scrap box very often for two reasons. I don't have a very good one, and it is a

McDonnell XP-67 Moonbat. This was the first original design from McDonnell Aircraft. Conceived as a "Destroyer," it was intended to attack enemy bombers, armed with six 37mm cannons. There was a prolonged period of development during which the plane experienced severe overheating problems. It was lost due to an engine fire in the summer of 1944 after flying fewer than 32 hours. (Dan Ormsby photo)

scratch project, isn't it? The downside of the heavy use of the scrapbox is that it kind of defeats the purpose of the do-it-yourself nature of scratch building. I've seen an awful lot of "scratch building" that was little more that a compilation of someone elses parts.

ASSEMBLY

The Betty was assembled from the various vacuform components that had been detailed from the inside out. I have found that the methods used in assemby of the real plane are often appropriate for a model—sometimes even better. A good solid wing spar not only holds the wing in place, it sets the correct dihedral. It also adds strength just as the real one did. I guess I must be a little different from many other builders in that over the past twenty or so years of doing this, I've only resorted to building an assembly jig once or twice. I may just be lazy. The decision to use a jig is up to the individual builder and the amount of challenge in getting the components to line up correctly. I often make up for the lack of a jig by the constant use of a good old ruler and more precise measuring tools (calipers, etc.). Nothing beats a square and your eyes to keep things straight and true, even if you are using a jig. Remember, if it looks right, the chances are that it is right.

SURFACE DETAILS

Once all of the major components were assembled into something that resembled the real thing, it was time to move on to the surface details. I like to do most of the surface scribing before the major components are assembled, so with the exception of panel lines that wrap around the fuselage and wing leading edges etc, most of the scribing was already in place. You do have a good scriber, don't you? This is probably one of the most important tools any modeler can have. Whether you scratch build or not, this tool is a must. My personal favorites are available from the Micro Mark catalog. They are reasonably priced and are double ended. Buy a couple.

Another essential is two part epoxy putty. Everyone has their favorite. Mine is white Milliput—expensive, but worth it. It is a very finely ground putty. It also has the highly desirable quality of not shrinking. I've been using this putty since it first went on the hobby market and over the years have never found it to be lacking in any respect. Once it has been blended, sanded, and feathered into the surrounding surfaces, I like to apply a coat of Mr. Surfacer 1000. This primer has the wonderful ability to blend to invisibility the transition between the putty and the plastic. The effect is quite striking. Sometimes the decision to use putty vs. molding the shape in vacuform is up to the individual. In the case of the Betty I elected to make the fairing that surrounds the bomb bay out of putty rather than mold it in styrene. This is typical of many of the decisions that the scratch builder has to make. I felt that making a mold, fitting it, and puttying it into position was more difficult and time consuming than molding and shaping the epoxy. This method also accomplished three other things: it resulted in the desired shape, added about two pounds to the weight of the model, and kept the Milliput folks in business for another year. It was also good for a lot more dust in the modelling room. I had so much fun using the putty on the bomb bay that I decided to make the tires out of the same material. It may be slow, but it does give you the shape you're after.

There will always be areas of virtually any project that defy documentation. One such area on the Betty was the bomb bay, and more specifically the mounting points for the Ohka. Even for a dedicated aviation historian this may be getting a little obscure! Through a little verifiable information and a lot of conjecture, I was able to hang the bomb in the opening. After all, how many places could it go? And something has to pull down that 85 percentile thing. The final detail assemblies and parts were added to the airframe before it was painted.

FINISHING

The person who suggested this awful project in the first place managed to find a photo of a rather rare two tone finish aircraft with the Ohka slung underneath. That was good enough for me. It also looks a lot more interesting than the overall green versions. One accidental discovery in the painting process occurred when I was painting the area directly behind the engine cowls. I had previously covered the sections behind the cowl flaps with metalizer. When these areas were later over painted with the green top coat, I gently used high-tack masking tape to remove small areas of paint to duplicate chipping. I believe it worked effectively. You need to use the tape shortly after the color is applied. Once the paint is dry you will not get it to work. Adding the final details is accomplished the same as with any normal kit assembly. It's just as easy to break parts off of a scratch project as a production piece! Typical kit finishing techniques were used with no departures from the norm.

REFLECTIONS

The only thing left to do was build a box to keep it in (that's the subject for another chapter) and put it in the attic with all the other long forgotten projects. Since I don't keep track of the hours on how long these things take, I can't pass on any information in this area. How relevant is it, anyway? I tend to build pretty quickly, and based on the complexity of a project a model takes me anywhere from a couple of months to a year plus. The biggest satisfaction that I derive from a project is a sense of accomplishment. The challenge of research and the application of that information into the final result is all part of that road to completion. The Betty project began over twenty years ago with the discovery of a photo of the cart that was used to move the Ohka around. I'd always seen it sitting on a couple of saw horses, and I thought the little cart really looked different. It provided a nudge in the direction that ended up twenty years later in a Betty. But when it's all said and done, every one of the efforts that I've put together over the past twenty years or so go back to that first impression I got from seeing that incredible A-20. That's the real "How I built the Betty" story. It put me on a path from which there is no turning back. Allow this book to give you the same inspiration.

Macchi MC 72. This twin-engined Italian aircraft was designed to contest the 1931 Schneider Trophy. Fortunately for the British contingent, the plane was not finished in time for the race. The Supermarine S6B went on to win and retire the trophy. Later that year, the MC 72 set the absolute world speed record for propeller driven sea planes at 440.68 MPH. This record has never been surpassed. (Dan Ormsby photo)

CHAPTER VIII
How I Built My Avro Lancaster
by Peter Cooke

PREFACE

In SB!, Chapter V: RESIN CASTING was prepared by co-author Peter Cooke. Therein, he explained the unusual and complex, yet very efficacious resin casting technique which he has evolved for producing his 1/24th scale models, mostly of W.W.-II subjects; in short series runs for various customers, including museums. These models are truly remarkable for their configurational accuracy, realistic appearance, and, incidentally, sturdiness/durability. To date, his fortunate customers have had their choice of SPITFIRE (several models), LANCASTER, MOSQUITO, Hawker SEA FURY, and P-51D MUSTANG. "In the works" at the time of writing (June 1998) is the Hawker HURRICANE Mk.I.

Peter has thoroughly researched each type prior to construction, to ensure that the aircraft configuration is correct in all respects, within the constraints of modelling practicality. Thus, while he began with the best available plans (multi-view drawings) of the type, in every case, he was obliged to make corrections, based upon supplemental documentation, period photographs of the type (and, when available, of a specific aircraft), and inspection/measurement/photography of surviving examples. As stated in his September 1989 AEROPLANE MONTHLY article on making the LANCASTER: "As usual, my biggest single problem was (obtaining) really accurate drawings. All the commercially available ones disagreed with each other, and some had errors that were obvious even at a casual glance."

Having damaged his right hand last year (1997) in a bad fall from a ladder, Peter was only able to resume serious modelling in January. Therefore, being too busy on HURRICANE production to do so himself, Peter has kindly given me (Alcorn) permission to edit his SB! chapter so that, while basically a repeat (for the sake of "stand-alone" completeness), it is directed explicitly towards his LANCASTER(s).

I had the great pleasure of visiting Peter's home/manufactory in Sonning-on-Thames during September 1990, at which time I was priviledged to witness LANCASTER production. Unfortunately, he had no completed models for me to admire. However, this situation was remedied 9,000 miles distant, and seven years later, following our move to Seattle, Washington. There, in Paul Ludwig's impressive scratch built model collection, are several of Peter's creations, including a SPITFIRE Mk.XIX, MOSQUITO FB VI, and P-51D MUSTANG. Incidentally, unlike most of us airplane enthusiasts, Paul is no "fantasy flier," having flown carrier-based Douglas AD SKYRAIDERs during the late '50s, and thereafter for NORTHWEST AIRLINES, retiring in 1994 as a 747 Command Pilot. But, Paul happens to be enamored of W.W.-II fighters—a not uncommon affliction.

INTRODUCTION

I have chosen 1/24th as the scale for all of my scratch built models, since I consider this to be the smallest in which I can represent all of the details visible on a full-size machine.

I cannot stress too much the need to closely examine real aircraft wherever possible. It is all too easy to develop in the mind an idealized image of what an aircraft should look like, based entirely upon study of other models. We have all seen numerous examples which, although beautiful works of art, are not convincing representations of the real aircraft, particularly when photographed. The difference between convincing replica and artful toy lies in such subtleties as surface finish, panel and rivet line representation, panel distortion (on occasion), "sit" of the undercarriage, colour "scale effect," degree of finish sheen, and "weathering" in all of its manifestations. I firmly believe in photography as the ultimate test of a model's effectiveness for simulation of reality. The close-up camera lens is a cruel judge.

MATERIALS USED FOR RESIN CASTING

Skinning:

Plasticard: Manufactured by firms like Slaters and readily available from model shops, this consists of polystyrene sheets from 5-60 thou in thickness. It can be easily formed after heating to 250-275F. It normally has a slightly rough surface, which means that it has to be rubbed down and polished before it can be used to represent alloy skinning. But it is perfect for fabric.

PVC (polyvinyl chloride) Sheet: This material is manufactured specifically for vacuforming. I obtain mine from a local firm that produces blister packaging. In a thickness of 10 thou, this material is ideal for producing clear cockpit canopies. In fact, I now use it for virtually all my skinning panels, as well. If a mistake is made in moulding, reheating will usually send it back into a flat sheet, ready for a second try.

Peter Cooke and "S for Sugar."

Moulding:

Plaster of Paris: This cavity mold material is available from any art supply store.

Silicone Rubber: This is a liquid with the consistency of cream. A catalytic hardener is added, and the mixture cures over a period of about 12 hours depending on temperature. The mould is flexible, yet stable dimensionally, and tough. It is eventually attacked by any resin, but is ideal for a batch of up to a dozen castings. Its one disadvantage is its high cost, but, if a mould is well designed, not much rubber is used. I am currently using two forms:

• R.T.V. 11 (white) available from Alec Tiranti Ltd., High Street, Theale, Reading, Berks; or General Electric R.T.V. 31. This is a fairly stiff rubber when set, and therefore ideal for large castings, or ones in which there is not too much undercut.

• Dow Corning Q3-3481. This is a softer rubber, but very tough and flexible. It is therefore ideal for situations where the mould has to be stretched to remove small castings of complex shape. It has a fairly thick consistency when poured, and therefore tends to entrap air bubbles unless great care is taken.

Vinamould: This has the consistency and feel of jelly cubes and melts at 170 degrees Celsius. It is cheap and re-usable. It cannot, of course, be used on any master pattern that might melt or crack with the heat as the mould material is poured on. It is normally only suitable for making one casting, since it tends to break up as the cast item is removed. Unlike with the other mould-making materials listed, it is best to cover the master-pattern with a release agent such as wax, so very fine detail cannot be produced.

Latex Rubber: This is a thin white creamy liquid that can be painted on to the master-pattern with a brush. This then cures in the air, although the processes can be very much speeded up with gentle heat in an oven (60 degrees Celsius is quite sufficient). Normally several layers will have to be built up to produce a strong mould which can then be peeled off the master-pattern like a glove. It is thus ideal for figures with an open base. Because of its great flexibility, a fair degree of "undercutting" can be incorporated in the master-pattern. It is not dimensionally stable enough for casting thin items like propeller blades.

Casting:

Polyester Resin: This is a strong smelling, normally clear liquid to which a small quantity of hardener is added. It then cures in about half an hour depending on temperature. It is the basic bonding material in most fibre glass construction. Consistency can be thickened by mixing in a filler such as talcum powder. This not only makes the resin more economical to use, but makes a casting

AVRO LANCASTER I "S for SUGAR." This, one of Bomber Command's most famous aircraft, now resides in the RAF Museum, Hendon. R5868 became "PO-S" upon joining No.467 Squadron RAAF in November 1943, with which it went on to complete 137 missions. Originally, it had served with No. 83 Squadron as "OL-Q," with which it logged 78 missions following its first, against Wilhelmshaven on 8/9 July 1942. It is depicted per its press coverage, following completion of 100 missions in May, 1944. -Cooke photo

AVRO LANCASTER I "DUMBO." This model represents ED953, PO-Q of No. 467 Squadron, RAAF. At 1/24th scale, its wingspread is 4 foot 3 inches (1.30 meters)! -Cooke photo

AVRO LANCASTER I "ADMIRAL PRUNE." Peter reports that he came into a colour photo of this RAF No. 106 Squadron machine. This photo, perhaps more than any other, shows the remarkably realistic appearance of his models, achieved through meticulously researched accuracy, fully detailed surface features, crisp clarity of glazed panels, and convincing finish. -Cooke photo

North American P-51D-5-NA MUSTANG. This model, built for Paul Ludwig, depicts the next to last mount of 8th Air Force ace Major George Preddy, who was tragically shot down and killed by "friendly" AA fire on Christmas Day, 1944. At this time, he was C.O. of the 328th Sqdn., 352nd Fighter Group. -Cooke photo

with slightly softer, less brittle machining characteristics. Castings made in this material are quite strong and rigid. The major disadvantages are that its quick setting does not always allow enough time to remove bubbles from the mould's surface after pouring in the resin, and also the material shrinks by about 2% during curing. This does not usually make a serious change in dimensions, but, since the shrinkage occurs before the resin is fully cured, the pulling away from the surface of a silicon rubber mould tends to mar any fine surface detail on the casting. For this reason, it is used primarily for master forms to which skinning will be attached.

Epoxy Resin: This is the material which I use for the actual cast model components. It is more expensive than polyester resin and can be more difficult to obtain: small boat building suppliers are probably the best source, especially for the small quantities which we require. I tend to use a product called WEST SYSTEMS "GOUGEON." It consists of a golden liquid resin to which a normally brown liquid hardener is added. Curing then takes place over a wide variety of different times, from about 1/2 hour to several days, depending on the type of hardener and the temperature (slight warming considerably speeds up the process). This control over the setting time can be very useful if complex castings are being poured. The final casting has a slightly rubbery, less brittle nature than polyester castings, particularly in thin sections. The degree of flexibility can be increased by using more hardener. Since negligible shrinkage occurs during curing, very fine surface detail can be incorporated in the mould, and an excellent surface finish obtained.

EPOXY CAST COMPONENTS

INTRODUCTION: My technique employs the following basic elements, each of which represents a process step.

- Pattern
- Plaster of Paris cast
- Solid polyester resin form
- Formed sheet ("skin") panels
- Skinned master form
- Master mould
- Resin cast component

This general approach offers three fundamental advantages, relative to vacuforming of shells:

First, casting the final product in a master mould allows the creation of subtle surface features (panel lines, hatches, rivet detail, pillowing, etc.) which are not obtainable through vacuforming, except by subsequent skinning, or later scribing, etc.

Second, "limited production runs" can be made from the master mould; and/or variations can be generated with relatively little extra effort by revising the formed sheet panels on the resin form, and casting another master mould.

Third, the final cast resin component is inherently strong and rigid, so that no internal structure is required. However, the flip side is that, if extensive interior structure is to be visible, such effects must be created by preparing cores for the final resin casting.

It should be emphasized at this point that my technique has been developed for production runs: for producing a single model, certain steps can be eliminated, as described below.

THE PATTERN: Certainly the basic component shape, a fuselage half, for example, can be carved from basswood, as described in Chapter I above for vacuforming. While this may be entirely appropriate for smaller 1/24th scale components, including the entire fuselage halves of single-engine fighters, I prefer the following approach for large components:

Cut out two identical fuselage side profiles from balsa sheet. Build up one fuselage half and then the other, as follows: Attach a side profile to a flat board of convenient size, using rubber cement or double sticky-sided "Sellotape." Pre-shaped balsa cross-section (half) formers are then glued to the profile. Their size must allow for the thickness of the side profile, as well as for the balsa stringers which are then applied in a generally fore and aft direction.

The number of formers used depends on the complexity of the fuselage curves and component size, but remember that the balsa stringers will automatically follow a smooth curve. Gaps between the stringers can now be filled with Interior Polyfilla. This has a similar consistency to balsa when sanding, making it easy to blend the two materials. It can be an advantage to insert a horizontal plasticard profile of the fin and rudder at a strategic point, as well as a similar vertical profile at the rear of the fin. With sandpaper wrapped around, or glued to a wood block, the entire fuselage can now be quickly smoothed to the correct shape. In the area of the fin, scraping of the hard plasticard inserts will warn when the correct shape has been obtained. The entire fuselage is now painted with catalyzed polyester resin, which will soak in and set hard, enabling a really smooth surface to be obtained by final sanding. This composite element is now fully equivalent to a solid hardwood pattern.

A variation on the above is to make the side profile and cross section formers out of plasticard, balsa blocks being placed in the interformer spaces (grain being perpendicular to the side profile).

P-51D MUSTANG. While Lt.Col. Glenn Eagleston of the 9th Air Force is usually thought of as flying P-47s, this depicts his P-51D of the 353rd Squadron, 354th Fighter Group, France, Spring 1945. This model was built for Roger Perks. -Cooke photo

P5lD MUSTANG. "TANGERINE" served with the 364th Squadron, 357th Fighter Group, 8th Air Force. -Cooke photo

"TANGERINE" Nose Detail. Here, we are afforded another intimate glimpse of Peter's panelling treatment. -Cooke photo

Chapter VIII: How I Built My Avro Lancaster

DeHavilland MOSQUITO Mk.IV. This model represents D2353, GB-E of RAF No. 105 Squadron, in 1942. These two MOSQUITO photos were run to very small format in SB!(-I), so bear repeating at this size. -Cooke photo

The balsa is then block-sanded just to the plasticard formers, at which point Interior Polyfilla is applied to fill the inevitable balsa to plasticard gaps. Then, the pattern is sanded smoothly down until the plasticard formers are again contacted, no stringers being employed. As before, the fuselage is now painted with catalyzed polyester resin, which is given a final sanding after setting.

The fuselage halves are now temporarily glued together with rubber cement or double sticky-sided Sellotape. Final light sanding is then performed across their common profile to assure a perfect match.

SOLID POLYESTER RESIN FORM: In principle, either the solid wood or composite patterns described above can be used for subsequent skinning. However, for some production runs, I cast a solid, single piece component, as follows:

Using rubber cement or double sticky-sided Sellotape, reattach the fuselage half to a flat board, with a piece of "cling film" in between ("Saran Wrap," or equivalent in the USA). The cling film must extend beyond the pattern far enough (approximately 2") so that its edges can be folded up to form a watertight "casting box." With a thin coating of wax mould release on the pattern, and its sides supported with books, the casting box can now be filled with Plaster of Paris.

After the plaster has set, remove the pattern and allow the cast to thoroughly dry before coating its cavity surface with Vaseline.

Catalyzed polyester resin, powder-filled to produce a porridge-like consistency, is now poured into the inverted mould, over which a flat, release agent coated board is placed. The two solid half fuselages made in this way can then be superglued together, smoothed, and polished to yield the final master form.

DeHavilland MOSQUITO B.XX of No. 139 Sqdn., RAF. -Cooke photo

WING PATTERNS AND FORMS: While the process for preparing the wing patterns and casting the master forms is similar to that for fuselages, numerous detail differences require explanation.

For smaller aircraft, including 1/24th scale single engine fighters, the wing patterns can be carved from basswood, as described in Chapter I. However, the following procedure is advisable for larger wings, as for the LANCASTER.

First, cut the wing planform from fairly thick plasticard. Ignore any dihedral break at this stage. If the wing is basically straight taper, cement two plasticard ribs at each end of the wing. More complex shapes will require more ribs to define their cross section. Fill the spaces between the ribs with balsa blocks. Stick a large sheet of sandpaper to a convenient table using double-sided tape. The wing can be rubbed quite vigorously over the sandpaper in the secure knowledge that scraping of the plasticard ribs will warn when sanding should stop, or the angle be altered. The balsa wing should now be painted with polyester resin and finely smoothed down, like the balsa fuselage.

If there is a dihedral break, the balsa should be sawn down on each side of the wing as far as the plasticard core. The dihedral angle can now be set by inserting a balsa wedge in the saw cut, and any remaining gap filled with Araldite or Plastic Padding and finally smoothed over. The ailerons and, if necessary, the wheel wells should now be cut out of the wing using a razor saw. The upper surface of the wheel wells can usually be skinned over with a single sheet, so loss of the wing shape in this area is not critical.

The wing could be skinned directly and built into the model, though a resin copy made via a plaster cast is stronger, and necessary for production runs. If the wheel well has been incorporated, a plaster cast will have to be made in two pieces. In this case, cover one side of the wing with double-sided tape and stick this down to a sheet of cling-film a couple of inches larger than the wing all around. Pull up the cling-film to form a watertight tray, as with the fuselage, and pour in the plaster mix. When set, turn the cast over

Master Form. The heat formed, 10 thou clear PVC panels, with surface detail embossed, have been attached to the solid wood form using double sticky sided Sellotape. Each panel was cut separately, so that the lap-joints of the actual aircraft could be represented.

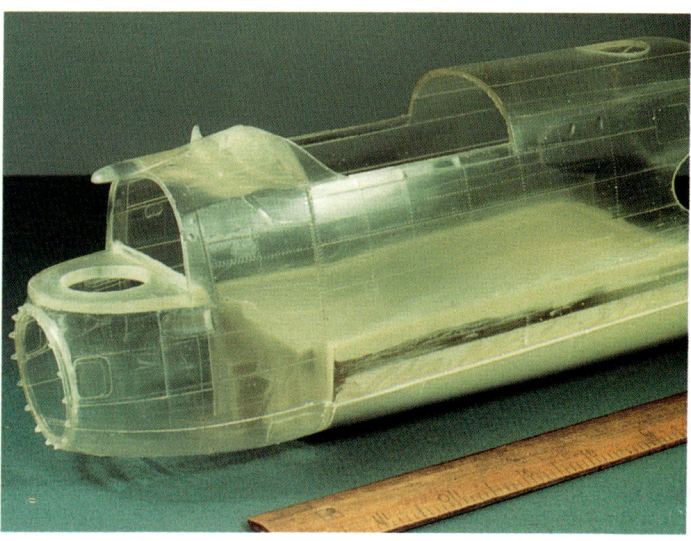

Epoxy Cast Shell. A silicone master mould had been cast from the master form, shown in the prior illustration. A core piece (similar to a master form, sans skin) was carefully located within the mould. Epoxy was slowly poured into the mould, resulting in this shell.

and pull the cling-film into a tray in the opposite direction and pour the other half of the plaster cast. When the cling-film and wing are removed, the two halves of the plaster cast should fit sufficiently tightly when held together with rubber bands for no seepage of polyester resin to occur, as long as it is a fairly stiff mix. The mould can usually be filled via the wing root. The resulting wing casting will be too thick by about 4 thou due to the double-sided tape. This does not matter, as it can easily be lost by final sanding.

Walls can now be built into the wheel wells using ten thou plasticard, with the riveting detail previously impressed into them. Where the wheel well is fairly large, it may be advisable to reinforce the upper surface with thick gauge plasticard to avoid sag in the final skinning.

In my smaller (i.e. all other) models, I cast the wings in solid epoxy resin, with an embedded steel mainspar for extra strength and rigidity. But, it was obvious that a 1/24th scale LANCASTER constructed in this manner would be excessively heavy. Therefore, for each model, I constructed a hollow wing core from 1mm thick artist's mounting card, with card internal reinforcements. The whole structure was seamed with epoxy resin and a spring steel leading edge incorporated, to form a mainspar. I was pleasantly surprised at how very strong and rigid this structure was, whilst being quite light. This core was placed in the silicone rubber mould, incorporating the external wing detail, which was then filled with epoxy resin. Thus, the entire wing was cast in one piece; by far the biggest casting I have ever made. The finished model weighs about 12 lb, yet lifting it by a finger beneath each wingtip causes no detectable flexing of the wing.

SKINNING THE FORMS: When contemplating the pattern of skinning on an aircraft you wish to model, remember that the problems you face are similar to those which the manufacturer of the full-sized aircraft had to solve. First decide which panels have double curvature, and will therefore have to be heat formed, and

Semi-Finished Nose Section. Interior detail, finish painting, and markings are added prior to final assembly of the primary model components.

which can simply be curved out of flat sheet. As well as being more realistic, use of separate panels is usually the easiest way to skin a model, although several panels can sometimes be combined and formed in one piece if realistic lap-jointing is not going to be attempted. In this case the panel joins can simply be represented by scribing after forming. This is easier if done against a flexible straight edge made from a strip of plasticard stuck to the panel with double-sided tape.

I used to form panels from 10 or 15 thou plasticard. This had to be rubbed down and polished smooth to produce a realistic representation of alloy skinning, so I now use the same 10 thou PVC sheet that I use for making transparencies. This is not only smooth, but is also fairly hard and scratch-resistant. It may seem obvious to state that the final paint finish can only be as good as the surface underneath, but it is a lesson I had to learn the hard way. Paint may enhance a blemish, but will certainly never cover it up.

While vacuforming can be employed, most skinning panels can be formed by simply holding the opposite ends of the PVC sheet in clamps made from double strips of balsa with a Sellotape hinge. A fair degree of force often has to be used in forming, and the PVC sheet will tend to pull out of the clamps unless it is attached to the inside with a strip of double-sided tape. The material, held in the clamps, should be heated in front of a fire until the sheet quivers when shaken. This is the point at which the sheet is soft enough to form well, but not so hot that it will over stretch. There is a tendency to feel that the actual forming must be accomplished quickly, before the sheet cools down. In practice, a slow steady pull works best. Always make at least one spare for each panel formed. Also make sure that the sheet is oversize by a reasonable amount to allow for trimming.

In the case of most wings, only the leading edge and wingtip panels will need to be formed. The rest of the wing skinning can usually be cut from a single sheet. Since adjacent panels are usually butt-jointed, the panel joins can simply be represented by scribing with a pin. After forming the wing tip in PVC sheet, any navigation lamp housing can be cut away from the wing core. Unless you possess genuine vacuforming facilities, moulding inside curves like the base of a fin can be difficult without wrinkling. One method is to tape the PVC sheet to one side, and then, after heating, ease it round the curve with a firmly held tissue.

Rivet Detail: The tool I use for this is a watch cog built into the handle of an old dressmaker's pattern-marking wheel. Run this alongside a plasticard straight edge using moderate pressure (a steel straight edge will chew up the brass teeth of the cog), and a neat row of "flush rivets" are impressed into the panel. On the reverse side is a row of mushroom rivets. In the case of plasticard, these tend to look more like pimples, but PVC sheet will produce crisp mushrooms. Don't worry if lines of rivets are not always perfectly straight; they aren't on full-size aircraft, either. When thin alloy sheet is riveted, the material "quilts" as a result of the stress, the degree of quilting depending on the gauge of alloy. This quilting will occur on the model panel if the "riveting" is done on a wood surface, the degree of quilting depending on the hardness of the wood.

Panel attachment to the forms: Panels are fixed into place with double-sided tape (In the USA, this could be 3M SCOTCH #136 Double-Stick). I usually seal the edges by allowing superglue to seep under and quickly wipe away the surplus, before there is time for the outer surface of the panel to be attacked. Panels should be trimmed and matched into place to form a close fit. This is easier to achieve with transparent skinning. When panels are lap-jointed, they are rarely thicker than two mm, and this is equivalent to thin sellotape in 1/24th scale. A thin strip of this sellotape should be applied to the underside of the appropriate panel edge to raise it slightly above the adjacent panel.

If necessary, panel joins can be finally made neater by rubbing in fine Surface Polyfilla. When set, the surplus can be wiped off with a damp tissue.

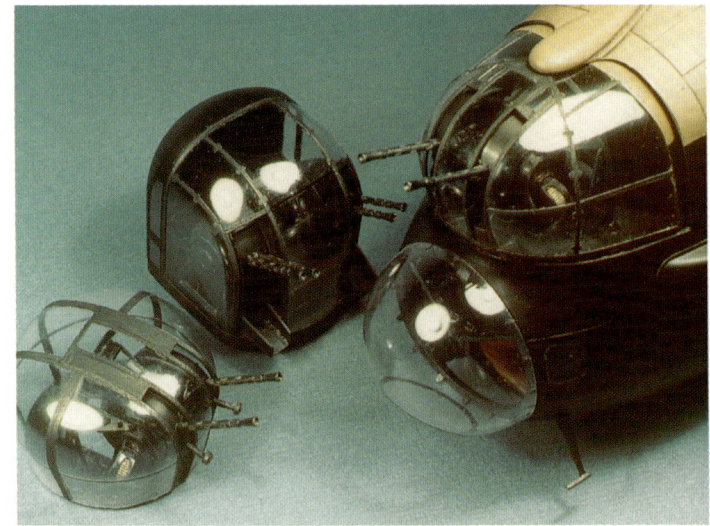

These gorgeous transparencies were epoxy-cast in a silicone mould; whose cavity was formed by a 10 thou PVC master skin, over which 5 thou framing had been applied with superglue.

Wing/Engine Subassembly. This 1.30 meter, 2 1/2 pound component is the largest ever made by Peter Cooke. Note the steel "mainspar."

Finishing Touches: Small fittings for the fuselage can either be moulded, or cast in resin using a rubber mould, as described in the next section. When making the master-patterns for items like airscoops, radiators, or cockpit canopies, I generally define the shape with a plasticard skeleton and then fill in with Plastic Padding. After smoothing down, a resin copy can be cast. This is essential for a cockpit canopy master, as it has to be completely smooth and flawless for a really clear transparency to be moulded.

Small wing-root fairings can be made by defining the edges of the fairing with plasticard or sellotape, and then contouring in between with Fine Surface Polyfilla. This is an ideal material, as it can be quickly worked and polished to a smooth surface. Larger fairings are best made by separate panels in imitation of full-size practice.

MASTER MOULD: At this point, the major "subassemblies" are represented by the master forms, covered by their rivet and panel detailled skin, with certain projecting features affixed.

A master mould is now prepared for each major component. Silicone rubber is used to capture the surface detail, while presenting the resiliency to permit removal of the form and subsequent final part.

Clearly, forethought is required to ensure that the master form and finish casting can be extracted from the mould without damage to either—and that interior cavities can be represented. Often, the best way to achieve this, as well as to work with manageably sized "subassemblies," is to cast the fuselage (or whatever) as multiple components, which will be joined at final assembly. Consideration must be given not only to the structural logic of major component division, but also to minimizing the difficulty of later "healing" of the joint: thus, an obvious division would be at a panel line. In the Lancaster model, the subassemblies corresponded to those of the actual aircraft, which could be unbolted for road shipment.

Almost any appropriately sized and shaped container can serve as the cavity into which the silicone is poured, so long as it can be separated after the material has cured. Since silicone rubber is expensive, one should be judicious in selecting enough wall thickness to ensure dimensional stability, but not so much as to be wasteful.

RESIN CAST COMPONENT: With the master form removed from the silicone mould, we are at last ready to consider subassembly production!

Interior cavities are of course created by insertion of core moulds, whose extraction from the final casting must be addressed.

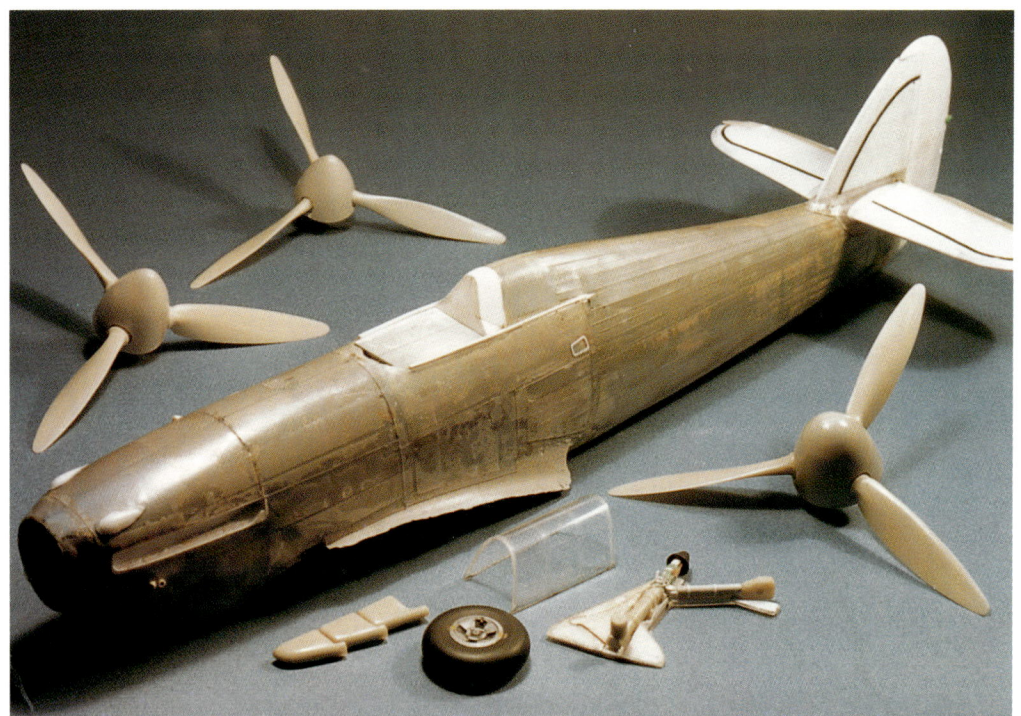

Hawker HURRICANE Mk.I. This composition shows some of the elements of Peter's ongoing production run. The wooden fuselage master pattern has been painted grey, so that the panel lines and other surface features can be marked in India ink. Note that the fabric tail surfaces have been simulated with 10 thou plasticard. The sprayed black lines represent tapes, which should only be visible when light catches the edges. Since he could not get moulded plasticard to look right on the rear fuselage, the fabric is represented by 10 thou transparent PVC, on which stringers have been represented by embossment on the inside surface. PVC is also used to represent plywood panelling around the cockpit, and the metal cowling panels. Evident here are master forms for the three different propellers used on Mk1 HURRICANES: early (blunt spinner) and late (longer spinner), wooden-bladed Rotols and DeHavilland metal-bladed type.

Various exotic approaches can be envisioned, including "lost wax" casting. But, usually the core mould (cavity) can be built up from plasticard, with inverse ("female") features added for interior detail, care being taken to assure later removal from the rigid casting. A variation here is to provide a relatively featureless cavity, whose detail is added later.

The core mould must be carefully inserted within the cavity of the silicone mould to ensure its correct relative position, even as the epoxy is being poured. This requires judicious placement of standoffs on the core, which will neither disfigure the final exterior surface nor obstruct core removal (they can be lightly attached for later breakaway from the core).

Finally, with the silicone mould back in its upright container for support, and the core(s) securely in place, the epoxy resin is admitted, slowly and evenly so as not to produce voids (trapped air bubbles). No mould release agent is used, nor is it required: it would inevitably obscure some of the surface detail, and would doubtless produce some surface topography of its own!

ONE-OFF MODELS: I again want to emphasize that the above technique is meant primarily for production runs, of, say, two to ten. For fuselages of a one-off model, one can simply skin the master form. This can also be done for wings. However, for thinner wings, such as a 1/24th scale SPITFIRE, I recommend casting of a polyester form, upon which the PVC skin is then applied.

An issue here is long-term integrity of double-sided sticky tape for skin attachment. My feeling is that, once the tape has been isolated from contact with air or sunlight, it should hold indefinitely. But, final judgement should be made by the modeller!

TRANSPARENCIES: Cockpit canopies, windscreens, turret housings, nose glazing, and such are key elements in establishing a model's appeal and realistic appearance. Crucial aspects to be addressed include correct shape, distortion-free optical clarity, crispness of framing, and scale thickness. Usually a weakness of kit models, scale thickness is necessary for imparting correct refraction characteristics; as well as offset from adjoining components. Since 1/4 inch is a typical thickness for actual transparencies, 10 thou is correct for a 1/24th scale model.

Most of my canopies, turret housings, and nose cones are epoxy cast, in the following manner:

First, I make a pattern, from solid wood, or built up, as described above for major components. From this I cast a master form, into a Plaster of Paris mould. I use epoxy for this application, due to its lack of shrinkage and superior surface relative to polyester. This I then polish to a high sheen.

I make the master using 10 thou PVC, vacuformed or heat pulled over the epoxy form. In the case of deep, complex three-dimensional shapes, such as the LANCASTER turrets, three separate elements are thus formed—being superglued together after trimming.

Framing is added to this as appropriate using strips of 5 thou plasticard. First, framing locations are accurately marked on the epoxy master form, from pin pricks located using my UNIMAT as an indexing tool. The assembled PVC master is placed over the form. One end of a framing strip is attached with superglue, after which glue is progressively applied to the strip over a short length (about 1 cm) at a time, which is laid down over the guidelines visible on the form.

Inner and outer moulds are then cast, using silicone rubber. With the PVC master removed, I reassemble the moulds; a few standoffs being added to ensure correct, uniform spacing—never at a glazing location, of course.

I mix the epoxy and let it sit until all of the bubbles have disappeared. This is facilitated by heating the volume somewhat to reduce its viscosity using a small, intense lamp. However, since heating also accelerates curing, pouring into the mould must commence promptly. This is performed evenly and slowly enough that the liquid in the mould remains fairly level, thus avoiding fresh bubble entrapment. Each canopy or turret is cast in one piece. A seeming difficulty was removal of the inner mould from the top turret casting of the LANC, which tapers inward towards its base. Fortunately, the slots for the gun traverse allowed the casting to be flexed just enough to permit mould removal.

For the almost hemispherical bomb-aimer's glazing, I simply used heat formed PVC: no subsequent epoxy casting being made.

PAINTING

Since my technique for painting resin cast models is very different from that usually employed for plastic models, I will explain it here. My motivation for developing this approach was to replicate as well as possible the actual silky sheen appearance of wartime camouflage on metal skinned surfaces, whilst preserving the intricate rivet/panel line detail achievable with PVC skin/resin cast construction.

PAINT CONSTITUENTS: By a long trial and error process, I arrived at the following rather bizarre formula:

- Mix matte HUMBROL from the tinlet with an equal quantity of enamel thinner; this prevents the paint from drying too quickly;
- Add about the same quantity of polyurethane varnish (or perhaps slightly less);
- Add somewhat more nitrocellulose thinner than for either of the other two constituents. I now mix until just a trace of color remains on the side of the container when touched by the mixing stick.

Polyurethane provides the correct sheen, tightens as it dries, and imparts a hard surface. It can later be rubbed down if necessary, with worn 1200 grade wet or dry. The nitrocellulose thinner ensures smooth flow through the airbrush and makes the paint dry more quickly. It seems to prevent coagulation of the mixed paint.

APPLICATION: Along with the aforementioned formula, the second key to achieving the desired result is a very thin air brush application of paint—only enough to impart opacity. Otherwise, the fine rivet and panel line indentations would become flooded.

But, no finish is better than the surface upon which it is laid. I have found that clear PVC sheet possesses an ideal surface for subsequent moulding and casting. All that is required is a brisk rub down with a clean cloth. Of course, the parent sheet must be carefully examined for surface flaws before use.

THE FINAL SURFACE: After two days, the polyurethane varnish will be dry, but not fully hard. At this point, black water color can be rubbed into the surface. When most of it has been wiped off, an oily "used" appearance is achieved. The black will also remain in panel lines and around rivet heads, highlighting those features, in the same way that dirt and oil collect on actual aircraft.

I do not like oversprayed varnish, since it always seems to give the paint an unrealistic depth, although I can see its advantage for hiding decal film. In any case, I airbrush all of my insignia/markings directly onto the surface, using masks cut from low tack frisket film.

CHAPTER IX
Model Research and Photography
by Clark Macomber

ABOUT CLARK MACOMBER

I was born in Chicago in 1930, and began modelling ten years later. My first effort was a prototype Hawker HURRICANE, carved in balsa from a kit bought at the local cigar/hobby shop. This was followed by many quarter-scale pine "solid" and control-line flying models from then through high school.

The next years included a confused college career, a Combat Infantryman's Badge for Korean service and, finally, a B.S. in Product Design from the Institute of Design at I.I.T. in 1956. Modeling resumed while product designing at Bell & Howell. This was followed by three years as an Assistant Professor of design at North Carolina State in Raleigh.

As my design career continued, I found that my hobby time was being spent more on correcting faulty three-view drawings than on the models themselves. I produced three-views for the NASM and the AAHS Journal during the '60s. The latter eventually resulted in acceptance of a design job at MONOGRAM Models in 1976. Since then, I've drawn many three-views, all unpublished, for model kits, no satisfactory representations existing at the time for such subjects as the P-51D, "razorback" P-47D, B-25, B-26, F-102 and F-105 for MONOGRAM; the KC-135 for ERTL; and the Il-2 for ACCURATE MINIATURES.

In the late '60s, I was a founder of the Chicago Scalemasters, a flying scale club. I was a judge of flying scale events at the AMA Nats, and other contests; formulated the still-used radio-control Sport Scale rules; and was Director of all scale events at the AMA Nats for three years.

Now back in North Carolina, as Director of Design for ACCURATE MINIATURES, I get to do still more three-views. Aviation "archeology" has, for me, become a way of life.

Clark Macomber.

MODEL PLANS

INTRODUCTION: Plans—multi-view drawings—are the foundation of any scratch built project. Indeed, no such model is any better than the plans upon which it was based. So, step one—well, after deciding what to build—is to find the best plans available, and then to determine whether these are accurate; can be made so with some revisions; or, whether you must prepare your own—from scratch.

Let all of your airplane enthusiast/modelling buddies know what you're looking for. All aircraft configuration research depends on finding some persons, institutions or publications that have the documentation you need—or, of working from an actual specimen. Get all the help you can in this search. You never know who might be, or know of, a source for useful material—or what great stuff may be available right in your own files.

Next, start rounding up the usual suspects. Get all the books and magazine articles about your passion (if it's not a passion, perhaps you should forget it) that can be found. In the case of subjects about which a really great monograph has been published, just one book may be all you'll need: but, this is rare! Photographs, not drawings, will be your first line of defense against the inaccuracies that might make your model ultimately unsatisfying, even though the craftsmanship is quite decent. Can you imagine someone saying that a photograph must be inaccurate because it doesn't look like the three-view you found? I think not, but many modelers (and model companies) aren't too bothered by drawings that are contradicted by the available photographs.

A prevailing attitude in modelling, common even among kit manufacturers who should know better, is that all three-views are created equal. The truth is that most drawings will take a little tinkering to be satisfactory and many, including drawings effusively praised by those who sell them, are not really of practical use in producing a satisfactory model. When we say "practical", this means that even though the drawing may have some valuable information, it would take an expert (you'll know when you are one) a great deal of effort and care to extract it.

What are you looking for in a three-view? First, you're looking for accurate shapes and outlines. These can, in fact, be found on many drawings that are, at first look, not too impressive. It's much easier to add details to a drawing that has basically accurate outlines and proportions than to correct the shapes on a highly detailed drawing with bad outlines.

SOURCES: At this point a few words about sources: There is only a small group of draftsmen of whose work it may be said: "Go ahead and make the usual checks against your collected photos, but it's almost certainly right." The late Peter Westburg in the U.S., Vladimir Voronin in Russia, Arthur Bentley in the UK, and Doug Carrick, a Scot now living in Sweden, are in this select group. There

Messerschmitt Bf 110G-4/R3/R2. This superbly rendered 1/24th scale model by Anthony Clements depicts a *nachtjaeger* of III/NJG 1, flown by Oblt. Martin Drewes. It was equipped with FuG 212 Lichtenstein C-l and FuG 220 Lichtenstein BC SN-2b radar; and armed with two Mk 108 30mm cannon in the nose, two MG 151/20 cannon in the lower fuselage, two MG/FF 20mm cannon in the *Schrage Musik* position, and twin MG 812 for rear defense. This model was Senior National Champion at the 1991 IPMS/UK Championships and Gold Medal winner at the 1991 Model Engineers Exhibition. (Ivor Fields photo)

are a number of others whose work is usually quite good, but whose occupational pressures precluded their devoting the huge amounts of time to each drawing that are necessary for almost flawless work. In this class would be found the late Paul Matt, G.A.G. Cox, the late Bergen Hardesty, and quite a few others whose output was individually small. One of the most influential and best drawings ever made was LeRoy Weber's P-38L for Superscale. It may have been the first of the nearly perfect and very complete drawings of the sort that Westburg, Bentley, and others did in later years. As far as I know he has never had another three-view published: the P-38 was his passion.

Be aware that drawings by the most famous, most advertised and most prolific sources should be approached with great caution. A decent three-view cannot be constructed in less than about 150 to 200 hours work. This does not include the research, which will likely range from 30 to 300 hours, or inking the drawing for publication, which adds a minimum of another 30 hours. A draftsman who has published at a rate of one or more drawings per month has either copied others' drawings (try always to find the primary source) or has short-changed the subjects. Several aviation draftsmen are famous for their output and at least two that I can think of should be infamous for their inaccuracy. In particular, be skeptical of drawings with copious dimensioning, unless the draftsman has given his sources for the dimensions. In the case of one famous three-view artist, he not only made up countless dimensions, apparently scaling from his own drawings, but also provided airfoil ordinates for non-existant airfoil sections. Occasionally, he even provided more than one measurement for the same dimension. Finally, do not be much impressed by style. Some of the prettiest drawings are among the most inaccurate. On the other hand, some quite useful three-views are the work of dedicated, conscientious nonprofessionals and look a little rough around the edges.

NOTE: The remainder of the SOURCES section is provided by your kindly editor.

Among the modern genre of multi-view drawings are those of Dai Nippon Kaiga's ongoing AERO DETAIL monograph series. Not surprisingly perhaps, one of their best efforts (#7) delineates the various marks of the Mitsubishi A6M "ZERO". Another especially praiseworthy set covers the Macchi C.200/202/205 series (#15). AERO DETAIL's photo coverage of subject aircraft are of great value, and the drawings in #7 and #15 appear to be excellent.

If the Ju-88A is your passion, you'll do no better than the multi-view drawings of it by Doug Carrick, which appeared in the 3/1998 issue of PIENOIS MALLI, a Finnish modelling magazine. In addition to other primary configuration sources, Doug was able to measure major Ju-88A components recovered in Scandanavia. Fuselage cross-sections, for example, were carefully defined. He has also rendered the Messerschmitt Bf 110C for MALLI; again, based upon reliable primary sources, including "measured from life." This publication has also featured excellent drawings of the Dornier Do17Z by Pentti Manninen, another well respected aircraft delineator.

Another source of apparently excellent drawings of Japanese aircraft was the periodical MARU MECHANIC. Here the Zero was also well delineated, as was its antecedent, the Mitsubishi A5M series. Other types covered included the Kawasaki Ki-61 Hien ("Tony", to us), Aichi D3A2 ("Val") and Nakajima Ki-43 Hayabusa ("Oscar").

Of the ongoing Polish AIRCRAFT MONOGRAPH series by AJ PRESS, #2 covering the Heinkel He111 is especially praiseworthy for its extensive multi-view drawings by Robert Michulec (with Witold Hazuka). Number 13 covering the Yakovlev-1 and -3 includes extensive and probably accurate drawings of these types, by Robert Bock and Jacek Jackiewicz. Besides, they're available in English! Their stablemates, the LaGG-3, MiG-3 and Lavochkin La-5 (and -5FN) were given proper treatment by Vladimir Voronin in a Russian volume which will, hopefully, be reissued in the near future.

Each WINDSOCK DATAFILE and DATAFILE SPECIAL includes multiview drawings of the W.W.-I aircraft type covered, usually rendered by Ian Stair. These drawings usually represent good to excellent representations of the type. In the classification of "ultimate" configuration material are the Rozendall Nieuport C.17 drawings in WINDSOCK DATAFILE #17, prepared through measurement of a captured example in 1917.

It is surprising—indeed, depressing—how many significant vintage aircraft have *not* been properly delineated by accurate, detailed multi-view drawings which are commercially or institutionally available to the dedicated modeller/enthusiast. Yet, in order not to become confrontational, we have not cited herein those aircraft which, in our view, are even now inadequately defined configurationally. Of major W.W.-II combat aircraft, for example, those properly done remain in the minority. This despite the fact that authentic survivors exist for most (excluding Soviet) and adequate archival documentation remains in museums, corporate and/or private archives for perhaps all. With distressing regularity, those producing "new" drawings simply rely upon some previously published, without making the effort to verify their authenticity through detail comparison with photos, primary source documents, and scaling from survivors, when possible.

In our view, the value of putatively authentic multi-view drawings is enhanced by inclusion of at least basic dimensions, comparable to those shown on the better tech manual illustrations. Far more important, the sources for the configuration basis *must* be given, in order for the potential user to assess its credentials. Even so, our admonition stands: *always* compare with independent sources.

No better opportunity for detailed scrutiny, including measurement, exists than during restoration of an authentic survivor. What better time, for example, to establish the contours of fuselage or nacelle cross-sections than when this component is disassembled? We submit this challenge to enthusiasts, to offer (inflict) their services during restorations for which they have great interest and potential access. It was Bob Waugh of Australia who finally set the

Bf 110G-4/R3 Closeup. This view emphasizes Clements' fine detailing of the cockpit area, nose, and port DB605B engine. (Ivor Fields photo)

configuration record straight on the Albatros DVa through his precise, detailed delineation of the Canberra machine during its restoration—after decades of gross misrepresentation in plans and kits. Ideally then, these drawings could be incorporated in a monograph which includes numerous detail photographs taken during restoration, supplemented by period photos, dimensions, specifications, etc. as appropriate to provide complete configuration documentation of the type. No better exemplar exists than the NASM publication ALBATROS DVa by Robert Mikesh, documenting restoration of their "STROPP"—including reproduction of the Waugh drawings.

One final admonition: if you as a dedicated and conscientious researcher have properly and thoroughly delineated some important aircraft, but lack the experience/skills to adequately translate your effort into "camera ready" drawings (e.g., you don't "do" ink), do not simply consign your valuable work to your files. Contact publications with a reputation for producing good plans: they may be willing to reformat and trace your penciled drawings for publication. (In this manner, I, Alcorn, was fortunate in having Arthur Bentley transform my A-20/BOSTON pencil drawings into MAP PLAN PACK 2989: Paul Matt did the same for the A-20G model in his HAA Volume XV.) It's your contribution, not just to the modelling community, but to aviation history.

PLANS ASSESSMENT: Next comes the stage where you evaluate the three-views you've been able to find using the photos and dimensions you've gathered. Some three-views may flunk the test quickly. Put them to one side, but don't throw them away. They may have details not to be found on the others.

Look at proportions first. Is the nose too long, the fuselage too shallow or too deep, the cowling too narrow or too wide; are the wings too tapered or not tapered enough or too far forward or back? Next, check angles. Is the slope up from the leading edge of the wing correct? How about the taper of the rear fuselage, the slope of the fuselage forward of the windshield and the rake of the windshield itself! Is the rear fuselage angled too up or too down; how about the landing gear struts, dihedral angle and, again, etceteras? Finally, because they're both most likely to be wrong and are the easiest to correct, check the curved profiles, such as vertical tails, wing tips, cowlings, etc. It's best to work these out on something where they can be changed as many times as it takes to get them right. You can trace over your chosen three-view on tracing paper. You can get an erasable electrostatic copy made at a drafting supply house and erase and redraw lines as necessary. Airfoils are just a special case of the curve family. Many otherwise excellent aviation draftsmen could never get a handle on them. If you can find what airfoil your subject had, the book "COMPREHENSIVE REF-

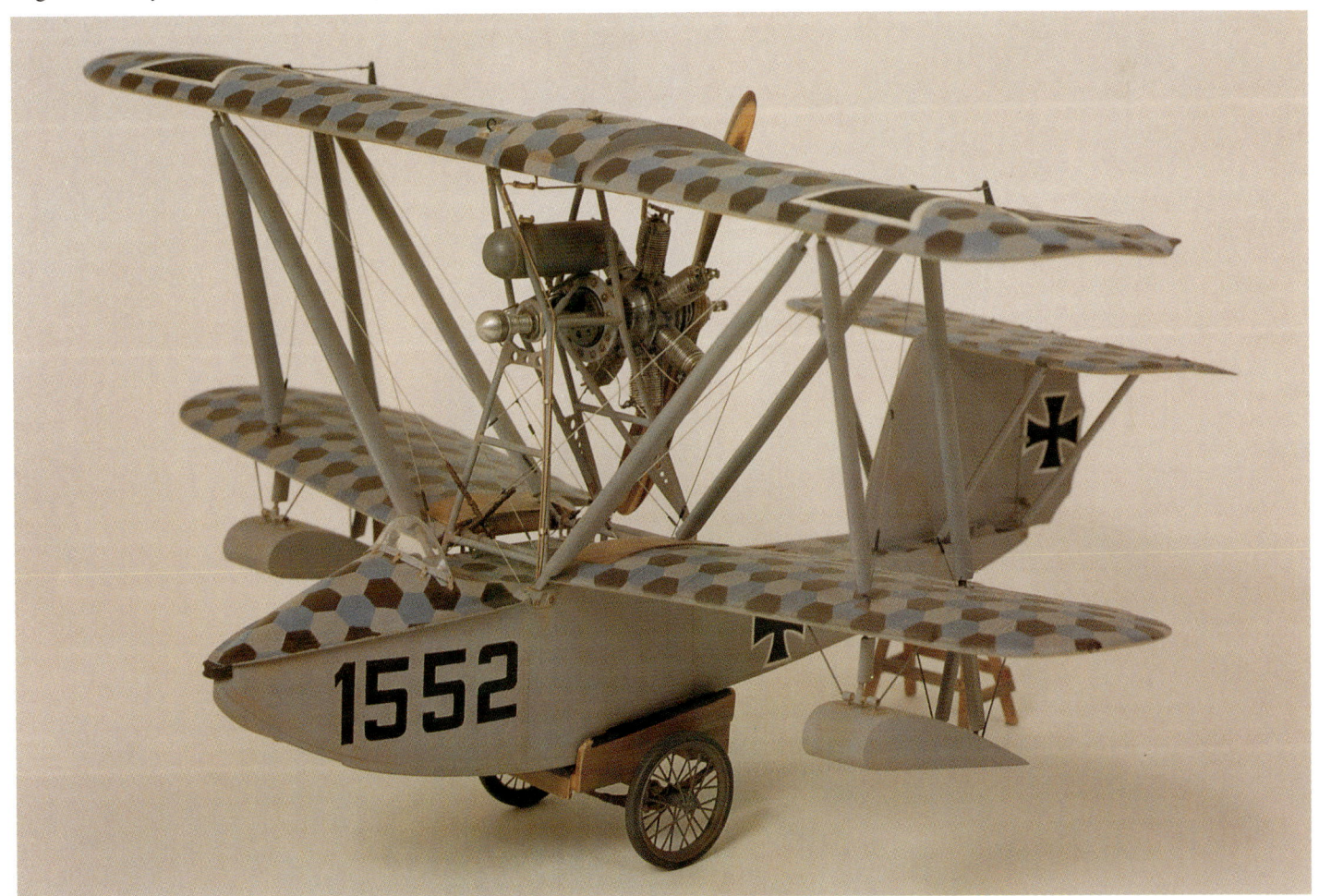

Hansa-Brandenburg W20, Werke Nr. 1552. This fascinating 1/24th scale gem by Tony Clements represents the second of three W20s, while undergoing testing at Warnemunde during March 1918. (Ivor Fields photo)

Hansa-Brandenburg W20. This compact little seaplane was designed for operation from special U-boats, to search for potential victims—or threats. In order to achieve this, it had to be capable of rapid assembly and subsequent breakdown, yet rugged enough to withstand takeoff and landing from normally encountered open waters. However, the project failed because: a. no submarine fitted with the requisite 6x20 foot internal space was constsucted, and: b. when the second prototype (#1552) was fitted with interplane struts of sufficient strength, it could not be assembled and broken down fast enough for practical operation. It was unarmed, and powered with an 80hp Oberursel rotary engine. Needless to say, considerable research was required to adequately define this aircraft's configuration. (Ivor Fields photo)

ERENCE GUIDE TO AIRFOIL SECTIONS FOR LIGHT AIRCRAFT" will not only show you what it looks like, but will give you the "ordinates" that the manufacturers used to generate wing sections.

When you're satisfied that no more differences can be massaged out of the three-view to make it look more like the prototype and dimensions match those given in reliable sources, you're ready to start building. Drawing debugging sounds tougher than it really is. Your working drawing doesn't have to be pretty enough to publish: it needs only to be readable by one person. If you have the manual dexterity required for building, you have enough for this, too. As with all human activities, the first time will be the hardest. And, don't be intimidated by the fact that the drawing you're modifying was PUBLISHED. Remember, the goal is to make great and truthful-looking scale models, not to reproduce someone else's drawing errors.

AlRCRAFT RESEARCH PHOTOGRAPHY

EDITOR'S NOTE: For the great majority of scratch built projects, "research photography" as described below will not be possible, or necessary, since: there is no surviving example of the subject; or, adequate plans, plus photo and other archival documentation exists; or, it is not possible (or practical) for the modeller to incur the expense, take off from work, or whatever, to journey to a distant subject for performance of the in-depth photography described. Clark's efforts of this nature were done professionally, for model companies as the basis for a production kit. Nonetheless,

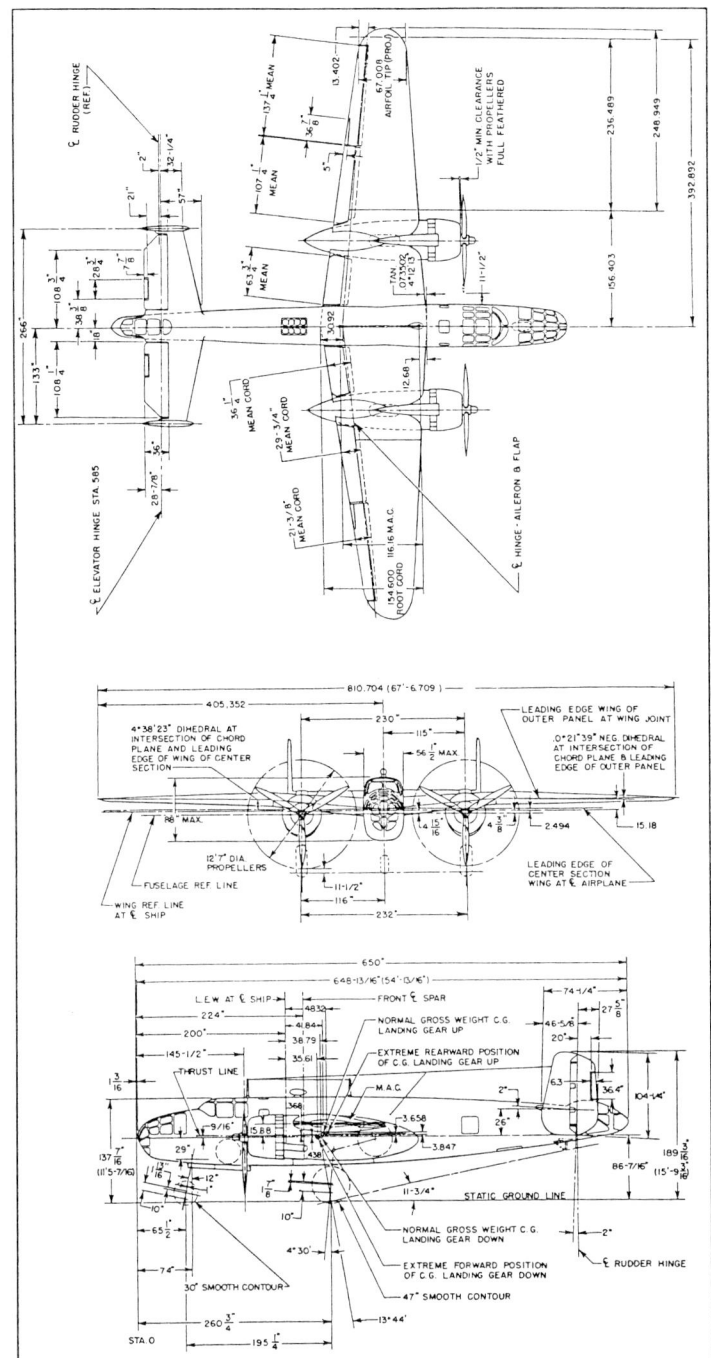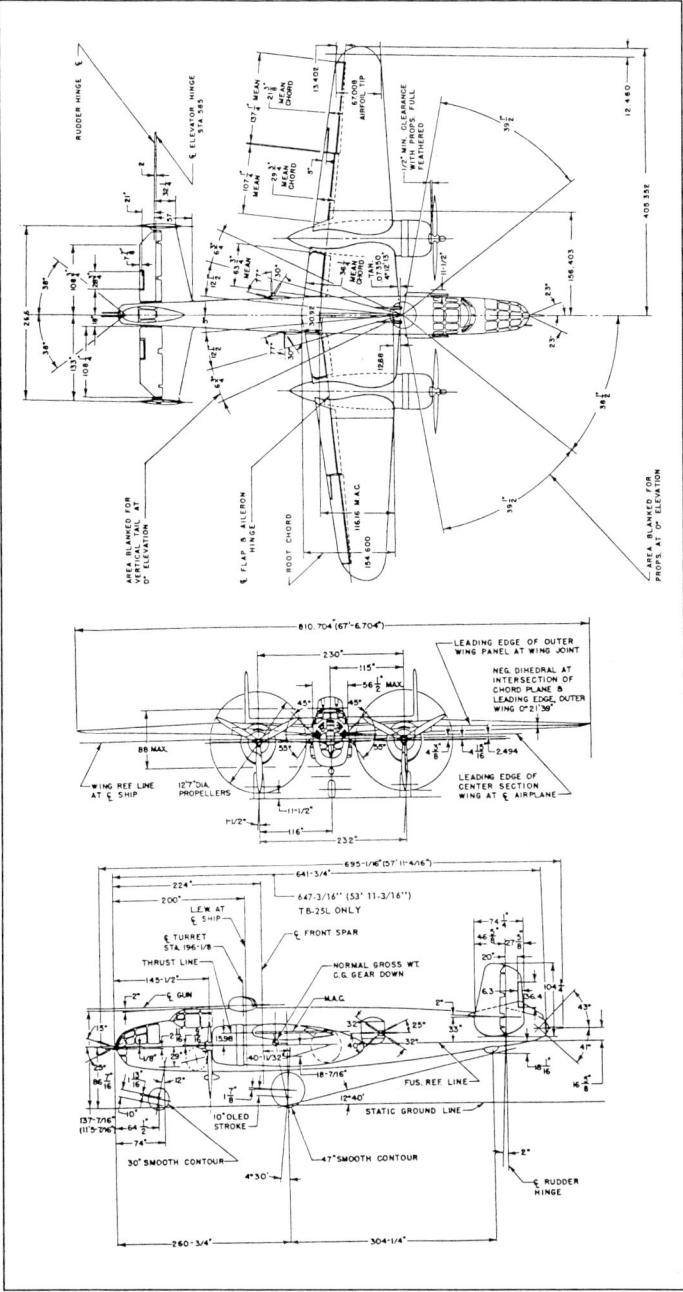

Tech Manual Drawings of the B-25A and G. These extensively dimensioned and annotated drawings are as good as any modeller/researcher could ever hope for, from such sources. Most have far fewer dimensions. Nonetheless, even these are far from complete as regards basic dimensions: for example, there is no setback dimension for the cockpit canopy. (photo courtesy of SPECIALTY PRESS)

sometimes it is possible—indeed, necessary—in order to adequately define some vintage airplane for faithful replication. Furthermore, even being aware of how such full treatment is done may be of help for assessing material which is available, and perhaps of augmenting it with one's own "research photography" of certain specific configuration aspects which may require further clarification.

INTRODUCTION: In aircraft configuration research two somewhat different types of photographs may be required. The majority serve as "general reference" for the aircraft configuration and details. Others are taken specifically as aids in making the classic three-view drawing. These "configuration research" photos, made for defining profiles, panel joints, markings, etc., are taken

Chapter IX: Model Research and Photography 121

in ways that minimize the effects of perspective distortion. More on this later. But before taking any research pictures you must have "the right stuff":

EQUIPMENT: The best camera type for the research photography to be described, in fact, the only one to be considered, is the 35mm single-lens-reflex (SLR). Only an SLR gives the precision of view-finding you need to avoid wasting film. The 35mm format gives all the image sharpness necessary, even with high-speed film: and since 250 to 350 pictures will be needed to do an adequate job, you won't want to use anything more expensive! Almost any SLR, from a thirty year old "relic" to the latest autofocus models will do the job. Cameras without through-the-lens (TTL) light metering will present some problems: TTL flashmetering and motorized film advance are both big advantages.

Much more important than having the latest camera body is having the lenses best suited for research photography. The single most useful focal length (f.l.) for research is a short "telephoto" of from 70mm to 90mm. Lenses in this range produce pictures that appear to have the least distortion of shape ("telephoto effect" or "wideangle effect" are terms often used to describe apparent distortion). F.l.s longer than 90mm make subjects appear to be flatter than they are. Shorter f.l.s, particularly those less than 50mm, introduce perceived distortion that makes it very difficult to assess shapes accurately from the photos made with them. If you must use a so-called "normal" 50mm to 55mm lens for your research work, don't crowd the subject. Stay back and keep the subject within the central two-thirds of the viewfinder. The images will be smaller, but perspective will be more like that from a short telephoto.

But, because you'll be shooting in the real world, you'll also need to have (or wish you had) a 35 to 42mm f.l. wideangle lense for times when you can't get any further back (or up), and a little distortion is better than no picture at all. For emergency use only, a 20-24mm lens can be a lifesaver if your back's against the wall (or floor, or bulkhead). Such a lens can provide useful coverage of the bottom of a wing, inside of a wheel well or overall cockpit views, to be used in conjunction with detail shots using longer f.l. lenses— and measurements.

The "three-views" used for all scale modelling show their subjects as seen from an infinite distance. So, a lens that pictures the subject as much like this as is practical will be very useful. Yet, even a 1000mm lens, with all of its bulk, cost and impractical working distances would have some "wide-angle" distortion. A good compromise telephoto lens for our work would be 200mm f.l. But, we rarely have the luxury of shooting from the distances required, especially in museums.

After the above, you may be asking, "What about zoom lenses?". Many otherwise attractive zoom lenses are marginal as research tools because they distort the image too much at one f.l. or another. But a good, almost distortion-free "zoom normal" lens can be invaluable. Two that I've used, with excellent results, to take about 90% of the shots on many dozens of research projects for Revell-Monogram, Ertl-AMT and Accurate Miniatures, are the now discontinued (but available used) Pentax 40 to 80mm and the large and expensive Nikon 35 to 70mm f2.8. New lenses are being introduced almost every day and just keep getting better, so there are probably others in this quality class now.

In addition to the camera and lens(es), you'll need a good electronic flash with automatic exposure control (preferably TTL) and a guide number of at least 100 for ISO 100/ft. A coil-cord extension will allow the flash to be used off the camera for more definition of surface detail or for photographing cockpit interiors when the canopy can't be opened. This last is done by holding the camera wherever the best views can be had and placing the flash right against the canopy so that all of its light goes inside the cockpit, with none reflecting back as glare from the canopy surfaces. This works almost as well as opening the canopy or for shooting into the nose area, as for a Ju-88.

If this listing of equipment sounds like more than your back or budget can stand, remember that useful work can be done with any SLR using just a 50-55mm "normal" lens, a good flash, and an understanding of what's required. Where you'd have used a wideangle or telephoto lens you'll just take more pictures to get the necessary coverage.

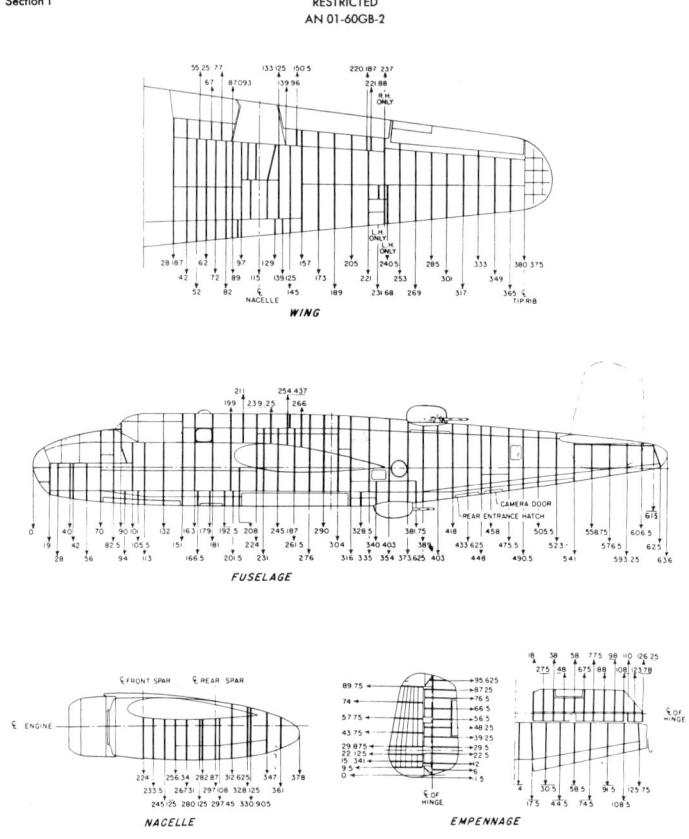

Stations Diagram of B-25C/D. This excellent diagram is from AN-01-60GB-2, the Erection and Maintenance Instructions for the type. It well complements the dimensioned drawings of the previous illustration. Sadly, however, such station diagrams rarely, if ever, provide any orthogonal stations; i.e., in the vertical plane, that would have pinned things down almost totally for us latter-day enthusiasts. Well, yes, they could also have provided us with engine cowling, wing leading edge, and turret centerline station numbers—clearly, these guys were not modellers, nor did they have our interests at heart.

FILM: The next decision is which film to use. Don't even think about black and white. There is about five times as much information in a color picture as in a black and white of the same subject. Use color print film because research often involves comparing several images, which is nearly impossible with slides. Film speed? Give yourself and your flash a break and use ISO 400, or even 800. Color print films of this speed are more than sharp enough for the relatively small prints you'll use (4x6 in./10x15cm) and allow reasonable exposures on the dark, flat-camouflaged subjects in badly lit museums that always seem to be my assignments.

Always take more film than you think will be needed. At least ten rolls of 36 exposures should be available for any project of normal size. Prints should be on glossy paper for best definition.

Last, don't forget to take spare batteries for your camera, flash, winder, etc. Take a spare camera body if you have one; you're usually working far from help. I take a spare flash and several extra lenses as well. I feel more secure with these back-ups when far from home. Now we're equipped for the next stage.

GENERAL REFERENCE PHOTOGRAPHS: For most photos, you'll be concerned with the forms and contours: the "sculptural" aspects of the subject. The pictures you take to capture the shapes of the aircraft will resemble most of those seen in publications. They will usually be taken at an angle to the main elements of the subject and from varying heights. Sometimes a photographer will circle a subject taking pictures every 20 or 30 degrees. As you view your subject, what you should be looking for are those angles that are most revealing of the shapes and details. Often the difference between a picture that shows critical shapes by means of highlights or light shading and one which doesn't is a change of about two inches in camera location. Remember, for all this "sculptural" photography, use a lens of near 80mm f.l. or keep your zoom lens as close to that as possible. Use shorter focal lengths only when forced to by space restrictions.

I usually begin a research project by walking around the subject for awhile, not taking any pictures, but just noting which shapes and details must be revealed by the photography. In your mind, break the subject down to its design elements; fuselage, wings, nacelles, canopies and enclosures, radomes, etc. Then take the pictures necessary to show the profiles, contours and details of each element.

CONFIGURATION RESEARCH PHOTOGRAPHS: For those photographs taken particularly to aid in making a three-view, you should use the longest focal-length lens that circumstances will allow. Since I usually change lenses for this part of the job, I often take these shots all in one block. For these pictures the axis of the lens should be kept as nearly perpendicular as possible to the primary plane of the subject: those at the center-line of the fuselage and to the planes of the wings and tail surfaces. Unless you are able to use a lens with an exceptionally long focal length, say more than 200mm, each picture must be considered to be useful only over a section of the subject about 3 to 4 feet (1m) square. To produce photos with inconsequential distortion it will thus be necessary to shoot a "mosaic" of overlapping pictures. On an average aircraft this would require starting at the tip of the nose and making an exposure every 3 to 4 feet along the horizontal center-line of the fuselage and then repeating this journey twice, once at the level of the top contour of the fuselage and once at the bottom. Used in conjunction with enough carefully selected measurements, this method can result in very accurate drawings.

If you are forced, for instance, to photograph the profile of a wing tip while lying on your back on the ground, your mosaic will have to be on a smaller scale, with the pictures taken on centers of 1 to 2 feet instead of 3 to 4 feet. A good rule might be that center to center distances of your mosaic should be one-fifth the shooting distance at a maximum. The method I use to avoid confusion about where in a particular mosaic photograph the camera was perpendicular to the main planes of the subject is to always put that point in the center of the frame. For example; those pictures taken at the same level as the top of the fuselage have the top of the fuselage in their center. Yes, some of your photos will be only half filled with the subject, but they will be more easily used as a result. Don't forget to take some photos from the ends of the fuselage and wings to show cross-sectional shapes as revealed by panel joints and painted markings. Also, remember to record both sides of the fuselage and both surfaces of wings and tailplanes, as they're probably different as regards surface detail.

Keep in mind when you're doing research photography that, when travel and equipment expenses are taken into consideration, film and processing are usually the least expensive parts of the job.

Messerschmitt Bf 109E. This almost perfect bottom view was taken for wartime recognition purposes. See discussion of it in the text. (NASM #3B-34688(USAF))

Chapter IX: Model Research and Photography   123

You're better off with 25 pictures more than you need rather than 5 fewer. Actually, you'll always have 5 fewer than you need; you're trying to avoid having 15!

Be prepared to take about 15% to 20% of the pictures lying on the ground. These are the views you can't find in books and magazines. Wear clothes that won't show dirt and are not too valuable to you. On my clipboard, under the pad of paper I use for recording measurements, I keep a folded piece of very heavy wrapping paper about 3x6 feet to lie on if it's too dirty for even old clothes.

Use the flash! If you're shooting in less than bright sunlight you'll need it to give enough contrast for details to be visible on your prints. In bright sunlight you'll need it to put enough light into shaded areas so that they won't just turn black. For research photography the flash is your best friend; even more important than the right lens!

Be adaptable and resourceful. If they let you up to shoot the cockpit, make sure to take the top of the fuselage and wings while you're up there. Take advantage of any special viewpoints; balconies, ladders, etc. that are available.

MEASURING

Measurements and photographs should work together to produce good research results. For this synergy to be effective keep two simple ideas in mind.

First, if time is limited, take bigger measurements rather than smaller ones. It's better to have only the width of an instrument panel than to have all the instrument sizes and not the width. Big, known dimensions can be broken down quite accurately with the aid of your photos to find sizes of details contained in them. The reverse is emphatically not true!

Second, try not to leave yourself with measurements that can't be related to each other. Measure the wing chord, but also make sure you have the distance from the leading edge to the nose and the trailing edge to the tail or to some equally known points. On large subjects, it's often useful to pick a "zero-point" somewhere near the center and measure in both directions from there. Just be sure you don't know the exact size of wheel wells or bomb-bays without knowing where they are.

This paragraph added by the editor: Whenever possible, measurements should be taken parallel to the plane of the profile to be defined. This can be challenging, and usually requires an assistant for any but short lengths. Suppose, for example, that you want to measure, or verify the length of a P-47D THUNDERBOLT cowling, which, of course, curves in toward the front. In principal, what one wants is a measurement from the cowl rear edge to the plane of its front edge and perpendicular to the latter. A great long straight-edge resting on both sides of the cowl front would be ideal—but that bloody propeller hub is in the way! Short of this, the fellow in the front will simply have to "eyeball" the cowl front plane, while holding the tape as parallel as possible to the fuselage "elevation and plan profiles."—i.e., the shortest length is correct. Sure, such work can be performed more accurately with surveying equipment, but you can probably get within 1/4 inch.

As with the photography, it usually helps to spend a few minutes thinking and planning before beginning. If a decent three-view can be found and enlarged to a comfortable size, this can be used to put your measurements on; thus saving making a sketch or drawing for the purpose. Some "shorthand" symbols can speed the process. For instance, I use a dot about 1mm (3/64") in diameter with a dimension next to it to indicate the width or thickness at the location of the dot. Different colors can also be used as indicators, but since much of my work has to be photocopied or faxed, I try to avoid this.

SCALING FROM PUBLISHED PHOTOS

This section was also added by your editor.

As mentioned above, for most modelling projects, even scratchbuilt, we haven't the luxury, time, money, skills, equipment or opportunity to fully define, through our own photographs and measurements, an airplane selected, but for which adequate drawings do not exist commercially—or which require extensive verification/correction. As also mentioned above, often no example survives.

For the sake of this discourse, I will take the Messerschmitt Bf 109E as an example. You say: "Oh, c'mon!: That airplane has been totally and accurately defined many times in multi-view drawings (and inaccurately many more times). What about those in AERO DETAIL 1, or the old MAP Plan Pack BH 2790, drawn by Doug Carrick?" O.K., since I know and have the greatest respect for him and his work, let's pick on Doug's MAP BH 2790. (My 1/24th scale print is tatty, yellowed and falling apart at the folds, but still valid as reference.)

A few years ago, despite ongoing work on the NINAK, I began thinking about a possible future 1/24th scale scratchbuilt Bf 109E project. (Yes, I am aware of the AIRFIX kit; I have one.) First, I wanted to verify the side view. So, I made a seven inch long transparency of it from his drawing. Then, I found an in-flight shot of a *schwarm* of Emils in which the nearest one was an almost perfect side view, from far enough away to have minimal perspective distortion. Using a copier with full-range enlargement/reduction capability, I fussed around until I obtained a copy which almost perfectly matched the drawing transparency as to size. Laying the transparency over this instantly revealed any differences—which, as Clark reminds us, must be errors in the drawing, not the photo!—allowance, of course, being made for slight perspective distortion. In fact, Doug's drawing was almost spot on, except for some slight nose contour errors just behind the spinner. As for plan view contours, and details; several years ago while at the NASM Archives in Washington, D.C. (coincidentally, while with Doug Carrick!), I stumbled across an almost perfect underside plan view (#21520AC, or 3B-34688) of a Bf109E—obviously taken for recognition purposes. As for precise wing geometry, Model Art's monograph on the Bf 109B-E features a profusely dimensioned line drawing of this element on page 71, evidently taken from a tech manual on the type (perhaps it says so, but I can't read Japanese). Although not dimensioned, fuselage side and top inboard profiles are also included, which may have come from the same source. While I haven't subjected them to rigorous (i.e. pre modelling) scrutiny, the Emil drawings in AERO DETAIL 1 also appear to be quite good.

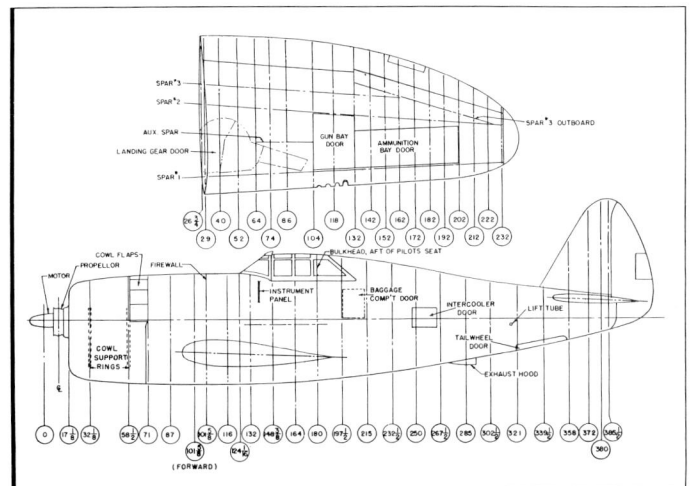

Stations Diagram, Republic P-47C-1-RE and up. This diagram is from T.O. No. 01-65BC-2: Erection and Maintenance Instructions. If not an actual error, the indication of two Station 101 5/8s is at least very confusing. They are in fact 8.00 inches apart, reflecting the "Quick Engine Change" modification embodied from the 57th P-47C. Although not indicated on the Stations Diagrams, the leading edge of the P-47B (and first 56 P-47Cs) was at approximately Station 86 1/2, so that for the later variants was at about Station 94 1/2. Compare this with various published plans—and with your favorite kit of the type. (The key direct measurement being from Station 71 at the cowling rear: i.e., 23 1/2 inches.)

I do an enormous amount of scaling from available photos during the course of a modelling project, often long after I have selected/corrected/made basic configuration drawings. These later measurements are usually made for the purpose of better defining some detail which I'm about to make. As Clark emphasizes, such scaling can only be performed with confidence for portions of the aircraft over which perspective is minimal in a perpendicular (orthogonal) view. What's then necessary is to have some known dimension within this (relatively) undistorted portion, in order to establish its scale. For example, for my NINAK, I know the cylinder spacing of the LIBERTY 12 engine: 6 1/2". I had a wonderful orthoganal view of the nose region, one of many detail photos kindly supplied by Peter McDermott, the world-class scale RC modeller in England. The carefully measured distance in the 4" x 6" photo from the same point (exhaust nut) on the forward to fifth cylinder is 1.24". So, 4 x 6 1/2"/1.24" = 21.0, the (inverse) scale of the photo. Thus, for any feature within the photo:

Model feature size (X) = photo feature size x photo scale inverse (21)
                        ──
                                  Model scale inverse (24)

I made hundreds of such scalings from my many detail and overall DH9A photos. O.K., so I used my old 12 inch K&E slide rule to do the "sums," instead of a calculator.

Even photos which are not minimum distortion orthogonal views can be used for some scaling. For example, suppose you have a 3/4 front view: if an exposed wheel is visible for which you know the diameter, this can be used to scale other elements in the vertical plane which passes through the axle.

A trick which I learned while still a kid was to hold a model in front of a larger scale photo (usually an AIR TRAILS color centerspread), at the same angle and relative distance. A serious error, such as wrong dihedral or fuselage contour will be revealed. Sure, it's not precise and the model must be well toward completion, but it does prevent glaring mistakes. (Over the years, one of the commonest errors which I have seen in—mostly kit—models is insufficient dihedral: this could be identified and corrected before completion by this simple method.)

INTERIOR CONFIGURATION

This section was also provided by your verbose editor.

Often a considerable challenge—and source of frustration—is establishing the nature and configuration of interior features: structure, instrument panels, "black boxes", controls, seats, bomb racks and the like. While good, or at least verifiable, external general arrangement drawings are available for many aircraft, interior drawings are much scarcer.

If you have only photos to work from, it's tough, because they are mostly perforce oblique, high perspective views. Often you can relate internal structure to external panel, rivet or nail lines of known location. This is where good tech manuals can sometimes be of great help, through photos and line drawings which enable one to identify components and their relationship to structure. However, it is usually necessary to prepare detail interior scale drawings in order to define these relationships to a degree of accuracy commensurate with that of the overall model. But, this takes time, patience and a great deal of detective work.

Occasionally your research is rewarded by discovery of an authentic and reasonably detailed "inboard profile," such as that for the Bristol BEAUFIGHTER which appeared in the March 1944 issue of AVIATION, in their "Design Analysis No. 5"—along with a great deal more excellent configuration information.

Sometimes, we're even blessed with good inboard profiles and supplemental interior views in recently published monographs, or still available plans. A shining example of the former is given in ALI D'ITALIA #1: FIAT CR 42, pp. 32-33 (probably extracted from a works document). An ideal presentation of cockpit layout is that on page 75 of AIRCRAFT MONOGRAPH 13: YAK-1, YAK-3, by AJ PRESS of Poland. To be sure, good perspective drawings of cockpit interiors are useful, but accurate scale multi-views are of greater value, so long as they are supplemented by "around-the-clock" interior photos.

A point which I hope to make here is that, since scale interior detail is also of great importance to the serious modeller, it should be included as an integral part of a multiview plans presentation whenever possible. Many vintage aircraft of major historical importance have yet to be accurately and thoroughly delineated for publication—and posterity. For those who take on such projects, don't neglect the interior!

CHAPTER X
Finishing
by Pete Chalmers

EDITOR'S NOTE

Pete is not a scratch builder, nor is he well known in the general modelling community. However, he is a fine and prolific modeller, whose finishes are superb in all respects.

His in-depth knowledge of aircraft, especially in the World War II era, is vast—as is his library of aviation books and periodicals. This is manifested in the authenticity of his models, especially as regards camouflage/marking schemes. Aside from crispness of such elements as painted-on markings and canopy frames, his deft rendering of complex camouflage schemes, such as those employed by German and Italian wartime aircraft, is especially impressive. Weathering—subtle, delicate, and convincing, is another Chalmers forte.

While his methods are very effective, and therefore relevant to scratch as well as kit building, they are complex, involving many materials and arcane techniques. But, they are well explained in the following narrative.

Pete comes from a strong aviation background:

His great uncle, William Wallace Chalmers, was a Nieuport 28 pilot in the famous 94th Pursuit Squadron during World War I, having the dubious honor of being shot down and captured on July 7, 1918, being claimed as a victory by no less than 3 German aces of Jasta 26.

His father, Don Chalmers, is retired after over 50 years of professional piloting as a flight instructor, flight school owner, and FAA examiner—with almost 50,000 flight hours.

Pete served for 5 years in the 1960's as a Navy flight and intelligence officer and instructor, with service aboard 5 different carriers, primarily in Douglas A-3 SKYWARRIORS, and ashore overseas in 3 countries. This gave him ample opportunities to observe aircraft finishes and weathering "in action."

Incidentally, I've known Pete since our "Sand Hill Club" days in the early 70's (Pete, George Lee, Pat Stein, John Jenkins, Pete Shirk, Chris Mikuriya, and myself). The SHC was a decidedly ad-hoc San Francisco Bay area IPMS Chapter.

INTRODUCTION

All of us "kit bashers" who have seen the marvelous scratch built models shown in this volume or at the IPMS Nationals have wondered at the tremendous patience necessary to bring some of these complex and superdetailed projects to completion. Conversations with John Alcorn, Bob Davies, or the late George Lee give some insight into one common characteristic of the best builders—a willingness to discard or do over a component or sub-assembly which doesn't quite measure up to their exacting demands. Many kit builders use more than one kit or part if they are dissatisfied with the results, but to rebuild an entire wing or fuselage from scratch because it's not precisely right still boggles my mind.

There is one area, however, where discarding a component ceases to be a viable option—the final finishing of the model. We are all faced with the prospect of only having one chance to "get it right." Kit builders and scratchbuilders alike come to the point when their models are essentially complete, and they can no longer defer the airbrushing, decaling, highlighting, and weathering which can either enhance or detract from all the laborious construction which has gone before. Since scratch builders usually render far fewer models than kit builders, they are often weakest at these most important skills—in some cases entire epochs of technological change take place in the years between models!

The following is a run-through of "How I do it." It assumes that the modeller is not a novice, but perhaps has had some problems from time to time with various aspects of finishing/decaling/weathering. It is by no means intended to be the "only" way to achieve good results, but I am comfortable that *any* modeller who is skilled enough to scratch build can achieve excellent results using the methods and materials which I describe. Many of my techniques were "borrowed" from many generous modellers over the years, as I have always been willing to try any method or material which can result in a better finish.

This chapter will be divided into two parts. In the first part, I'll discuss the equipment and supplies I have on hand before starting, as well as some useful tips and techniques. In the second part, I'll give a run-through of the process I use to finish and weather a model, with much digression on the "whys" of my choices. Sources of some of the tools and materials will be found in the chapter covering that subject.

PART 1: EQUIPMENT, PAINTS, MATERIALS, SAFETY, USEFUL TIPS

EQUIPMENT

Air Sources: I use a silent piston compressor and ballast tank with the usual pressure gauges, air filter, moisture trap, and adjustable

Macchi C.202. Pete Chalmers finished this 1/48th scale Hasegawa kit as a C.202 Serie I of the 168th Squadriglia, 16 Gruppo, based at Palermo, Sicily, in mid-1943. Per his photo references, it was still in its original livery of Verde/Bruno/Jiallo. -Dan Ormsby photo

Macchi C.202. These two views reveal Chalmers' deft and authentic application of such challenging camouflage schemes. He relates that both the fasces national insignia on the fuselage and the House of Savoy crest on the rudder were decals even on the actual aircraft. -Dan Ormsby photo

Chapter X: Finishing

pressure regulator. A more economical alternative would be a compressed CO2 bottle with a pressure regulator. I would NOT recommend a diaphragm-type compressor because of the inability to regulate the pressure and pulsation of the output air. Whatever set-up you use MUST have the ability to supply clean, dry, unpulsed propellant at a constant selected air pressure. This is much more important than the type of airbrush you have.

Air Brushes: There are many excellent airbrush brands. I have seen outstanding work done with some of the least expensive. A good source of propellant and correctly mixed paint are more important than the exact airbrush brand or type—an expensive airbrush, if anything, will be less forgiving than a simple, less expensive design. A quality "single action" airbrush is necessary for priming, general painting, and overcoating. A more expensive and maintenance heavy "double action" is necessary for fine work. I believe you need both.

I use a Paasche H-1 (Fine head) Siphon Feed Single Action External Mix for priming, general painting, and overcoating/sealing. The Paasche H is economical, reliable, easy to clean, and parts are available at most hobby or art supply outlets, as well as by mail order (See "Sources"). I use it with a 1/4 oz. color cup or even put a drop or two of paint right in the back of the needle assembly for small jobs. For large models, the H-3 (Medium) head assembly may be suitable. I rarely use a bottle assembly—just don't need that much paint: but for large jobs one may be convenient.

For fine-line detailing (separation of camouflage colors with minimum overspray) or Luftwaffe-type mottling, I prefer an internal-mix double-action airbrush because of its ability to spray very small and fine patterns or lines. I started with a Paasche VL-1 Double Action Siphon Feed and then switched to a Paasche VJR Double Action Gravity Feed. I have found that elimination of the weight and bulk of the cup/bottle used with a siphon-feed allows me much finer control and the ability to get the tip of the airbrush very close to the model and into tight corners, which gives superior results in the 1:48 scale I prefer. The gravity-feed is also superior when using very thin paint mixes. The Badger 100SG or 100G, Iwata HP-A or HP-B, and Thayer and Chandler "Nailaire" are all of the internal-mix gravity-feed double-action types with either a small "cavity" or built-in color cup of 1/16 oz. or less capacity, and are good alternatives—and all use the "guts" from other airbrushes in their respective lines, so parts availability is no problem. I would not recommend the hybrid "single-action internal-mix" type of airbrush. Although having similar internals to the 100, the inability to "rock" the trigger back and forth to "clear" the needle while painting makes it much more difficult to use.

All internal mix airbrushes are much more difficult to clean than the simpler external-mix single-actions, so I only use them when I must have very fine detail. A good single-action airbrush will provide just as smooth a finish, as long as the paint is properly thinned and sprayed at an appropriate distance and air pressure. I also prefer the H-1 for the acrylic sealers and oversprays I use, again for the ease of cleaning.

PAINTS

Like many modellers who have been at it for many years, I've tried numerous brands of paint, including some not designed for model building. After much trial and error, I'm convinced that the current

Dewoitine D.520. This Chalmers-built 1/48th scale Tamiya kit depicts aircraft serial No.423 in Vichy service, with 2 Escadrille, GC II/3, Algeria, 1942. -Dan Ormsby photo

generation of Floquil enamels (and the Aeromaster enamels made by Floquil) are the best paints available. The Floquil Military, Rail, Marine, and Aeromaster lines total about 340 colors—even eliminating duplicates there are over 300, including many subtle variations of greens, olives, browns, and grays. They are all intermiscable, have extremely fine pigment, thin readily with either their proprietary thinner or odorless Mineral Spirits (my choice), and spray and adhere beautifully, drying hard to the touch in only a few minutes and very hard in 24 hours. They also have a long shelf life, are readily available, and are easy to mix and use.

At one time, Floquil paints used a "hotter" base containing both xylol and toluol, which was more toxic and lacquer-like in its effect on plastic. This is no longer the case—they are now truly enamels and can be hand painted on plastic with no ill effect. You can tell if you have the new or the old formula by the label—the oldest formula states "contains xylene," which changed to "contains xylol and petroleum distillates," and now states "contains petroleum distillates." The latter two formulas are still on the shelves, and are what I use. They are also excellent for hand painting if well thinned with turpenoid or mineral spirits.

I continue to use Humbrol paints, which are especially good for hand painting—but they are not as finely ground as the Floquil paints, tend to separate in the can and can be hard to mix. Humbrol has recently revised their formulation, but has chosen to reduce the number of available colors—a retrograde step, in my opinion. They are also becoming harder to find in the U.S.

I also use Testors Model Master Gloss Black, Gloss White, and especially Chrome Silver.

I also use water-based acrylics, but not as my basic paint. Although I have seen other modellers achieve excellent results using Polly Scale (made by Floquil), Tamiya, or Gunze Sangyo, I have found them to be more difficult to master, and tougher to clean up than enamels. For sealing and clear-coating, however, they are essential. I also like the Polly S "Metalline" metallic acrylics for small details, Tamiya clear (red, blue, green, orange, smoke), and Future acrylic floor polish.

MATERIALS

Brushes - good quality red sable artists brushes—sizes from 2/0 to 10/0 round and spotters, plus flat 1/8 to 1/4 inch for dry brushing.

"Palettes" - two pieces of 9" x 4" x 3/4" plywood drilled with 5 equally-spaced 1/2" holes. I use one to secure bottles and mix paint for airbrushing; the second has a two-hole piece cut from one of those cheap 3 1/2" x 5 1/4" white plastic palettes taped to the end two holes; this I use for hand painting and oil "washing."

Artists Oils - Top quality tube oil paints (I use Windsor & Newton); Burnt Sienna, Raw Sienna, Burnt Umber, Raw Umber, Black, White, Yellow Ochre. Use the more expensive "Artists" quality versus "Students" quality.

Artists Tones - Top Quality pastel chalks—Grey and Earth Pastel

Artists Tone - Berol Prismacolor—Silver, Grey, and Earth Pencil

Stir Wires - 4" to 6" pieces of coat hanger or piano wire.

Mix Bottles - 1 3/8" dia. (Mixing) and 2" dia. (Thinner) Badger bottles with caps.

Eye Droppers - 5 or 6, with identical diameter tips.

Thinners - Odorless Mineral Spirits, Lacquer Thinner, Turpenoid, lighter fluid, rubber cement thinner, plus Polly S and Tamiya acrylic thinners.

Cleaners - Clear Ammonia and Liquid Citrus Cleaner ("Citrus Magic" or "Goo Gone Citrus Power") in spray bottles.

Masking - 3-M "218" Fine Line Tape (1/16" & larger)*
3-M "471" Plastic tape (1/8" & larger)*
3-M "ReMount" repositionable adhesive spray
Drafting tape, various widths
"Long Mask" tape
Post-It note pads
Bare Metal Foil
Masking liquid

Sanding - Wet-dry sandpaper (1000 to 2500 grit)*
& Filling 3-M Softback Sanding Sponges (Super Fine, Ultra-Fine, Micro-Fine)*
"Kiss" F222 manicure sticks (or similar 4- grit manicure stick)
Gunze Sangyo Mr. Surfacer 500 & 1000

Polishing - Swirl remover auto polish*
Carnauba wax*
Micro-mesh

Other stuff - Paper towels, Q-Tips, round and flat toothpicks, cotton wool, toilet tissue, old t-shirts or diaper cotton, ultra fine point "Sharpie" red permanent magic marker, #11 scalpel, fly tieing or surgical scissors, fine tweezers, 3 x 5 index cards, black artists paper, plate glass piece or ceramic tile, cloth photographer's gloves, plastic grocery bags (for sniffing glue maybe, Peter?-ed.).

*(these items can be found at stores listed under "Automobile Body Shop Equipment & Supplies in the Yellow Pages)

SAFETY

Whenever I spray organic solvent paints, I take the following safety precautions:

(1) Respirator: I use a 3-M "Easi-Air" 7019ES dual-cartridge respirator with 7251 Organic Vapor cartridges and prefilters. It works so well you can't smell the thinner, (which is the test to see if it's working right). Inexpensive and available at any home improvement store—I got mine at Home Depot.

(2) Spray booth/exhaust fan: I use a Badger spray booth with an explosion-proof exhaust fan venting to the outside of the house via a dryer vent kit/window insert. The fan works fine, but the booth is way too small to paint inside of. I spray directly in front of the booth and spray inside of the booth when flushing my airbrush. A bigger home-built booth would be more practical and is on my "to-do" list.

(3) Fan: I keep a small fan blowing directly at me to dissipate any fumes which don't get vented outside.

(4) Cleanup: I put any cleanup paper towels, rags, or Q-tips in a plastic grocery bag and knot up and dispose of the bag in the outside garbage bin at the close of each days session.

(5) Personal: I use a citrus cleaner to clean any paint or thinner residue off my hands at the end of each session.

I feel that these are the minimum precautions necessary.

PAINTING AND AIRBRUSHING TIPS

All of us have heard the term "scale color," i.e. the toning down of colors with white or a lighter color to compensate for the scale of the model. I would propose two extensions of this concept—"scale thinning" and "scale spraying."

Most paint manufacturers recommend that you thin your paint for airbrushing 20-25%, i.e. 4-5 parts paint to 1 part thinner. This may be fine for paint sales, but this mixture is too thick—it can obscure fine detail and easily "orange peel."

My method is as follows:

(1) "Standard" Mix: 1 part paint to 2-3 parts mineral spirits, plus a touch of Floquil "Glaze," as follows (for a typical small batch of paint):

Put 20-25 drops of mineral spirits in your mix bottle, then 1 drop of Glaze. After thoroughly mixing your paint, add 10 drops—taken from near the bottom of the paint bottle to get sufficient "flatting" agent. This is really important with Floquil—the flatting agent seems to settle out very quickly, so re-stir the paint frequently. Squeeze your eyedropper out as completely as you can into the paint bottle and then use this "paint" eyedropper in your mix bottle as a stirrer and to put paint in the airbrush.

To achieve a "Thin" mix for mottling and very fine work, go to 30-35 drops thinner, 2 drops Glaze, and 10 drops paint.

Ilyushin Il-2. If this model looks familiar, then you must have the ACCURATE MINIATURES 1/48th scale release of the single-seat STORMOVIK (or STURMOVIK to some of us)—this was the box art model, by Pete Chalmers. Even we scratchbuilders applaud AM's thoroughly researched and faithfully rendered W.W.-II Soviet subjects (even though I, Alcorn, had always meant to do a 1/24th Il-2). Few aircraft of that conflict were more important than the STURMOVIK: no others were built in such numbers (about 40,000) during that time. (I have been informed that the Po-2 was the aircraft built in the greatest numbers ever, though some were post-W.W.-II.) -Dan Ormsby photo

(Glaze is a clear slightly amber liquid which adds resins and hardeners to the mix—it seems to cause the paint to dry harder and smoother, flow better, and retards the drying time slightly—some folks simply use a bit of turpentine in their mix and get the same result)

(2) Put only enough mix in your cup or receptacle to fill it half full or so—and be careful not to spill on the model.

(3) Start at about 25 psi with your external-mix or 20 psi with your internal-mix. The simpler external-mix airbrush seems to require more air pressure. I like to use as little air pressure as I can but you must be careful—at too low a pressure you may experience flow problems or spatter. Adjust as you practice.

(4) Practice on a sheet of clean styrene (.040 Evergreen is perfect—you can wipe it clean with mineral spirits and use it indefinitely), on a quickly put together kit you'll otherwise never build, or on a fresh 3 x 5 index card—don't make errors on the model itself.

Use a "scale distance" for spraying. Hold the tip of the airbrush very close to the surface—1" or less, and practice until you can get no spatter and an absolutely smooth coat. The thinner the mix, the closer you go. Adjust the paint-air mix/distance/air pressure to walk the fine line between running and air drying. You'll paint a much smaller area at a time, and this may feel tedious, but the effect will be more to scale.

(5) You want the paint to be wet when it hits the model, not to run, and to dry almost immediately. With the typical Floquil flat color, you should see the shine fade in a few seconds. Floquil paint has such fine pigments that it will cover with surprisingly little paint—don't overdo it. Your goal is to put as little paint on the model as you can get away with—you do not want to obscure any of that fine detail you've worked so hard on. You should not see any visible spattering or droplets—just a soft fogging of the paint. As the area you spray gets larger, you'll be able to see if you are covering the plastic adequately—again, just enough to cover evenly.

(6) If you get a run (too wet) or some pebbling (too dry), don't panic—you can easily fix small runs or orange peel after the paint is dry. Adjust distance and your air/paint mix and air pressure to get that "fogging" effect.

(7) Keep your eye on the quantity of paint in your airbrush—don't run it dry. I usually flush out the airbrush at this time by blowing some lacquer thinner through it each time it gets close to dry, and cleaning out the cup or receptacle with a Q-tip and thinner. This only takes a few minutes, and will help prevent a clog or spatter.

Some tips before starting

(1) Observe the "Rule of 24"—wait AT LEAST 24 hours between the major steps I describe to assure ample curing time for paints, sealers, and washes.

(2) Keep your hands as clean as possible—wash often and wear gloves while handling the model. I often spray a tiny bit of citrus cleaner on my hands and wipe while working, which removes oil and thinner residue.

(3) Try polishing the needle of your single-action airbrush with the finest Micromesh or 3-M pad between sessions—this aids the flow of the spray and improves the results. Inspect the needle, head, and O-rings/gaskets of either type airbrush each time you break it down for cleaning and replace parts before they fail while you are painting the model. Keep a good supply of these parts on hand.

(4) Clean your airbrush thoroughly after each session.

(5) Don't hurry!!

(6) Practice, practice, practice!!

PART II: FINISHING

I build mostly camouflaged, "flat" finished 1:48 aircraft models, and the following is an outline of how I do it. For natural metal finishes I would recommend some of the excellent articles which have appeared in "Fine Scale Modeller": for gloss finishes "Scale Auto Enthusiast" is the bible.

MASKING

For covering cockpit openings, I put pieces of drafting or long-mask tape on my cutting glass and cut small pieces to fit, measuring the relevant cockpit area with caliper dividers. I use multiple pieces and seal the dividing lines with liquid masker. I use two types of liquid masker—the latex/ammonia-based type (Humbrol "Maskol," Grumbacher "Miskit," or latex mold builder—remains flexible and is not water-soluble when dry) or the water-based type (Micromask—inflexible and remains water-soluble when dry). Each has its uses—but always keep in mind that ammonia will attack any acrylic finish.

For already painted wheel wells, I carefully cut small pieces of toilet tissue and place them dry in the opening with tweezers. Wetting the T.P. as I go, I CAREFULLY fill up the well, using a Q-tip, toothpick, or old paint brush to shape the wet "paper mache" to the well edges. When I'm satisfied, I use a bit of dry paper towel to suck up the excess water, and then let the mask dry. When dry, I seal up the edges with latex masker and chisel back any slop over with a sharpened toothpick. Rewetting the tissue when finished makes removal a snap (well, sog.-ed.).

CLEANING AND SURFACE PREPARATION

Next step is to thoroughly clean all surfaces with a strong cleaner. I use either clear household ammonia in a spray bottle or a liquid citrus household cleaner. Usually, I spray a little on a piece of old t-shirt, and clean one wing thoroughly. Then, wearing cloth photographers gloves, I clean the balance of the model, holding the cleaned wing. Q-tips are used for the small nooks and crannies. Either one of these cleaners will cut through any finger oils, dirt, or grime left on the model during the long building process. I then use another piece of cotton wet with clean water to wipe the model. From this stage on, I try never to handle the model unless I have gloves on. I also try not to have too highly polished a surface—a slight sanding with the Micro Fine 3-M pad will add a little "tooth" to the surface which will help paint adhesion.

PRIMING

I rarely prime the entire model—only those areas where I have filled seams, patched, or added detail. This would normally include the top and bottom of the fuselage, and edges of the wings and tail surfaces, wing roots, and any filled areas.

For primer, I make a standard mix (no glaze) using Floquil's light gray "009" primer or the underside color of the model, and spray it with the Paasche H. I don't observe the "Wait 24" rule here—just let it dry a few hours. I then carefully examine all the primed areas, looking for ridges, pits, gaps, etc. I put on my 4.00 half frame reading glasses and look over each primed area at a low angle, holding the model between myself and the light, or I use a pen light held at a low angle to reveal any shadows indicating low spots or ridges. Normally, I don't find any major flaws here—I've fixed most of them during the construction phase—but I always find a few divots, cracks, low or high spots, etc. I mark those with the red magic marker—a dot or small mark is sufficient. Red is very translucent and will paint over easily, a permanent marker dries immediately and is water proof and non-bleeding.

I then pull out my favorite liquid filler—Gunze Sangyo Mr. Surfacer. This is one of those must-have products—it's a thick lacquer-based primer in a 40 ml square bottle with a narrow blue cap that looks like it belongs on a magic marker.

"500" is the most useful, while "1000" is finer and suitable for the finest cracks. Mr. Surfacer is applied with a small paint brush, and is perfect for filling sink marks, scratches, and any small cracks or holes. I put some on the spot to be filled—it's like a thick paint, and will flow into the hole and be dry to the touch in a few minutes. I repeat the application until I get a build-up above the surrounding surface. When all the flaws are filled, I put the model aside for 24 to 48 hours. Although hard to the point of workability in an hour or so, Mr. Surfacer continues to cure and shrink slightly for a day. When it is thoroughly cured, it is very hard but less so than styrene—perfect as a small area filler. Floquil primer also works for very fine cracks, but is not quite as hard.

Next step is to use two other must-have products to smooth down the filler. First, I use a manicurists sanding/buffing pad to cut down the filled area to the original surface level. Squadron sells a "Tri Grit Sanding Stick," Micro-Mark sells a "Triple Grit Flex Pad"—they'll work, but a much better choice is a "Kiss" brand F222 "Hawaiian Shine" manicure pad—a 7" x 3/4" x 1/8" semi soft flexible stick with 4 grits from fine to polishing—at less than half the price of the "Hobby" sticks—check your drug store fingernail area. I use a Sears Handi-Cut to cut square or pointed ends or smaller pieces to fit into tight areas, and use the blue and pink areas (the most coarse).

When I've taken the filled area down almost to the original level, I switch to a 3-M Softback Sanding Sponge (a "miracle product" according to John Alcorn!). These are 5 1/2" x 4 1/2" x 1/4" closed-cell foam pads with adhesive permanently bonded to one side. There are 5 grades—only the 3 finest are useable for modelling—Super Fine (500-600 Grit), Ultra Fine (2000-2500 Grit), and Micro Fine (6000-8000 Grit). I cut them into 1" squares—they can be used wet or dry—and are perfect for the final cutting of the filler. They will conform to curved surfaces without creating any flat areas. I use the Ultra Fine to smooth the filler down to the original surface level and the Micro fine to polish all the primed areas.

Once this step is complete, shoot another coat of primer on the areas you've filled and put the model aside for another 24.

PAINTING

(1) Mix a standard batch of the underside color, and paint the underside of all surfaces, edges of all flying surfaces, and (if doing a Luftwaffe-type mottled fuselage) the fuselage and vertical tail surfaces. I take an appropriately-sized box and drape an old T-shirt to rest the model upon while painting. During painting, I am alert for runs and coverage. I remove any "serious" runs with a Q-tip damp with mineral spirits, and paint over immediately. When satisfied, I put the model aside for the usual 24 hours plus.

(2) If I'm doing a fuselage mottle, I'll mix up thin batches of the 2 or 3 required colors. I then wrap one wing of the model carefully with an old T-shirt piece and lightly hold it on edge in a Panavise with round base set on an old TV cart, so that I am looking down at one side of the model, top toward me. Using my internal-mix airbrush, I carefully do one color at a time, reversing sides as necessary and flushing the brush between each color. I use the lowest air pressure I can, and try for "clean" spots smaller than a pin head, "randomizing" the pattern by overlapping and varying the distance of the airbrush from the surface. Runs sometimes happen, but the thin mix allows you to simply paint over them. A similar technique is used for "wave mirror" or Italian WWII mottling. When satisfied, I put the model aside for the usual wait.

(3) For the typical multi-color "pattern" type upper-surface camouflage found partially or overall on many WWII aircraft, I first paint the lightest color, bringing the color lower than the final line on the fuselage and wing leading edges (unless I'm doing a sharp-edged scheme, in which case I mask off the bottom as described in the next section.) I find it easier to go back with the underside color at the end to "touch up" to the correct line, or do "scallops" on leading edges, etc. When finished this first color, I again put the model aside for the usual wait.

(4) The procedure now varies with the type of camouflage finish desired.

a. Sharp-edged divisions (straight lines)

For a sharply-divided multi-colored camouflage pattern with straight-line edges, like a Saab "Viggen" or pre-war Luftwaffe 2 or 3 color "splinter" scheme, I use 3-M "218" fine-line tape to mask. I always have a camouflage drawing copied at the same size as the model as a guide. I cut pieces of 1/16" tape and put them on my cutting glass. Then I cut and trim pieces to measure using dividers and a scalpel and carefully build the outlines of the lightest colored areas on the model. When I'm satisfied with placement, I burnish the tape down with a wet toothpick or Q-tip. "218" tape is a translucent beige plastic and will show darker or lighter when burnished, depending on the underlying color. Burnishing assures a sharp edge. I then fill in the balance of the area with pieces of drafting or long mask tape (both are fairly lo-tack) cut to size on the glass. Small gaps can be filled with masking fluid. I then paint the second color, wait the usual period, and repeat the process for the third color, if any.

This method is also used for any stripes, leading- edge I.D. markings, anti-glare panels, etc. I sometimes substitute "471" tape, which is like blue plastic electrical tape, for the "218" tape, if complex curves are encountered, as this tape is more flexible laterally.

When the entire model is done, and the last coat has completely dried, I remove the masking and fix any minor bleeding or overspray where tape has lifted by using the edge of a small piece of new 2000 or higher sandpaper.

b. Sharp-edged divisions (curved lines)

For a Spitfire/Hurricane type camouflage where the actual aircraft was painted using rubber masking mats, I cut curved pieces of drafting tape to match the pattern from my drawings. These are then "fitted" to the model, trimming so that the curved piece is only about 1/4" to 1/2" wide, in order to ease the problem of compound curves. Centers of areas to be protected are treated as mentioned earlier. An alternative is artist's Friskit paper, which is easy for wing tops and areas without compound curves.

This is a tedious, time-consuming job—thankfully, most aircraft using this type camouflage have only 2 upper colors !

Cleanup as described earlier.

c. Semi-sharp edged divisions

As in the last section, but I don't burnish the tape—I "pick up" the edges of the tape carefully with a sharpened toothpick so that a little "fuzz" will appear when sprayed—and I am careful to spray vertically. I have also used patterns cut from my camo drawings and "raised" with bits of tape placed on the inner sides about 1/16" in from the edges and sprayed with 3-M ReMount adhesive, which is similar to the adhesive found on Post-it note pads.

Another useful masking medium which deserves mention is "Parafilm." Some of my modelling associates stretch and roll lengths of this elastic and tacky film and use it to edge camouflage areas, getting sharp or semi-sharp divisions by varying the diameter of the "roll," and using Long mask tape to protect the sides of the "roll" not to be painted.

d. Soft-edged divisions

I very carefully draw the outlines of the pattern on the model with dashes of my red magic marker—the red ink, although permanent, is very translucent and easily covered—and then spray a spot of the second color in the center of the correct areas. I then

Yakovlev Ib. This was built by Pete for the 1/48th scale ACCURATE MINIATURES kit box art. It represents an aircraft of the 270 IAP (Fighter Regiment) of the 203 IAD (Fighter Division), Ukraine, late 1943. The inscription reads: "To the Hero of Soviet Union Sergei Luganski from the Komsomol members and youth of Alma-Ata city." The "b" was the final variant of the Yak-1, remaining in production alongside the -3 and -9 at at least one factory until 1945. -Dan Ormsby photo

carefully overspray the outlines with the second color, using either my external- or internal-mix airbrush depending on how sharp I want the edges to be, and then fill in the centers. If I'm doing the top of a mottled fuselage, I'm very careful not to carry the solid colors on the spine too far down, but for solid top colors, I carry them lower on the fuselage and wing leading edges than they should be. I then come back with the bottom color in my internal-mix airbrush and adjust the line, do scallops, etc., as my final step.

After waiting through the final drying period, I remove all masks, except for the cockpit, and carefully examine the model for any flaws in the paint, making any necessary corrections. I don't hesitate to "adjust" any color lines or fix any flaws I have somehow overlooked. At this time, I usually paint and finish any non-attached parts, such as wheels and canopies—I'll have some tips on these at the end.

DECALS

The next step is to prepare the model for decal application. I use waterslide decals as they are available in incredible profusion and quality for the models I build.

The first step is to apply a gloss finish to the entire model.

My pre-decal gloss finish of choice is Polly Scale Clear Gloss acrylic (Aeromaster Gloss Clear acrylic is functionally identical). I make a standard mix using Polly S acrylic airbrush thinner and apply with my external mix airbrush. I apply a few thin coats rather than one thick one.

An alternative is Johnson's "Future" acrylic floor polish, applied with an airbrush straight from the bottle. I only use this if I know that the decals I'm using will NOT require a strong decal setting solution such as "Solvaset," as Future seems incompatible with any alcohol-based setting solution.

Future can be a bit "tricky," but it's property of being resistant to mineral spirits and other solvents used in the "washing" and weathering sections to follow makes it a good final sealent for that purpose.

Future has the following handicaps:

(1) Although almost instantly hard, it takes a long time to totally cure—48 hours plus is common, and I have heard times of up to a week from some modellers

(2) Even after curing, it can get "milky" from an application of decal setting solution or water. This normally disappears with drying (always with a re-spray) but it's disconcerting.

(3) Some batches appear yellow in the bottle, and this may slightly discolor white areas.

The Polly Scale seems to resist Solvaset much better than Future, but should also be allowed to cure at least 48 hours. I immediately clean my airbrush after using any of the acrylics by spraying ammonia through it.

I apply the gloss until the finish is shiny in appearance, but I don't try to achieve a mirror finish—just enough to prevent "silvering" of the decals.

I generally use the "Microscale" or "Superscale" method of decal application—but I NEVER pre-wet the model or the decal with even the weakest of the setting solutions (Microset or Superset—acetic acid based). The Aeromaster or Superscale decals I use (or any decals printed by Microscale) are very thin and can be easily stretched and distorted—they can't handle much repositioning once softened. What I do instead is use a trick learned from applying sun-screen window film—I mix 1/4 teaspoon of baby shampoo in 1 quart of distilled water, which makes a non-foaming wetting agent perfect for applying decals. I wet the decals with this solution at room temperature and apply the solution to the surface of the model—the baby shampoo removes any surface tension from the water so it will spread and lay down beautifully without negatively effecting the adhesive.

Dip the decal in the solution and then remove it as soon as you can—don't leave the decal submerged too long as this causes the adhesive to float off. I set the decal on my plate glass and wait until the "curl" goes out of the paper, slide off the decal, and then apply.

After applying and positioning the decal, I carefully wick away the water with a large soft sable brush and small bits of paper towel. For small stencils, I usually immediately apply some setting solution to an area quite a bit larger than the decal. Stencils, because they are small and have large clear areas, are prone to silvering, and this lessens that possibility.

I carefully watch each decal as it dries. If it becomes apparent that some setting solution is necessary, normally because the decal doesn't want to settle into a panel line or similar uneven surface, I apply setting solution only to the affected area with a small brush. I start with the weakest solutions and move up to Microsol/Supersol, and finally to the strongest, Solvaset (both alcohol-based), only if the weaker doesn't work.

When satisfied, I put the model aside for a few days. If I then find a decal which has failed to blend into the paint properly, I rectify minor lifts and bubbles using the methods described on the decal sheets or solutions. If the decal is hopelessly misapplied, I'll pull it off with masking tape and start over—luckily this does not happen too often.

When all decals are on to my satisfaction, I clean the model with a clean rag using my decal wetting solution.

SURFACE SEALING

The next step is to overseal the decals with a clear coat which will be resistant to oil washes. I normally use Polly Scale Clear Gloss Acrylic as described earlier. Again, THIN is the word—enough to cover thoroughly but not too thickly. (If I've used Future, I continue with it in this step.) I usually coat with gloss as I normally want a very lightly weathered final appearance, and the cleanup after "washing" is easier.

If I'm building a model that is going to have a well-weathered or "dirty" appearance, I will skip the gloss sealer and go immediately to the final flat sealer. The Il-2 illustrated with this article was done this way. For this I use Polly Scale Clear Flat Acrylic, thinned 3 parts Polly S thinner to 1 part clear, or I mix 1 part Gloss with 4 parts Flat, then thin the mix 3:1. This provides a smoother finish with just a touch of sheen. I have found this flat coat to be absolutely the best I've tried—but it is important to put on only a very thin coat—otherwise you will get a milky appearance. (This is also my final coat if I "wash" after the glosscoat stage.)

When finished, I put the model aside for 48 hours or more to make sure the sealer has cured completely.

WEATHERING AND SHADING

Many builders are uncomfortable with "dirtying" the finish of the model which they have worked so long to complete. All of us have seen many models at the IPMS Nationals or other contests which are either so "clean" or so over-weathered that they appear unrealistic. I believe that there is a middle ground—that subtle weathering, like panel line enhancing, can add to the realistic appearance of the model.

Photographs of the actual aircraft should be the guideline—careful study of photographs of most in-service aircraft reveal many tonal variations in both the color and reflectivity of the paint surface—and my goal has always been to try and emulate this. Doing this properly means walking a very fine line—it is very easy to overdo.

Enhancing panel lines and other detail: This step is usually called "applying washes," but this implies too heavy a process for my taste.

The purpose of this step is to add artificial shadows to the model. Real aircraft are usually seen and photographed in natural light (the sun) which comes from one direction. Models, on the other hand, are usually seen under artificial light—which comes from multiple directions. The net effect of artificial light is to "wash out" shadows—panel lines and raised or sunken detail seem to disappear, and the model appears toy-like and unrealistic. By judiciously adding the optical illusion of shadow, the detail reappears, and the net effect is a more realistic appearing model.

This technique, as well as some weathering techniques, are easily overdone, so I try to go very lightly.

I prefer to use thinned artist's oil paints for this process. They have exceptionally fine pigments, are color-fast, and have a relatively long working period. Some modellers use ground pastels, inks, or even acrylics—these have their uses, but don't provide the control in application which I like. Here's how it's done:

Ilyushin Il-2. Another ACCURATE MINIATURES STURMOVIK, this one by Ted Holowchuck of Seattle. This single-seater on skis deservedly took first place in the Aircraft, 1/48th scale, Small Prop, Single Engine, Split: Allied Non-US Airframe category at the 1998 IPMS/USA Nationals. The white distemper paint and weathering are very convincingly performed, and the snow-covered base provides an effective setting for this fine interpretation. (Jim Schubert photo)

(1) I take my hand-painting "palette," and put a tiny bit of either Raw Umber (a dark brown) or medium to dark grey (mixed black & white) in the end cup. Use a lighter color on the underside if the paint is a light color—I usually use a medium grey. I rarely if ever use black—it's just too dark. I then put a few drops of thinner—turpenoid, or lighter fluid—in the cup, and a few more drops in the next cup. I mix up the paint and thinner so that I have "tinted" thinner—I use a toothpick to mix, and I add thinner as it evaporates to maintain consistency. Turpenoid gives a decently long working period, whereas lighter fluid is much more volatile and enables you to "clean up" quicker, but is not as workable. Its quicker action doesn't allow the thinner to soften the sealer—which could happen if you put on too much. Neither thinner has any residue—my preference is turpenoid, because I'm not in a hurry.

(2) Taking a small round "spotter" brush—5/O, 7/O, or even 10/O, I paint all the panel lines with the oil mix—capillary action will "draw" the oil mix along panel lines, around the edges of raised detail, around fasteners, etc. Go very lightly—use as little as possible, and try not to overdo it. I take a lot of time—I enjoy this part of the building process more than any other, as the model begins to take on the appearance of a real aircraft.

If you get it on too heavy, don't worry. Go on until you have finished, and then put the model aside overnight. This allows any minor softening of the sealer coat to re-harden.

The oil wash will have a dull "flat" appearance when completely dry.

(3) The next step is to remove any excess and blend the oil mix.

Dampen a new Q-tip in mineral spirits and blot it almost dry. Then carefully rub off any spots left where you touched your brush. I also wet a brush with pure thinner and equalize any uneven lines. Again, I do this slowly and methodically, using new Q-tips as necessary.

If you are doing this on a gloss sealer, the process will go quickly, and you can usually dampen your Q-tips with water. On a flat sealer, you will have to rub a bit harder—be careful, as you can rub through the sealer, and you will notice that the sealer will polish up a bit—not an undesirable effect on panel lines in the engine area.

When you are satisfied with the end result, wait the usual 24.

If you started with a gloss sealer, you can now airbrush your flat mix overall to give the model a final overcoat. If you started with a flat sealer, you can "touch up" any shiny areas.

Shading during the painting process: One effective technique is the subtle variation of the upper surface color applied with the airbrush during painting. This is especially effective with solid upper colors, especially U.S. Olive Drab, as follows:

(1) Airbrush a slightly lighter shade of the base color to the top of the fuselage and centers of wing panels.

Boeing B-17G. This 1/72nd HASEGAWA "FORTRESS" by Ted Holowchuck displays a very convincing treatment of camouflage paint weathering, as well as fine all-around workmanship. (Jim Schubert photo)

(2) (or) Airbrush a slightly darker shade along panel lines.

(3) (or) Airbrush a slightly lighter shade behind and below panel lines, masking with an index card or post-it paper.

(4) (or) Before painting the top color, prime the model with a pale grey and then airbrush a dark grey along panel lines. Airbrush the top color, leaving a light enough top coat so that the light/dark primer "shows through" as lighter or darker top color. This would obviously also work with multi-colored upper surfaces.

These techniques should be so subtle so as to only be slightly noticeable.

Using pastels: Artists pastels are also very useful. I use earth and brown tones, powdered and rubbed in with a Q-tip, along wing roots and other areas which would be walked on, to simulate ground-in dirt.

Pastels also provide one of the best ways to simulate exhaust stains. I first make sure that the area to be stained has an airbrushed coat of Polly S flat. I then use dark brown, black, tan, and light grey ground pastels applied with a 3/O or smaller brush until I am satisfied. I tend to exaggerate, as I then "fix" the pastels with a very light airbrush coat of Polly S flat. Pastels tend to almost disappear when overcoated, but they cannot be handled if not overcoated—your choice.

Chipped and worn paint: This area is so often overdone that I have rarely seen a model with any chipping that looks right. Here are some techniques I've used—but use caution !

(1) Underpaint the upper surface in the areas you want to chip with Floquil "Old Silver" or Testors "Chrome," or with yellow zinc chromate or other primer if the prototype aircraft was so primed. Apply tiny drops of white glue before you airbrush the top coat. Remove the white glue chips after the top coat has dried. Further remove the top coat, if desired, using a Micro Fine sanding pad, so that the metal shows through. Subtlety rules!

(2) Use an artists silver pencil—I use a Berol Prismacolor Silver 949 or a Berol Verithin Silver 753. Using a sharp point, "draw" your wear and tear on the wing roots, panel edges, fasteners, gun muzzles, etc. You can blend with a Q-tip and remove with a water dampened Q-tip or toothpick. This leaves a very effective dull aluminum in the "pores" of your flat finish—especially effective on wing root "walk" areas, canopy frames, panel lines, or fasteners. You can also use Berol earth or grey toned pencils and blend/remove as above. These pencils are basically solid water color, so you can achieve very subtle effects by blending and removing with water.

(3) Use a paint brush if you must—I sometimes dry-brush prop leading edges—but NEVER put little "chips" of silver paint on anything—it never looks right.

Dry Brushing: I use a dry-brushing technique as an adjunct to shading with oils to enhance relief in raised detail, or to show wear on leading edges, etc. I normally use a light grey, tan, or earth (rarely silver) on darker colors. I use a soft 3/O brush or 1/4" flat brush and Floquil or Humbrol enamels. I wet the brush with straight paint, then squeeze it almost dry with paper towels. I then test on a piece of black artists paper to assure that I'm getting only the slightest color, before I go to the model, lightly brushing with only the tip of the brush until a "hint" of the color begins to appear. This can be especially effective on cockpits, instrument panels, wheels, tires, and exhausts, which I will discuss later. Again, be subtle.

THE SMALL DETAILS

Finally, I'd like to discuss those small subassemblies and parts that lend themselves to similar finishing techniques described earlier. They are the components which tend to draw the eye, and are sometimes ignored by even the best modellers.

(1) Exhausts

First, I paint the exhausts a dark purpley brown—Humbrol No. 173 "Track Color" or Floquil No. 303353 "Nato Tricolor Brown," let dry 24, and overcoat with Polly Scale flat, and let cure.

I then oil wash with black, emphasizing the inside of the pipe ends, any welded seams, and the base.

Next, I apply a Burnt Sienna (rust color) oil wash, especially to the tops of the pipes, to represent rust—going easy, since steel usually doesn't show too much pure iron oxide.

I may use a little dark blue or purple oil wash as those colors often are present in heat-discolored steel.

I will use straight turpenoid to wash and blend the colors as necessary.

Finally, after the oils have cured overnight, I dry brush the ends of the pipes and the sides with light grey to represent the lead oxide residue from the fuel, in order to "pop out" the pipe ends and weld seams.

(2) Wheels, tires, and struts

The Accurate Miniatures Il-2 Stormovik pictured in this article has black wheels and tires. I painted them as follows:

The wheel rims were painted black and the tires were painted with Floquil No. 303123 Panzer Dark Gray. After drying, the tires were dry brushed with Floquil No. 303386 Mud, heaviest on the portion of the tread closest to the ground, but not on the bottoms. The bottoms were dry brushed heavily with Floquil No. 303384 Grimy Black, to represent rubber that has been "cleaned" by surface contact. The wheel rims were dry brushed with a light grey. Then the whole assembly was given a coat of Polly Scale flat and let cure at least 24.

The engraved treads on the bottoms of the tires were washed with thinned "Mud," while the balance of the tire/wheel assembly was oil washed with Raw Umber. A tiny bit of Burnt Sienna wash was used on the wheels, as I assumed that they were steel.

Landing gear struts were washed with raw umber, and left fairly "dirty" as they were in the prototype.

(3) Cockpits and instrument panels
Taking a page from the figure painters, and after practice using the after-market resin cockpit sets now so common, I complete all super detailing of seats, cockpit walls, and instrument panels before I paint anything. I then airbrush the primary component color, wait for drying, and then hand paint all detail, using enamels, oils, acrylics, and drawing ink. I drybrush as necessary, usually with light grey. I usually use decal instruments—either from the kit, if good, or from Reheat or ProModeller decal sheets, cut or Waldron-punched individually to fit each instrument.

When I'm satisfied with the components, and they have dried thoroughly, I airbrush all components with Polly Scale flat, and let dry.

I then proceed to very carefully apply an oil wash, usually black, to pop out the detail—but very delicately. After this is dry, I go back and gloss the instruments and any components which should be glossed using Future or Polly S gloss, thinned as necessary and applied with a 5/O to 10/O spotter brush.

(4) Canopies
Much has been written about the use of Future to give a high gloss to canopies. I don't like it, as I cannot control the thickness of the Future.

Here's a method that works very well for kit canopies—the scratch builder may be able to use some of it.

First, I polish out any scratches, using a Micro Fine sanding pad, then 8000 or 12000 grit Micromesh, and finally a "swirl remover" auto polish, which is the finest auto polish and does not contain any wax or silicones. I use Q-tips and diaper cotton for this purpose.

When satisfied, I make sure no polish residue remains. I then polish the canopy with pure automotive paste Carnauba wax containing no abrasives. This brings up a brilliant shine and does not seem to effect adhesion of the paint.

I then mask the canopy using dull-finished "Bare Metal Foil," which is a very thin adhesive-backed foil used by car modellers. I apply the foil to the canopy in sections, burnishing it down with a Q-tip or wet round tooth pick. The foil is very delicate, so be careful. The foil will conform to any compound curve and into engraved frame lines or up against raised frame lines.

I then take a new #11 scalpel blade, and cover it with masking tape except for the tip, so I can use the blade without a handle. I very carefully and gently run the tip along the edges of the "glass" areas I wish to mask and then, using a sharpened toothpick and fine tweezers, I remove the foil from the frames and any other areas I want painted. I then re-burnish the edges if necessary. I then wipe the frames with a Q-Tip slightly dampened with citrus cleaner to assist in paint adhesion.

I then airbrush the canopy with interior and exterior colors. If necessary, I will already have masked and air brushed, or

MiG 15. "But, wait!," you cavil, "We thought no jets were allowed in this book! "But, recall," I reply "the Heinkel He 162 VOLKSJAEGER, by Bill Bosworth, in SB!—Consistency is the hobgoblin of little minds." The notable, and appropriate aspect of this 1/48th scale MONOGRAM kit by Dr. Raleigh Williams, of Tucson, is the outstanding treatment of its natural metal finish.

used painted clear decal, to represent any interior framework. After the usual wait, I spray the final sealer coat to match the rest of the model.

After an overnight rest, I carefully remove the foil using a sharpened toothpick "chisel" and tweezers. Some of the foil adhesive will always adhere to the clear areas. I take some regular masking tape and fold it into a tiny wedge, adhesive side out, and carefully pull off the residue—which can take a while. Rubber cement thinner will also work, but should only be used as a last resort—it may soften the paint or sealer.

When satisfied, I take a "micro Q-tip" (made by notching the end of a round toothpick and wrapping it in a tiny bit of cotton wool) and re-apply wax as necessary, buffing as before.

(5) Temporary finishes

Many military aircraft during World War II were hastily overpainted with black for night work or white for winter. My Il-2 illustrates the latter finish. I wanted to achieve the appearance of a weather-worn hand-painted whitewashed finish, which was common on Soviet winter schemes—and apparent on the two known photos of the actual aircraft depicted.

First, I completed the model through decaling and the flat sealer coat.

I then mixed Polly Scale White acrylic with a drop of Black, thinned about 3:1 paint:thinner with distilled water, as I did not want any alcohol (present in Polly S thinner) to effect the sealer coat. I then hand painted the white areas using No. 1 or 2 flat shader brushes (1/8" and 3/16" wide, respectively), which are a scale 6" to 9" wide. This very thin mix resulted in a lot of brush marks and show through, which I wanted, but no surface roughness. When satisfied, I immediately gently abraded the whitewash, especially from the edges of wings and armament panels, using my ever-useful Micro Fine sanding pad.

(5) Prototype paint sequencing

The Macchi C.202 illustrated represents a very early Serie I aircraft built in 1941. Although it appears to have the upper side

MiG 15. Dr. Williams relates that, following considerable frustration in attempting to obtain a convincing natural metal finish, he made the acquaintance of, and learned from Les Sundt of Tacoma, Washington (now deceased). Although the Sundt/Williams technique is quite complex, it is very effective when done properly; this model garnering "BEST NATURAL METAL FINISH" at the 1998 IPMS/USA Nationals. Les Sundt's technique for "FINISHING NATURAL-METAL AIRCRAFT (Using Metallic Powders and Oil-Based Varnish)" is explained in the March 1996 issue of FINE SCALE MODELER, which also features a "PORTFOLIO of Les Sundt's dazzling aircraft." Dr. Raleigh Williams' copyrighted technique is reproduced herein, with his kind permission.

Chapter X: Finishing 139

painted first in green with the sand-yellow and red-brown added afterward, photos of the real aircraft and Italian references indicate that it was first painted sand-yellow, the red-brown splotches added, with the green very carefully "netted" around the blotches, leaving a variegated appearance. Although obviously more difficult to apply, this method results in a finish which very closely duplicates the original. Since this particular airplane represents a long-term survivor, pictured in 1943, I weathered away some of the green and brown in critical areas using very fine sandpaper—a 3-M pad would be ideal for this.

Conclusion

I have outlined the steps I take to paint and finish a model. I want to emphasize that I am always trying to find new and better or easier methods—and there are alternatives to many of those which I have described which many modellers use to achieve equally pleasing results. Hopefully, these tips will help you to get the finish you want.

CREATING A NATURAL METAL FINISH FOR MODEL AIRCRAFT
by Raleigh Williams

BASIC RULES OF METALIZING

A. Use only oil-based, clear, gloss varnish.

B. Varnish is thinned 60/40 with mineral spirits, plus 10 drops retarder per 1/2 ounce of mixture.

C. Adherence to the specified varnish curing times will greatly reduce chances of a disastrous tape lift-off.

D. When airbrushing use 30 psi air pressure.

E. Keep a log! It will provide continuously needed information on both the step involved and the elapsed curing time.

F. Use a test piece, along with the model, for deciding exactly when to start Step 3.

G. For safety's sake, minimize taping, maximize decaling.

H. After every powder buffing a sealer coat of varnish must be applied.

I. After each sealer coat, lightly wet sand with 6000 grit micromesh pad. Wipe dry to eliminate water spots.

THE NINE BASIC STEPS

1. Remove all kit panel lines by filling or sanding. Natural metalized panels will take their place. Layout views of the aircraft panels are necessary.

2. To begin the natural metalizing procedure, prepare all plastic with a soap wash. Let dry. Then apply a basic coat of Brush & Leaf silver lacquer, thinned 50/50 with lacquer thinner, plus one drop of retarder per 1/2 oz of mixture. Fix any surface flaws and reapply lacquer. When cured, after four hours, it is ready for Step 3.

3. Apply FIRST coat of varnish. The first coat acts as a primer, nothing more. Let cure for 48 hours, then lightly wet sand.

4. Apply SECOND coat of varnish. Allow approximatly 2 to 2 1/2 hours curing time. Then, when a finger is pulled along the surface of the test piece and a very, repeat very, slight drag is felt, lightly buff the entire model with aluminum powder using a wool rag. Buff with a light pressure. If the buffing was commenced at the right moment the surface will look just slightly shiny. Buff too soon and the surface will look too dull, like an aluminum cooking pot; buff too late and the surface will look too shiny, like chromium. It's a choice! Let cure 48 hours; one to two weeks is even better, because the longer the curing period the less the dulling effect of the subsequent sealer coat. This is a general rule.

5. Apply a THIRD coat of varnish as the first sealer coat. Let cure 48 hours.

6. Apply a FOURTH coat of varnish as a second sealer coat. Let cure 48 hours.

7. Apply a FIFTH coat of varnish as a third sealer coat. The last of these three sealer coats should be allowed to cure a minimum of 5 hours, but not more than 8 hours, because it now becomes the basis for "differential buffing" in producing chrome-like panels:

(a) To chromatize selected panels they must be masked off with tape. To minimize tape lift-off in this step, observe the specified curing times. Use the absolute lowest tack tape available, and never, ever use masking tape! 3M-811 tape seems to meet this requirement best. It is recomnended that even its tackiness be reduced by the old T-shirt trick. It will not cause varnish lift-off if care is taken when removing it. A low, slow pull, at 90 degrees to its length is recommended. Also recommended is very light pressure when applying, as it sometimes tends to leave residual adhesive upon removal. The latter is water soluble and is easily removed with soap, water, and a flat paint brush. If residual adhesive is not removed, subsequent varnish sealer coats may bead up rather than flow out level. Bob Dively's Liquid Masking Film also can be used effectively to mask off selected, irregular surfaces without fear of lift-off; provided, of course, that specified varnish curing times have been observed.

(b) After masking off panels, "differentially" buff them with aluminum powder and a wool rag. But buff a little more vigorously and faster than in the basic metalizing process. Remember, the more one buffs, the more chrome-like the panel will become. Soon, the finish will turn darker, more reflective and more chrome-like. Buff with graphite or even copy-toner for gun ports and jet cans. Mixtures of graphite and aluminum powder can also be used for different, intermediate shades. If, at any time, the panels get so complex that further handling and masking might disturb them, cease attempts and let the 48 hour curing process complete itself. Then, seal with varnish, and 5 to 8 hours later complete another cycle of "differential" panel buffing. After each masking and "differential" panel buffing session—and it may take several sessions—remove masking tapes. Clean up loose and random specks of loose aluminum powder with the air brush and, if needed, cautiously use a Q-

Tip moistened with soap and water. Use care not to drag a wet Q-Tip over a new "differentially" buffed panel, as such action will remove some aluminum powder from the incompletely cured, unsealed, hence unprotected, panel, and the whole process will have to be repeated—panel masking, spraying, and buffing.

(c) Now is the time to replicate rivet lines if you want to do so. With a Stim-U-Dent and a bit of aluminum powder on its knife-like edge and using a subtle touch, run it alongside a vacuum cleaner belt or straight-edge. For softer, wider rivet lines use an artist's blending stump.

(d) After "differential" paneling, decal paneling, 1/64 decal panel lines and Stim-U-Dent rivet lines are completed, let cure for 48 hours.

(e) Then seal with a SIXTH coat of varnish and let cure another 48 hours.

8. For additional paneling effects proceed as follows:

(a) Mask and airbrush selected, large area panels with various shades of Testors Metalizer paints. Also mask off the entire remainder of the plane with Glad Cling Wrap to guard against overspray.

(b) To make small area panels, apply pieces of clear decal film previously airbrushed with various shades of Testors Metalizer paints and sealed with Testors Metalizer Sealant.

(c) Note: Steps (a) and (b) will take on the high gloss of all other panels after the final varnish sealing coat of Step 9, the next coat.

(d) Replicate individual rivets with a Rapidograph or Staedtler pen using a 4x0 or 3x0 point along with gray waterproof ink. A .005 Pigma pen will do this very nicely, too, but comes in black only, which may be too dark for some modelers' tastes.

9. Apply a SEVENTH coat of varnish to seal all the preceding steps.

(a) Repeat Step 8(a) now for a matte finish to a panel.
(b) Repeat Step 8(b) now for a matte finish to a panel.

© - 1998 Dr. Raleigh Williams

North American P-51B "MUSTANG." This outstanding model by Rodney Williams is a massive conversion from the 1/24th scale AIRFIX P-51D kit. It represents an aircraft of the 361st Fighter Group, 8th Air Force. Beginning in the November 1993 IPMS/USA JOURNAL, a five part feature described Rodney's construction/conversion methods. The model is now in the Paul Ludwig collection. (Jim Schubert photo)

CHAPTER XI
Tools, Supplies, Materials, Services and Workplaces
by John Alcorn

One may logically question whether this topic is unique to scratchbuilding, rather than simply generic to aircraft modelling, kit or otherwise. While there is much overlap to be sure, the extent and nature of tools, materials, and services required for scratchbuilding is inevitably greater and somewhat different. As for workplaces, it just seemed like fun to throw in this aspect.

TOOLS
Scratchbuilding requires a broader array of tools than kit construction, most notably a vacuforming rig: this apparatus and its use are covered in Chapter I. Since no two builders employ all of the same tools, this section is biased somewhat toward those used by me, John Alcorn.

SOURCES: While most modelling tools can be purchased at hardware stores and the better hobby shops, I order some specialty items—tools and supplies—from the following sources:

SMALL PARTS INC. (SPI)
13980 N.W. 58th Court
P.O. Box 4650
Miami Lakes, Florida 33014-0650
Tel: (800) 220-4242

MICRO-MARK (MM)
340 Snyder Avenue
Berkeley Heights, NJ 07922-1595
Tel: (800) 225-1066

Grumman XF5F-1 SKYROCKET. This 1/24th scale scale model was constructed by Bob Rice. The SKYROCKET was a hot topic when he and I (Alcorn) were kids, so its appeal has remained with airplane enthusiasts of our generation. Desiring a next generation fighter/interceptor with high top speed and climb, yet having acceptable carrier takeoff/landing characteristics, plus potent armament, BuAer solicited proposals for such a machine in February 1938. Vought tendered with the XF4U-1, based upon the then unproven P&W R2800; and Bell with the Allison V-1710 engined XFL-1. Grumman based its submittal upon twin (but supercharged) engines of proven design: first the 750hp P&W R-1535; then the P&W R-1820 of 1200hp. Heavy corporate commitment to the high priority F4F program delayed completion of the XF5F-1, which first flew on April Fools Day 1940. Correction of various problems resulted in the prototype not being delivered to Anacostia for BuAer evaluation until February 1941. By this time, however, since the great potential of Vought's 400mph XF4U was becoming manifest, the Navy began to lose interest in the XF5F. Despite further development effort by Grumman, the SKYROCKET fizzled.

POWER TOOLS: Aside from the oven and vacuum cleaner required for vacuforming, I use no power tools: not even for airbrushing, now that I have begun using bottled CO2. While I have a Dremel type miniature rotary power tool, I rarely use it. Just personal style, I suppose, but I find its material removal too fast for my reactions. Some modellers, including Peter Cooke, employ a UNIMAT 3 type machine tool. A combination lathe, drill, and milling machine, its fortunate possessors find it indispensible for generating many precision components, especially metal requiring turned or radially indexed features.

HAND TOOLS: The accompanying figure shows most of my tool kit.

Knives: These are at the...errr...cutting edge of modelling. While the time-honored X-Acto type small handle with its many blades remains the standard, I now primarily use surgical blades, mounted in the flat #3 stainless steel scalpel handle. The straight-edged, very pointed #11 blade is by far the most used, supplemented for certain operations by the quarter round-edged #15. Surgeons blades (and handles) can be obtained from medical supply outlets (consult your doctor or the Yellow Pages) and from MICRO-MARK. For heavy wood carving (e.g. making basswood vacuform molds), any good, very sharp pocket knife can be used: I now use a VICTORINOX Swiss Army knife (with minimal "gee whiz" accessory gadgets). Also good for this purpose is a fat (No.6) X-Acto type handle, with a long "whittler's blade." It is well to keep a small, fine grit whetstone handy, to maintain sharp blade edges. Incidentally, I keep an X-Acto type handle with #11 blade in my kit, especially for cutting sandpaper. Since this dulls the blade quickly, better to whetstone sharpen it periodically than to constantly change blades.

Swiss Needle Files: These are another modelling essential, available in coarse, medium, and fine cuts. I rely primarily upon the fine (#6) cut needle file variety, made by GROBET in Switzerland: a somewhat smaller variant (with square cross-section handles), well suited to our needs, is called "Escapement File"—obviously tailored for watchmakers. GROBET needle and escapement files come in twelve shapes: perhaps the most useful for our purposes are "Barrette" (pointed end, one side cutting), "Equalling" (rectangular cross-section, all sides cutting), "Round" ("rat tail") and "Three-Square" (triangular, all sides cutting). The Swiss (GROBET) Single Cut Needle Files, Fine (#6) Cut are, I believe, available from SPI, as item #FSC-774/6. The available shapes are pictured in their catalogue. The #6 cut needle and escapement files are not cheap—about $20 a pop! But, hey!—are we serious about

RAF BE2C. This 1/72nd scale, 1970s vintage model by Ray Rimell depicts a single-seat modification of the BE2C, for home defense duties against the dreaded Zeppelin menace. Its purpose-built development, the BE-12, did achieve a measure of success against the "Monsters of the Purple Twilight." Ray Rimell has earned our everlasting admiration and gratitude for his ALBATROS Productions. Enthusiast/modelling community interest in W.W.-I aircraft has been rekindled and nurtured by its WINDSOCK magazine and DATAFILE monographs. The latter, including DATAFILE SPECIALS, are covering every significant type of the "Great War," through development/operations summary, copious photographic coverage, excellent multi-view drawings and colour profiles—the latter by Ray himself. Each is prepared by an eminent authority on such matters, primarily Jack Bruce for Allied and Peter Grosz for Central Powers types. We of the modelling community are especially grateful for this stimulus to our hobby: clearly the great increase in W.W.-I subject kits and supporting aftermarket infrastructure over the past decade has been due in large part to the WINDSOCK output. Ray himself is a modeller of considerable talent. His efforts have been featured many times in WINDSOCK and before that in SCALE MODELS, generally for the primary purpose of demonstrating construction technique and/or highlighting a new kit issue. While generally he has been far too busy with publication schedules to scratch build, he has done so on occasion, this BE2C being one.

our hobby or not? Personally, I couldn't model without these items. These files are also available in #4 Cut (medium), which are useful for coarser work. Obviously, large wood files are a necessity for making vacuform moulds.

Pin Vises: These are another essential for all modelling. While I have several types and brands of pin vises in my kit, those made by STARRETT cannot be beat for chuck precision and durability—at least to my knowledge. They come in four sizes, holding drill diameters from 0.000" to 0.200". While I have them all, I find the most useful to be the smallest; #240-A, holding drills from 0.000" to 0.055". These are available from SPI, the smallest as O-PV-5. In fact, it is desirable to have several of the smallest size, to minimize drill changing while making progressively larger holes. Pin vises are also handy for holding small metal parts during fabrication, and for holding wire or tubing while its ends are being dressed with Swiss files.

Twist Drills: Many sizes of these are, of course, required. Those from #60(0.0400) on up can be obtained from almost any hardware store. Those from #80(0.0135") to #61(0.0390") are usually found on modeller's tables in the traditional metal case made by HUOT and available in better hardware stores and hobby shops. But, I find it a constant source of amazement that so many modellers are unaware that high speed twist drills are available down to #97(0.0059" dia.). My source for the smaller sizes is SPI, as their O-HSD-X parts:"X" being the drill size.

Hand Saws: These are used for everything from cutting wire and tubing, plus metal and plastic sheet, to notching small components. Once again, the old X-Acto type long reinforced saw is ubiquitous on the modeller's table. AIRWAYS of England now markets a photoetched blade, and toothed #11 blades are available from MM and elsewhere—all at ten thou thickness. But, while I have a few precious thinner blades obtained a few years ago from a private source, to my knowledge, none down to, say 5 thou thickness, are available commercially—other than jeweller's hacksaw blades, which are difficult to use on delicate, small parts.

Tweezers: Every modeller has his own favorite tweezer. Some are straight, some curved at the ends, some blunt and some sharp ended, some scissors style, some cross-locking, but most simply pinch style; most are of stainless steel, some of titanium; some are worthy of a heart surgeon's table, while others appear to have sur-

Gotha G.IV. This impressive 1/32nd scale Gotha was constructed bp Robert Karr of Westminster, California. It represents Werk Nr. 991/16 (LVG built) of Kagohl 3. Though not visible here, this machine carried the dramatic and colorful fuselage marking "MoRoTa," as depicted in the Windsock DATAFILE SPECIAL "GOTHA." Robert Karr reports that its wings were constructed as for a flying model: silkspan tissue over a wooden rib and spar frame. The fuselage was built up of 1/64th inch thick birch plywood. The very convincing looking and, in fact, structural, rigging is monofilament nylon fishing line.

vived Stalingrad. (Hey, I once worked with a wizard technician at SLAC, many of whose tools he had while a Wehrmacht weapons technician in the Crimea, 1942.) My favorite is a stainless steel pinch type, angled end, with rather blunt tips (General#7). But, for some holding jobs, I also use a common old first aid type, replete with embossed "+" on the sides; having straight ends and mating, smooth, rectangular jaws.

Scribes: These are another hand tool without which modelling simply cannot be practiced. I have two, one (from George Lee) consisting of a MARS STAEDTLER#788 handle, mit chuck to hold a very sharp, compass-like point (but rather thick for strength). The other, (PEER #21-456), has a fixed, conical, carbide tip in a metal handle.

Pliers: These come in many sizes, styles, and standards of quality. Every kit must include a pair of miniature diagonal cutting pliers, of high quality (sharp edges, hardened steel) for wire cutting and such. A set of long, needle-nose miniature pliers is also essential for holding work beyond the capability of fingers and tweezers. I find that two sets of regular household pliers are necessary for tightening pin vises (I admit it, I'm losing my grip).

Embossing Tools: I was introduced to these tools by George Lee, who gave me the ones I use, primarily for producing rib edges on the polystyrene sheet skin of "fabric covered" wings. These are similar to a scribing tool, except that, instead of coming to a sharp point, the tapered end terminates in a small ball; 20 thou for one, 30 thou for the other (SP2 and SP3 respectively, by GESTETNER). Recall that embossing tools indent (deform) the material; scribing tools remove it.

Sanding Blocks: For me, at least, these are homemade items: perhaps not tools in the strictest sense, but as indispensable for material shaping as knives and files. I keep a small box on my table with an assortment of about a dozen small wood sanding blocks, of varying shapes and sizes and faced with sandpaper from 280 to 1000 grit. I attach the paper to the flat, rectangular block with

Handley Page 0/400. Robert Karr built this 1/48th scale rendition of the "Bloody Paralyzer," which equipped the RAF's first true strategic bombing force. This represents C.9707 of the Independent Force, Summer 1918. The wings were construed using the wood core/plasticard skin technique, as described elsewhere in MSB. The fuselage structure is made of HO scale miniature lumber, also skinned with 15 thou plasticard—except for the nose area, which is covered with 1/64th inch birch plywood.

TESTORS wood cement (green tube). Needless to say, the sandpaper needs periodic replacement: the worn stuff is removed with knife and fingernails, having been loosened with brush-applied lacquer thinner. Jim Schubert sez "But, John, why not simply attach the sandpaper with double (sticky) sided tape?"—uhhh... never thought of it! I also have about six large sanding blocks, from 3x8" to 2x4". These are faced with rather coarse sandpaper, 80-180 grit, for truing large surfaces such as wing edges, and making wood vacuform moulds.

Rulers, Straightedges, and Squares: These are always present in a modeller's kit. For making countless measurements, I use an old 12" long boxwood K&E ruler, left over from my engineering days—and, perhaps from my father's. The most used scale is that with 0.10 and 0.020 inch marks. I could, of course, use my 30 centimeter ruler, but remain committed to the system even abandoned by its English perpetrators. Too late to change now, though I did as an engineer. My 6" long (GENERAL) stainless steel rule is used primarily as a straightedge, for cutting and engraving: it is in almost constant use. I have a small 6" rule carpenters square, frequently used for obtaining and verifying right angles. This is supplemented with a piece of 40 thou plasticard, having external and internal right angles.

Drafting Compasses: I have six "A" frame (bow) drafting compasses, used for a variety of purposes. A small one, with a very sharp circulating point, is used almost exclusively for cutting out smallish holes in plasticard, using the hallowed thumb and forefinger twirl method. Another is permanently fitted with a GRIFHOLD #20 blade: while occasionally used on plastic, it serves primarily to cut discs in frisket paper, for masking (mainly British) national insignia (roundels). Two others, a bow and a drop type, are inking compasses, which I use mainly in preparing dry transfer (or decal) and photoetch "art work." Finally, two other bow compasses are used exclusively for pencil work; i.e., drawing airplane plans. This embarrassment of bow compass riches stems from my, and my father's, engineering careers. For, antediluvian as it may seem to younger folk weaned on computer games, older engineers actually used pen and ink, bow compasses, triangles, tee squares, circle templates, rulers, dividers, protractors, vellum, pounce, slide rules, trig and log tables, Roark (3rd ed.), and hand calculations to design things—including almost all of the airplanes which dominate our hobby.

SUPPLIES

This section covers expendable items, such as sandpaper, other than those used for painting.

SHEET SANDPAPER: O.K., so this is not a very scintillating topic—hardly worth mentioning in a specialist tome like this, right? Not quite. Sure, we all know about the sheet sandpaper available at ACE hardware, normally in 80 to 600 grit, WETORDRY and PRODUCTION—whatever that means. But, would you believe that an old, George Lee-trained practitioner like me didn't discover grits beyond 600 until 1996? If you know me personally, you would (right, Pat Stein?). It took my newly acquired modelling buddies in

Fokker D.VIII (E.V). This lovely 1/72nd scale "Flying Razor" was scratchbuilt by Jim Schubert. It won First Place, Scratchbuilt Aircraft, 1/72 and smaller, at the 1998 IPMS/USA Nationals. (Jim Schubert photo)

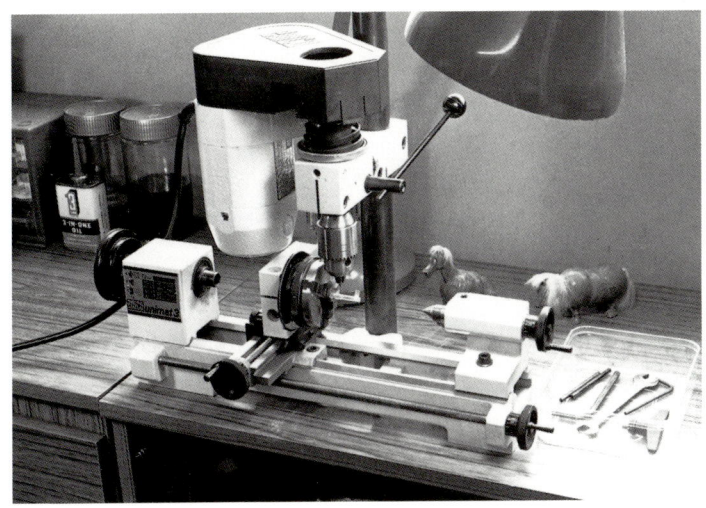

This is Peter Cook's UNIMAT 3: a combination lathe, drill, and milling machine; it is especially useful for generating precision metal components having turned and/or radially indexed features.

the Seattle area to remind me that #1000, 1500 and 2000 grit is available at any auto finishing store. Me, who restored three vintage American automobiles, including bodywork and painting. Suffice it to say, I now tend to use #1000 where I once used #600. But, that's not all. Having surmounted this technological hurdle, I was scarcely prepared for the next revelation: "Oh, by the way, it's also available in grits down to #12000." That's true grit. So, gritting (more at gnashing) my teeth, I asked where. "Well, at hobby shops, in small, multi-grit packets for one, but also from MM by the 4X6 inch sheet." Technically, it's known as MICRO-MESH Cushioned Abrasive, available in 6000, 8000 and 12000 grit.

SANDING SPONGE: But, it took my old modelling cronie, Pete Chalmers, to introduce me to 3M Softback Sanding Sponge, available in Super Fine-500/600 grit; Ultra Fine-2000/2500 grit; and Micro Fine-6000/8000 grit—a sample packet of which he kindly gave me at the 1997 IPMS/USA Nats. This stuff is especially useful for general cleanup of many curved areas having surface "topography," due to its great compliance.

ADHESIVES: Typically, we use only three kinds of adhesive during model construction: liquid styrene cement; 5-minute epoxy; and superglue. Although I used to use MEK, I now exclusively use TESTORS Plastic Cement #3502, in those little, one fluid ounce cubical glass bottles. It's convenient, and though still partly MEK, is somewhat less volitile than the straight stuff. Sure, it's more expensive than buying a can of MEK, but, how much can you use? Quite a bit, if you include spillage, but now I spill smaller bottles. Five minute epoxy needs no introduction. Several good brands are available in hardware stores and hobby shops. "Superglue," or cyanoacrylate, is one of those miracle products which we don't know how we ever got along without. Since, once opened, it deteriorates rather quickly (i.e., thickens), it should be purchased in those little 0.07 ounce (gram) tubes. Even then, it must usually be discarded before empty. Sure, other adhesives are sometimes used, such as

lacquer thinner and plastic cement in tubes, but these are the Big Three.

PUTTIES AND FILLERS: Are these supplies (expendable items) or construction materials? I'm arbitrarily putting them here, on the premise that most of it ends as dust; on the workbench, floor, or clothes. "But, hold it!," you cavil; "Sheet plastic, which is a construction material, ends up mostly as scrap, or dust, also." "Shuddup!," I say: "Life itself is mostly compromise, arbitration, plea bargaining, and befuddlement. So, this is where it goes and that's that." - *Dixi*

As mentioned in HOW I BUILT MY DH9A, and in SB!, I exclusively use a paste made of polystyrene dust and MEK (or liquid glue). However, for forming extensive, relatively large volume shapes, such as wing to fuselage fillets, it would expose the base material to too much solvent, unless built up little by little: a very time-consuming process—besides, it would take forever to dry. This can, however, be circumvented by slabbing on roughly shaped scrap plastic, which is squeezed into place when softened by paste in the interstices.

MILLIPUT two-part putty is the choice of many fine modellers: it comes in standard grain (grey) and superfine (white).

3M ACRYL auto spot filler, RED or BLUE is popular among modellers, at least in the Seattle area! It is available at auto supply houses—in handy one pound tubes, so we squeeze out lengths for our buddies, on a "Just in Time" basis.

MASKING MATERIALS: OK, so we're drifting into the realm of painting—tough it.

The most common traditional masking material is frisket paper, used by countless artists and craftsmen around the world. As related in SB!, our favorite for years was a product called REDI FRISKET, which I have been unable to find recently. So, although there are numerous brands available, I have settled upon FRISK

Hand Tools. This assemblage of Steel Age artefacts represents most of my (Alcorn) modelling tools.

FILM Low Tack Soft Peel Masking Film—matt finish. It is good for area masking, including that for airbrushed insignia/ markings.

I now make extensive use of 3M 218 Fine Line Tape, a flexible mylar material, available in 1/16th and 1/4 inch wide rolls at automotive painting stores. But, beware!: it is very sticky, so can pull up less-than-well-adhered paint.

POST ITs: These ubiquitous little yellow squares (and larger rectangles) are the cat's meoow for countless masking jobs; one of their great virtues being their low, non-residue tack. We just wish they had adhesive all over the back.

BRASS BLACK: Selenium dioxide solution, available in small bottles from Birchwood-Casey, is the stuff you can use to blacken the surface of brass parts, in particular photoetched: it also works on the nickel alloy used by FOTOCUT.

MATERIALS

This section covers plastic, wood, metal, and other materials which become part of the model structure, aside from elements simply left as residue, such as adhesives and fillers. Casting resins are excluded, being covered elsewhere.

ALCORN WORKSHOP#1: This "...In Action" shot, taken in early 1998 by Jim Schubert, reveals my developed concept of a mini-museum/workshop. Note the compressed C02 bottle; and stowed cardboard box which, when "deployed," serves as a spray booth. The wall decor reveals a few of my favorite airplanes: including the prototype for my ongoing NINAK model. Two heroes are also in evidence: Messrs. George Guynemer and Lee. The "solid" P-38F in the right lower foreground was built in about 1948 (high school).

POLYSTYRENE SHEET: This material, technically known as high impact polystyrene, and to the Brits as plastic card, is the basic ingredient of most vacuformed and built-up construction scratchbuilt models. However, in this tome, I use the term "plasticard." (After all, that's one way that our English language evolves new words: first, two words; then a hyphen between them; finally, a new, often compacted word. "Plastic card" is begging to be called "plasticard." This, by the way, is how "vacuformed" came to be.) Vacuformed, it becomes the shells of curved surface fuselages, nacelles, booms, wings, and often tail elements. Simply cut out from sheet stock are the slab sides, tops and bottoms, of many older planes; wing skins; bulkheads; plus countless small parts, many of which become three-dimensional shapes by filing, sanding, and laminating. Large 4 X 4 foot flat sheets, in thicknesses from 1/8" to 0.125", can be obtained from plastics retail outlets. 5, 10, 15 and 20 thou stock, in 6 X 12 inch sheets, are marketed by EVERGREEN and sold in most good hobby shops.

WARNING!!!: To my horror and amazement, I have found that this material has a finite shelf-life! Some 20 odd years ago, George Lee and I purchased a large, "lifetime" supply of polystyrene sheet, in 10, 20, 30, and 40 thou thicknesses, from a reputable dealer in the San Francisco area. Recently (1998), I found that my 10 and 20 thou stock at any rate has become imbrittled, evidently due to surface oxidation. (If I attempt to bend it back on itself, it breaks.) This actually caused the loss of an almost completed rudder, which failed when I inadvertantly pressed too hard between rib stiffeners. This revelation, of course, has sinister implications for the longevity of our creations. I can only take comfort in the hope that, once painted, oxidation degredation is retarded. (I won't even think about the fact that the inside surface of many skins, as for example, wings, is unpainted.) - *Praemonitus, Praemunitus*

POLYSTYRENE STRIP: EVERGREEN Scale Models of Kirkland, Washington, markets a line of Strip Styrene packets, containing 12" lengths of rectangular shapes (and tubes), in thicknesses and widths from 10 to 125 thou. These are extremely useful for interior structure and countless details. For convenience and efficiency, it is well to keep a wide selection of such packets on hand.

PLASTIC STRUCTURAL SHAPES: PLASTSTRUCT markets a line of "I" and "H" beams, "T"s channels and "angle irons" for architectural modelling, which can be useful.

TELESCOPING TUBING: This invaluable material, supplied by K&S, is available in brass and aluminum (aluminium), from 1/16" to 1/2" diameter from most hobby shops. It is also available in square, hex, "U" and other shapes.

FINE BRASS TUBING: Picking up where K&S left off, Stone McPherson's HOBBY HANGER (P.O. Box 472, New Carlisle, Indiana 46552) markets an amazing line of 6" long brass "Micro Tube" in 57 sizes, from 8 to 63 thou outside diameter. It's one of those products we don't know how we ever got along without.

BRASS SHIM STOCK: K&S Engineering Co. of Chicago packages this material in small sheets as thin as 1 thou. It is also available from SPI in larger sheets.

BRASS WIRE: DETAIL ASSOCIATES, in their HO Scale line markets a wide variety of straight brass wire down to 6 thou diameter, aimed at the steam and whistle trade. So, it's usually found in railroad hobby shops. As Karl Malden would have said: "Don't stay home without it."

STAINLESS STEEL WIRE: Straight 30" lengths of precision, spring-tempered 304V stainless steel wire, in diameters from 5 to 104 thou, are available from SPI. They also sell stainless steel hypodermic tubing.

STEEL MUSIC WIRE: SPI also has straight lengths (18" and 36") of hardened spring steel Music Wire, in diameters from 5 to 250 thou. This has a variety of modelling uses, including "set in place" rigging wire. It is also available at flying model shops.

FLATTENED STAINLESS STEEL WIRE: UNITEK/3M supplies orthodontic materials to the dental industry. George Lee employed rectangular (8X22 thou) "Permachrome" stainless steel wire for the flying and landing wires of his Keystone B4A. But, see Chapter IV: HOW I BUILT MY DH9A, section THE DREADED RIGGING for availibility.

SERVICES

Typically, the scratch builder requires two services (aside from psychotherapy): photoetching and decal/dry transfer. While resin casting is done by some modellers, most of us require the services of someone proficient in this technique.

PHOTOETCHING: Preparing "artwork" for photoetching is described in the chapter HOW I BUILT MY DH9A. I, John Alcorn, have my photoetching done by Fred Hultberg of FOTOCUT, as does Bob Davies. However, he does not widely advertise his custom services, due to the difficulty of educating people in the submission of camera-ready artwork. In any case, photoetch (or photoengraving) services are available from many sources: the trick is to find one who does small lot jobs of high quality at reasonable prices—like Fred. His address is:

ALCORN WORKSHOP#2: This view, taken in Williamsburg two years earlier, is dominated by the Plaistow poster of the Mk.V SPITFIRE of No.222 Sqdn., taken in 1942 by Charles E. Brown. A stahlhelm M35, mit Luftwaffe logo, is in evidence; as is George Lee, Billy Bishop and Grp.Capt. James Pelly-Fry, with whom I corresponded for over 15 years (and visited twice)—he commanded No.88 Sqdn. RAF during 1942/early'43 (BOSTON IIIs).

DAVIES WORKSHOP#1: This and #2 show Control Central of Bob Davies' workshop: the epitome of orderly efficiency. Really, it's a shrine to scratchbuilding; with the workspace below and resulting trophies above.

FOTOCUT
(Fred Hultberg)
Box 120
Erieville, NY 13061
Tel: (315) 662-3356

Contact him first, to find out what he needs to give you what you need.

I have recently discovered a good West Coast photoetcher:
ACU-LINE
(Greg Krueger)
462 N. 35th Street
Seattle, Washington 98103
(206) 634-1618

Both of these sources will accept small lot custom work: if your artwork is acceptable! They can provide photoetched parts from 2 to 20 thou, in brass, nickel/silver alloy and stainless steel—but, check with them for availability. For FOTOCUT, the elements of your artwork can be entirely separate: the parts are held in place on a rubberized backing. ACU-LINE requires that the individual parts of an array be connected by thin lines (sprue to us), so they don't end up at the bottom of the etching bath.

DECALS/DRY TRANSFERS:
A good source for custom dry transfers is:
    ARCHER Fine Transfers (Woody Vondracek)
    1205 Silvershire Way
    Knightdale, North Carolina 27545

A good source for custom decals is Lloyd Jones':
    SCALEMASTER
    929 Jasmine Circle
    Costa Mesa, California 92626-1721

Although they deal primarily in commercial decal sheets, custom work can also be done by:

DAVIES WORKSHOP#3: More of those suspect magazines, beneath his copier. Imagine the luxury of not having to drive down to KINKOS for every print required.

MICROSCALE INDUSTRIES, INC.
P.O. Box 11950
Costa Mesa, California 92627

The trendy way to make decals is by yourself, using any good computer graphics program and an ALPS MD 1000 (or 1300) "MICRODRY" color printer. Its waterproof ink process, which includes white plus metallic silver and gold, allows you to print onto water transfer decal paper. Thanks, Norm Filer.

WORKPLACES
While this section was added primarily as a diversion, it may be of some value to see scratchbuilder "manufactories." Really, though, there is no fundamental reason why our pigstys should differ from those of kit builders, other than the lack of floor-to-ceiling shelves of unbuilt (or, half built) kits.

ALCORN: My workshop is basically a "liberated" bedroom, the bed being replaced by a large wooden drafting table. While it is usually littered with tools in use, most are stored in a wond'rous GESTETNER wooden tool box; a hugely appreciated Christmas gift from my wife several years ago.

DAVIES WORKSHOP#2: To the left, we have the video to the Starship ENTERPRISE Bridge; or perhaps simply to the kitchen. But, Bob, about that neat stack of magazines on the right hand shelf—sure they aren't Playboys?

DAVIES WORKSHOP#4: Bob's built-in model cabinet.

DAVIES WORKSHOP#5: Wot, Bob!: no CAD CAM workstation?

Additional tools, paint, sandpaper, styrene strip packets, wire, frisket, photoetched sheets and the like are stored in the large, shallow drawers of my model display case; a custom made affair which, in retrospect, is less than ideal for its primary role. Magazines, monographs, books and lore-packed loose-leaf notebooks repose upon shelves of a large, wall-to-wall closet. A similar closet in the hallway contains more of the same, plus AAHS and CROSS & COCKADE Journals, plus great stacks of older magazines, including W.W.-II vintage FLYING, AIR NEWS, AIR TRAILS, and MODEL AIRPLANE NEWS. Two metal file cabinets beside my work table house folders of aircraft lore (plans, photos, clipped articles, etc.), by type. As can be seen in the accompanying photos, all available wall space in the workshop is covered with framed prints of my favorite airplanes, slowly gathered over the years from many sources. Then, of course, there is the modest military helmet and rifle collection, wooden solid models which survived from my youth, my Shirley Temple milk pitcher, die-cast TEXACO airplane models, my old bottle collection, Soviet Union memoribilia, an Edison Jem phonograph, a tuner/amplifier and 50s vintage Garrard turntable for playing my 78 rpm "golden oldies" (2000 of which repose downstairs, along with the bulk of my phonograph/gramophone collection)...on down to a full bottle of HADACOL (anyone outside of Loosiana recall Dudley J. LeBlanc?) In short, my own private mini-museum.

Perhaps the biggest problem of a modelling room is accomodation of airbrushing, without filling the house—and one's lungs—with paint fumes. Many solve this by doing their painting out in the garage. But, this is awkward: also, since such places are typically neither heated nor air-conditioned, they become unusable during much of the winter, and summer in some locales. A precious few plutocrats have the luxury of a full-on paint booth, as an adjunct to their workshop. I finally solved it by having an exhaust fan installed in the ceiling of my new Seattle workroom; and by simply using a large, tall cardboard box, cut open on one side, to contain the overspray and direct it upwards toward the fan. When not in use, I take it off the workbench and stow it beneath; where Belle the cat often hangs out. Note the CO_2 bottle beneath the workbench. Incidentally, another practical feature is the large plastic floor mat covering the carpet beneath the work area. It has prevented many a paint/thinner catastrophe—and saved many a tiny part from carpet pile oblivion. (Nevertheless, many must repose therein.)

BOB DAVIES: His work room is the epitome of purposeful orderliness: what else would you expect from an architect, W.W.-II flight instructor, cabinet maker, and world class scratchbuilder? Modeller's Valhalla; the ultimate workplace—and the accompanying photos don't even show his fully equipped workshop!

But, despair not, younger modellers. We haven't always had it so good. What's the old expression, usually attributed to the Germans: "Too soon ve bekommen alt, und too late ve bekommen schmart." You could add "und vell equipped." I, Alcorn, built my Douglas A-20A on the dining room table, which consisted of a hollow core door, mounted on two sawhorses—and, I was around 40 years old at the time. Only when I began my DH9A did I have a really proper workplace. It's like the other old saw: "It only takes two stools to make a school—with a good teacher on one and a receptive student on the other."

CHAPTER 12
Trio Diverso

This final chapter showcases the very diverse models of three scratch builders, from equally diverse corners of our ever shrinking planet: Dr. Dennis Collins, of England (20s British air racers); Mauro Cescutti, of Italy (W.W.-I and before); and Kevin Clayton-Greene, of...Tasmania! (W.W.-II).

MAURO CESCUTTI

I am a 42 year-old native of Trieste, a nice town on the Adriatic Sea, where I live with my wife, Rita. I have a High School Certificate in "Aircraft-Building," and I am employed by a large insurance firm. An aviation enthusiast since age 6, I began modelling at the same time—aircraft , of course!

My principal modelling interest is WW-I aircraft: I have long researched, for model projects (mostly 1/48th scale), the history and whereabouts of vintage aircraft in Italy, especially those employed during W.W.-I on the Isonzo front and around my town.

I am a member of G.A.V.S. (Gruppo Amici Velivoli Storici), a non-profit Italian Association for the preservation, restoration, and increase of Italy's historic aviation heritage.

Many of my models are entirely scratchbuilt; I like very much super-details: improving features provides interesting challenges!

Another diverse hobby is Minerals Collection: I am fascinated by natural shapes and colours. When I am not building models, I spend my leisure time in physical training and other sports, like skiing in winter, or basketball (not at N.B.A. level 4).

My "secret dream" would be to build a real aircraft. Now I am working on a 1/8th scale Nieuport-Macchi Ni 11 (strictly scratchbuilt!), but that is another story...

Mauro Cescutti.

ETRICH TAUBE: My 1/48th scale "Taube" depicts the machine flown by Ltn. G. Gavotti. It represents the aircraft as used on November 1, 1911: during the flight, bombs were released from an aircraft for the first time over an objective (one over Ain Zara and three over Tagiura oasis).

The scratchbuilt model is made from the usual composite materials, with only the spoked wheels and propeller being commercial parts. Fuselage, tail unit, and wing were from thin plastic sheet scored inside to represent ribs and frames, the surface dry-sanded to obtain a canvas effect. Aeroclub supplied the more powerful Mercedes 185 hp motor. Complete interior, struts, fuel tank, radiators, etc., were all scratchbuilt. Brass sheet and rods were used for the undercarriage; 0.14 mm fishing filament (dark metal painted) for rigging: inside the trasparency behind the pilot were homing-pigeons for communication!

A yellow sand Humbrol mix achieved the canvas colour for all the surfaces; clear varnish to simulate the connection between the upper wing fabric and the bottom wing fabric along the scalloped trailing edge. Stains around the engine area and chalk pastel weathering concluded the paintwork.

My initial inspiration for this model was the colour drawings of it by Pino dell'Orco, which appeared in Volume VI of STORIA DELL'AVIAZIONE. (This volume appeared in an English language edition entitled COLOR PROFILES OF WORLD WAR 1 COMBAT PLANES.-ed.)

OEFFAG Mickl type "H" -A II "Blau Vogel": This 1/48th scale seaplane depicts the famous boat "A11" as flown by Gottfried Banfield during 1916- 1918 at the Trieste Naval Air Station.

The scratchbuilt work began with drawings extrapolated from various sources (see references) compared with photographs available. The drawings did not match the photos in certain areas: I corrected them by proportional enlargement from photographs using dividers and common sense!

Construction was of the usual composite materials and started with the fuselage, which is of plasticard box section; balsa core. The front upper coaming to the cockpit was moulded from plasticard over a wood former; other items were added from plastic sheet, wood, and brass. The cockpit work was based on contemporary photographs of A.H. aircraft: all internal structure was fashioned from wood strip and sheet. Seat and throttle quadrant come from spares; Schwarzlose, control column, rudder pedals, instruments, etc., were all fabricated from plastic sheet, rod, and strip. The complex cabane and W struts were constructed from various plastic section; the fin, rudder, and tailplane were all made using the well known method of "rib embossing."

Wings were made by reworking the 1/48th Monogram" Wright Flyer," with ribbing effect obtained using the usual Evergreen products for each rib, sanding the whole down to scale. The lower wings fitted into the fuselage easily, but the fit of the top struts and upper

Etrich TAUBE-1: This is Mauro's lovely 1/48th scale TAUBE, depicting the machine flown by Ltn. Jiulio Gavotti, when he dropped the first bombs ever in anger, on 1 November 1911, upon recalcitrant Libyan tribesmen during the Italian-Turkish War. Construction details of Mauro's model are given in the text. He points out that the transparency behind the cockpit housed homing pigeons for air-to-ground communication!

OEFFAG Mickl type "H", A-ll "Blau Vogel": This 1/48th scale mode by Mauro Cescutti represents the famous "boat" flown by Ltn. Gottfried Banfield during 1916-18, based at the Trieste Naval Air Station.

Hansa-Brandenburg CC: Scratch built by Mauro Cescutti, this 1/28th scale model depicts "A.24" of Ltn. G. Banfield, defending Trieste in 1917, against the Italians—who, even then, represented the majority population of the city! Such is the madness of war. Especially noteworthy are the Hiero engine and translucent wings.

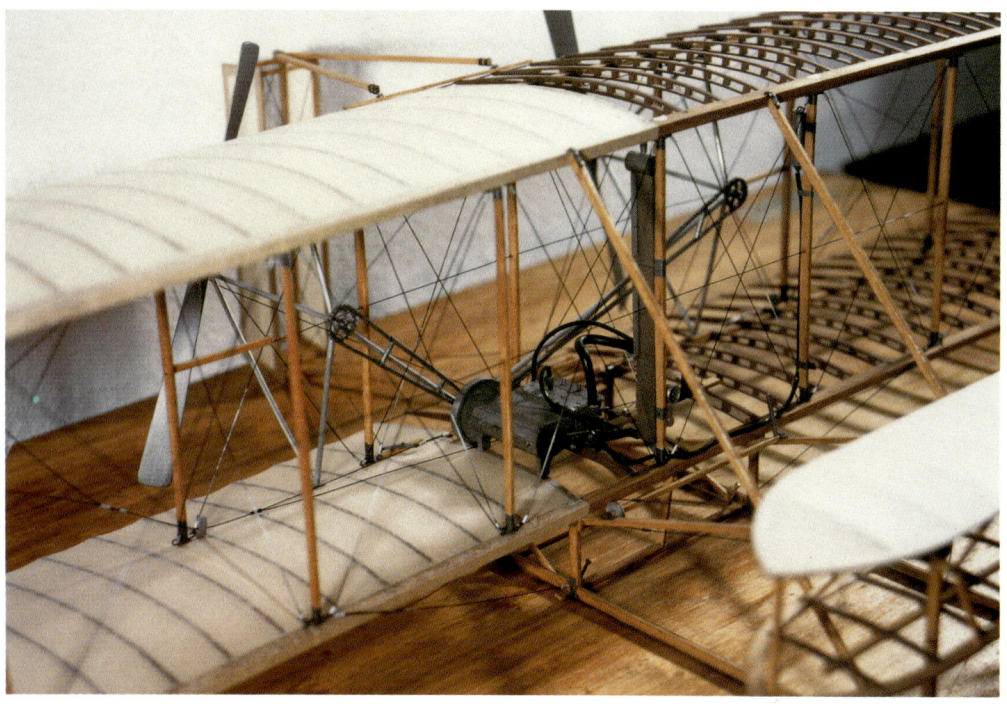

Wright "FLIER": Mauro's outstanding workmanship is especially evident in this wonderful replication of the first aeroplane to achieve manned, controlled, powered flight. This is an extensive rework of the 1/16th scale Hasegawa kit.

Chance-Vought F4U-1D: This impressive 1/24th scale scratch built CORSAIR is the work of Kevin Clayton-Greene, of... Penguin, Tasmania. It is finished in the livery of No.2 Servicing Unit RNZAF, based at Piva, Bougainville, during November 1944; as shown, having just returned from a mission during which a Japanese sniper deftly shot off one of its antennae. Kevin's construction methods for this, largely vacuformed, model are thoroughly explained in the text.

wing sections needed some adjustment: tabs and template provide for a jig. Tailplanes were added (rudder and elevator not yet fitted), and the entire airframe given a coat of light gray for inspection. At this stage I started work on the engine: an Hiero 200 PS entirely scatchbuilt using plastic rod, brass, and Milliput.

The beaching trolley was produced from plastic with the exception of the wheels, which were cast in resin, copied from spares; trestles were made from wood strip.

Before painting the model, I carefully studied articles and scale drawings by both M. O'Connor and R. Rimell on the subject. The main color used was Methuen Blue 23C7, as close as I could mix

Hawker TEMPEST V. Kevin's 1/24th scale model depicts "Le Grand Charles", the final mount of Wing Cdr. Pierre Closterman, C.O. of No. 3 Squadron RAF, 1945.

Chapter XII: Trio Diverso   155

Humbrol MC8, MG10, 109, 198, 157. Home made decals and light weathering effected with pastels finished off what is to me a very satisfying model.

HANSA-BRANDENBURG CC-A 24: This 1/28th scratchbuilt model is finished in the markings of A.24 when flown by G. Banfield in defense of Trieste during 1917.

Fuselage and floats are constructed of hard balsa covered with 0.5 mm birch. Rudder bar and mixture control are from brass and about 20 pieces make up the joystick; the frames and the floorboards are plywood. The single MG08/15 comes from Fotocut with sheet plastic for cartridge feed. The Hiero engine contains about 160 pieces with Milliput for crankcase, various sizes of plastic rod and tube for cylinders, plastic sheet brass and copper for the other little details. The propeller is made from six layers of plywood, the radiator is plastic with the front and rear surfaces from Trimaster. Realistic wings use real wood for the ribs and spars—covered with special paper from Hasegawa; tail surfaces are scratchbuilt in plasticard. The model, except for the white and red national colours, is in natural finish, and all the markings are cut out from Tauro Model decal sheet.

WRIGHT FLYER: This 1/16th scale Wright "Flyer" is an extensive rework of the Hasegawa kit, based upon drawings, photos, and documentation from the journal W.W.-I AERO.

KEVIN CLAYTON-GREENE

ABOUT KEVIN: I asked Kevin to provide some biographical background.

I was born in Hamilton (a dairy farming town) on New Zealand's North Island in 1952. I grew up continually pestering my father to take me out to the large aircraft storage depot at Rukuhia (pronounced Rook oo hee ah). This was where New Zealand's former WWII aircraft awaited their turn for the blowtorch. To a young aircraft fanatic they presented a tantalising site parked on the other side of the town's airport. I remember sitting in a F4U parked in the local garage when I was about 10 and have loved Corsairs ever since.

In 1975 I moved to Australia to take up a position at Melbourne University, where I completed a PhD in plant ecophysiology. Subsequently, I worked as a researcher in pome fruit physiology. For the last five years I have been working in private enterprise as a senior manager with a vegetable packer/exporter in Tasmania. I have three children, none of whom have the slightest interest in their father's interest, which is a pity, as now I have no one to give all my unbuilt kits and other modelling materials. They live in fear of the day that they will have to sort through all that stuff!

HOW I CAME TO MODELLING: I started building kits at the age of ten, and I think my first model was a 1/100 scale Bristol Beaufighter, produced, I believe, by Lincoln Industries in NZ under license from Marusan. Their entire range comprised three kits; the aforementioned Beaufighter, a Lancaster, and a Liberator. All were in rather plain plastic bags with I think three colour artwork. Due to its highly regulated economy, it used to be very difficult to buy model aeoplane kits in New Zealand, especially in a provincial town. I can remember my excitement when I first saw a Revell 1/72 scale P-40 Kittyhawk—in a box no less—with wonderful artwork. Occasionally one could also find the odd Aurora airliner kit or a Merit WW1 1/48 or 1/50 scale kit. Paint that adhered to plastic was even more scarce and restricted to six colours; red, yellow, blue, black, white, and clear (all very bright and very glossy!).

After finding Revell and Airfix kits, which appeared in stores from time to time, I was hooked, and modelling was how I spent much of my spare time and a lot of not so spare time. I might add that in between the irregular appearance of plastic aeroplane kits I

Hawker DH 103 HORNET F.3. Kevin is not alone in admiring this elegant machine, shown here as "F" of No. 33 Squadron RAF, serving in Malaya against Communist insurgents, 1954. As with all of Kevin's models, all markings are hand painted, except for small stencils, which are rub-on dry transfers.

spent a lot of time carving and constructing model boats out of wood. Despite the continual chiding of adults, I persisted with this behaviour throughout childhood, my teens, and shock horror, as an "adult."

AND TO SCRATCH BUILDING: Scratchbuilding for me came about as a progression from constructing model kits. Somehow the markings or variants produced in the kit were never quite right, and thus conversions gradually became the norm and also increasingly complex. It was, I think, whilst converting a 1/24 scale Me 109E into an F version, that I realized that building an entire component (in this case a fuselage) would be one hell of a lot easier than sticking large quantities of filler and plastic onto kit parts and then spending several days sanding and filling until I had worn out my fingertips. I had by now mastered the art of plunge moulding for my conversions and canopies, and thus inspired by Peter Cooke's magnificent set of drawings of a Mk XIV Spitfire I began my first scratchbuilding project. Harry Woodman's seminal work was also highly influential in heading down the scratchbuilding path. The relief was enormous! No longer did I have to worry about stuffing up a valuable kit if I made a mistake as I could now just cast or mould another component. In fact, for my first model, so distrustful was I of my abilities that I moulded six fuselages, two sets of wings, and six canopies!

I was also fortunate in having contact with a number of experienced modellers through IPMS, who provided considerable advice on things such as casting rubber tires, etc. In particular, Fred Harris from IPMS Australia deserves acknowledgement.

I enjoy the researching and planning of a model as much as the building. The only part that I find very tedious is wheel well detailing. Conversely, surface detailing I very much enjoy, perhaps because it is so obvious and important in capturing the final look.

In building models I believe that every aircraft has its own unique character and that it is important to try and capture this when constructing a model. This does not mean compromising accuracy, but just ensuring that the features which characterize an individual aircraft are well captured.

I also do not believe in displaying the model as if it is undergoing a major overhaul. Most aircraft have an elegance of line and a degree of aesthetic appeal. To me it is almost a travesty to cut away most of the aircraft's skin panels and thus destroy the elegance and nature of the subject. If massive quantities of wires, engines, tubes, etc. are one's thing, then maybe trains, tractors, or sailing ships might make better subject material? However, to each their own! Similarly, I feel that drooped flaps, etc. should be displayed only if that was the norm for the aircraft when parked.

SPITFIRE Mk. XIV: Before building the Spitfire, I constructed three vacuform boxes using wood and an old tractor grill (ideal, as the stout mesh provides a perfect porous base). The largest box is approximately 45 x 30cm (dimensions determined by the size of the oven in the house in which I then lived). Unfortunately I have since shifted several times, and much to my chagrin, all subsequent houses have been equipped with smaller ovens. The largest vacuform box I use for the fuselages and wings, the smaller sizes for tailplanes, canopies, etc. These vacuforms are simple in the extreme but have performed valiant service over many years and are still going strong. The largest has two outlet holes so that I can attach two vacuum cleaners and thus improve the suction.

In preparing the male patterns I use a backing piece cut to the correct profile/outline from 3-4mm three ply onto which the pattern is attached. This ensures both accuracy and also that the moulded plastic part will have a nice clean edge after separation from the plastic sheet and subsequent cleaning up (the actual edge of the

Supermarine SPITFIRE Mk. XIV. This 1/24th scale model represents a No. 139 Squadron machine, operating in Malaya, 1945. This was Kevin's first scratch built project, completed in 1985. The once snug-fitting gun cover was warped open by exposure to the sun.

part is 3-4mm from the curved vacuformed edge). I have also found that slightly raising the pattern above the surface of the vacuform machine produces a very neat and tightly moulded part. I thus place the pattern on blocks about 4-5mm high which means that the part has an undercut of plastic when first removed from the vacuform. As a consequence the plastic is thus sitting very snugly over the pattern, further enhancing the accuracy of the part being produced. For moulding fuselages and wings, I generally use 1mm or 1.5mm styrene card. For smaller components 0.5, 0.75, or 0.25mm is utilized.

The greatest problem that I encountered when building the Spitfire (or any other scratch built model) was translating the two-dimensional measurements from drawings onto the three dimensional vacuformed fuselage half. I use a number of approaches to this problem. When constructing the pattern, I make some fine holes at key places on the pattern to act as reference points for subsequent marking out and removal/addition of various features. Typically these points are the location of the main spars for the wing, tailplane, and fin, as well as the cockpit cutout. Other places to be considered are a couple of points along the datum line and the exhaust stack location on inline-engined aircraft. After vacuforming, these holes appear as small dimples on the inside of the fuselage, etc. I then drill a hole with a fine twist drill (#80) in the centre of each dimple. These quickly become filled with detritus when cleaning up the model and thus are easy to see. Marking of datum lines then is simply a matter of joining the dots!

Were I to have a lathe, this process would be considerably easier, as one could use the cross-slide and a sharp object mounted in the vertical drill to mark the various points of reference. I have subsequently made a small 'tool' that more or less duplicates the function of a cross slide. This consists of a board with a reference line along the bottom edge. The part (ie, a fuselage) is then placed above this line so that two of the above mentioned holes are parallel to this line. The 'tool' is then placed along the reference line and a fine pin/pencil held in a device—which I think can best be described as a small tower crane with boom—that is then moved along the reference line and marks made at appropriate intervals on the model. Any holes or imperfections can be either subsequently filled or covered during the plating/finishing process. I also use the template method described earlier by John.

Tires are moulded from silicone rubber dyed dark grey using carbon black. To make tires I use a process very similar to that employed by Gerald Wingrove and described in his books on car modelling. I first construct a male pattern of one side (split vertically) of the wheel (both if it is cross-treaded). This pattern is then used to produce a silicone rubber female mould. Wax is then poured into the silicone rubber to produce a master pattern of each side of the tire. The two wax masters are then correctly aligned and separated by cling-wrap or other extremely thin material that will not adhere too strongly to the cured resin. The wax tire is then used to produce a resin master mould. It is important to have some asymmetrically placed key points to enable the two halves of the tire to be correctly aligned. When cured the resin mould is inverted and the other half of the tire placed on top of the piece while it is still in the mould using the aforementioned alignment pegs. A second mould is then made around this tire using the already prepared half mould as a base. Thorough use of a separating compound is obviously a prerequisite at this juncture. At the conclusion of this procedure one should have two resin moulds that when joined together will result in a female impression of the tire. In some location, which will not be visible on the final item, it will be necessary to have a hole through which excess silicone can escape when the tire is cast. A mixture of silicone RTV and carbon black is then prepared and carefully poured into each half mould. The material is then left to sit for several hours or else placed in a vacuum container to extract excess air. Before the silicone begins to solidify the two halves are then joined and clamped tightly together. After 24hrs curing the moulds are separated and the result should be a complete tire. The process is then repeated for the other tire.

Undercarriage legs are constructed from either brass or copper tube, sheet or other sections etc. In attaching the undercarriage to the aircraft I always try to emulate the structure and appearance of the original. This can usually be done without compromising strength. Whilst this makes for a slightly more complicated model, I feel that it adds to the authenticity. *(No wonder I hate wheel wells)*

Propeller blades are cast from resin in a silicon mould after first making a master pattern from Ferropre. This is a black, two part, epoxy pipe-jointing compound available in Australia from plumbing supply shops. I presume there are equivalent compounds available in other countries. I use this as a filler and also as a pattern making material. It has the advantage that it is a lot cheaper than proprietary brand specialist fillers and is available in 1kg packs (500g per part). It sets rock hard and sands and polishes to a very smooth finish. For parts such as propellers I insert a metal reinforcing rod into the resin to provide strength during handling and also to act as a key into the propeller shaft.

Instrument panels are made from Litho-plate and the bezel rims cut from metal tube and epoxied in place. To make the instrument faces I prepare my own artwork and have them printed on heavy card. Instrument glass is either from clear sheet, or sometimes if non-circular from optically clear resin.

The Spitfire was painted using a formula developed and described by Peter Cooke: a mixture of paint, turpentine, lacquer thinners, and polyurethane varnish. All markings are hand painted, and stencils, etc. are applied using dry transfer sheets which I have prepared from my own artwork.

The aircraft modelled is finished in the colours of No.132 Sqdn, serving in Malaya during 1945.

The Hawker Tempest was constructed using similar techniques to that employed on the Spitfire. The aircraft is finished in the markings of Pierre Closterman and is constructed along similar lines to the Spitfire. Once again all markings are hand painted using either frisket or etched brass stencils.

The DH 103 Hornet has always been a favourite of mine, and the aircraft provided me with my first experience of building a complex multi-engined aircraft. The aircraft was built along similar lines to the Spitfire and Tempest and constructed from plastic card, metal, silicone rubber, and epoxy resin. It is a F Mk 3 finished in the colours of a machine serving with 33 Sqdn in Malaya during 1954. The colour scheme was provided by Mr Bob Stynes who served with the squadron during that time. I must also acknowledge British Aerospace, who provided extensive background material drawings, etc.

Breakdown of parts was as follows; vacuformed fuselage in halves split vertically, as were the fin, engine nacelles, and rudder, wings in four pieces split laterally as were ailerons, tailplanes, and elevators. The wing was then constructed into a single piece and inserted into a cutout made in the lower fuselage. The main spar was bolted onto bulkheads glued into the fuselage. Both the fuselage and wings (complete with nacelles) were largely complete when mated. The undercarriage attachments and bracing, etc. were also built before attaching to fuselage. Thus, only the wheels and parts below the oleo were required to finish this area.

HOW I BUILT MY CHANCE VOUGHT F4U-1D CORSAIR: The F4U-1D Corsair is an aircraft that I have always liked. It is also an aircraft that has a distinctive character: that large radial engine driving a huge propeller, followed by a long cowling and those impressive cranked wings with their fabric covered panels. Of course, it also had an impressive service record with several nations.

I determined to build a variant operated by the RNZAF in the Pacific during W.W.-II. The RNZAF purchased 424 of these powerful aircraft, becoming the third largest operator of the type. Unfortunately, General Douglas MacArthur's rather blinkered approach to the deployment of allied forces in the South West Pacific meant that the RNZAF only operated the aircraft in remote backwaters during the later stages of the war. This was a source of considerable frustration to both Australian and New Zealand aircrews during that period. This, despite the highly regarded efforts of RNZAF pilots operating P-40s on Guadalcanal during 1943; to say nothing of their record with KITTYHAWKS in the Western Desert from 1941 on.

The airframe was vacuformed out of 1.5mm plasticard after first carving the master patterns from wood. It comprised the following parts breakdown: a single piece cowling ring, a 2 piece rear cowling (engine covers), fuselage split vertically, 2 piece fin, 2 piece rudder, tailplane of 8 pieces, and wings comprising 6 major pieces, but with separate ailerons, flaps, and "fabric covered" outer panels. The fin needed to be moulded separately on this model, as it was offset 2° to counteract engine torque.

The construction sequence I follow always begins with the wings. There are two reasons for this. The first is that this is usually the area of an aircraft that provides a lot of its character and thus needs to be got right. Secondly, they contain the wheel wells, and as I hate detailing these areas I like to get them over and done with. To obtain the correct dihedral and to facilitate alignment I always make the wings in one piece, separating them later if required and using a jig for final assembly.

Here is Kevin Clayton-Greene as Mephistopheles. In a prior incarnation, he had served gallantly with Vercingctorix's gaulois at Alesia, against Centaurian Leonardo Cescutti's V Cohort of the VI "Ferrata" Legion. Small world.

Normally to represent fabric covering I use the time honoured method of fine embossing with a blunt instrument on the back of the part. However, on the Corsair the fabric covering was quite pronounced with reasonably prominent sagging between the ribs. On both the rudder and wings this fabric covering is one of the characteristic features of the Corsair to which I alluded above.

I thus made patterns out of card for each of the fabric covered surfaces and then vacuformed the parts from 0.25mm styrene. The patterns had fine ribs that were made thinner than actual size in order to make allowance for the thickness of the card. The secret with this technique is to just soften the plastic so that it only very subtly conforms to the ribs underneath. Several test runs were required, as it is very important to get the "sagging" just right because it could easily be overdone.

The Pratt & Whitney R2800 18-cylinder engine was subdivided into a number of sub-assemblies comprising block, reduction gear housing, crankcase, and cylinders. Patterns were then constructed and silicone rubber moulds prepared. The most complicated was the finned cylinder, which was built in two halves split vertically. Once the moulds were finished, it was then merely a case of making the required number of parts. In total, the engine comprised approximately 100 parts, but as it is such a prominent feature of the aircraft, it was important to get it right.

A master pattern of the propeller boss and blade were prepared and also used for casting the final parts.

Deperdussin 1913 "Monocoque": 1/20th scale model by Dr. Dennis Collins. This machine, designed by Louis Bechereau, was the fastest of all prewar aircraft; due to its elegant monoplane streamlining; Gnome 14 cylinder, twin row, 160hp rotary engine; and lightweight plywood monocoque construction. Bechereau had the good fortune to be financed by Armand Deperdussin, the flamboyant Lyonnaise silk merchant, who founded the Societe pour les Appareils Deperdussin (SPAD). Sporting the hastily-fitted short wings designed by the firm's "chief carpenter," young Andre Herbemont, this aircraft easily won the coveted 1913 James Gordon Bennett Cup Race, at the then phenomenal average speed of 200 kmh, over the 200 km closed course—piloted by Maurice Prevost, who had earlier in the year won the Schneider Trophy in a floatplane Deperdussin. However, by this time, Deperdussin was in prison, having been convicted of grand larceny, to the tune of some 28M francs. When Louis Bleriot later acquired the firm (including Bechereau and Herbemont) for a song, the acronym SPAD remained, but the "D" now stood for the bland "et ses Derives."

Gloucestershire Mars I "BAMEL." The woodworking firm/aviation works of Gloucestershire (GAC) had built fuselages for AirCo (DeHavilland) and Bristol during the war. Near the end of that conflict, they were awarded a huge contract for Nieuport NIGHTHAWKs: soon canceled, but leaving them with a large component inventory. Fifty Bentley B.R.2 rotary engined aircraft, renamed SPARROWHAWK, were sold to Japan: the necessary modifications were performed by Folland (HPF), still with Nieuport and General, but acting independently as an engineering consultant. In this capacity, he also designed the Mars I racer for GAC. Its airframe was based upon the Nighthawk, but was powered by the brilliant new "broad arrow" Napier LION II, which developed 530hp. The rather odd-looking little racer soon acquired the sobriquet "BAMEL"—half bear, half camel. Completed just four weeks from commencement of design, the BAMEL first flew, from Hucclecote, on 20 June 1921. Intended for the Aerial Derby in July, it suffered considerable damage just four days before the event. Following frantic repairs, against seemingly hopeless odds, it managed to win the Derby. Dr. Collins' model depicts BAMEL's appearance when it won the 1922 Aerial Derby, now fitted with a Lamblin radiator, and shortened wings employing the Folland-patented High Lift Biplane (HLB) airfoil.

To enable ease of transportation, the propeller was made removable. A brass screw was threaded in the boss, and a matching nut fixed in place in the reduction gear housing.

The 1,000lb bomb was also cast in resin after making a pattern out of card and Ferropre. The bomb rack is from copper tube, as are the undercarriage legs, exhaust stacks, and collector tubes.

(*left*) **Nieuport and General L.S.3 "GOSHAWK"**: another 1/20th scale model by Dr. Dennis Collins. Henry Phillip Folland's genius first found expression in the immortal SE5a, while employed at the Royal Aircraft Factory. Yet, something of an enigma, he remained "soundly conservative," eschewing monoplanes, all-metal structures, and even variable pitch propellers for much of his career. In 1917, he went to Nieuport and General as chief designer, following the demise of the Royal Aircraft Factory. "HPF"'s excellent NIGHTHAWK fighter of 1918 was meant to rival the Sopwiths, but was too late for wartime service: the ABC Dragonfly-powered design was slightly modified for civilian service—including racing—as the "Land Commercial type one," or L.C.1. In 1920, HPF designed the "Land Sporting 3" (L.S.3) purely for racing, still powered by a 340 hp upgrade of the unreliable Dragonfly radial. Following an almost comic-opera series of mishaps, the L.S.3 failed to even enter the 1920 Gordon Bennett Cup Race. Dr. Dennis Collins' model is shown in the L.S.3's colourful blue and yellow checkered livery. The next year, Harry Hawker was killed in this benighted aircraft, while preparing for the Aerial Derby.

For all major structural features where strength is required I like to use metal. I generally attach the main spar to the fuselage with a couple of small bolts. Perhaps this is over engineering, but I regard it as important to provide as rigid a structure as possible in order to prevent gaps appearing when one is handling the model during construction. It has been my experience that no matter how well joints are glued, it is almost inevitable that they eventually open up if subjected to regular stress. This is particularly true of the wing to fuselage joint due to the large amount of leverage which can be exerted on it.

The canopy framework is metal, built up over a pattern made from plasticard and Ferropre, tailor fitted to the cutout for the cockpit. The canopy is from vacuformed clear sheet over the pattern which is already covered by an initial vacuformed sheet to ensure as smooth a surface as possible. Whether or not the canopy is movable depends to some extent on my mood at the time and also on the type of hood. On the Corsair it is fixed in place.

The undercarriage doors were made from card. The stiffening grooves on the inside of the doors were machined in the plastic using a round headed dentist burr mounted in a hand held Dremel type drill which was guided by a metal straight edge. (I do not pos-

Bristol 32 "BULLET." This pugnacious affair sported a grotesquely oversize spinner and radically clipped wings for the 1921 Aerial Derby. It was flown to second place by Cyril Unwins—without the troublesome spinner. The BULLET's engine was an early Bristol JUPITER of 450 hp; whose designer, Roy Fedden, persuaded Frank Barnwell to build a racer around it, in the hope of furthering the engine's then unrealized—and indeed, precarious fortunes. Though a nice airplane, the BULLET's first manifestation was unable to best the winning Martinsyde in the 1920 Aerial Derby. It was almost totally rebuilt for 1921, but was deprived of First Place in the Aerial Derby by the BAMEL.

sess a lathe: therefore I sometimes have to resort to fairly odd methods to obtain the desired result).

The aircraft was painted in the colours of No 2 Servicing Unit RNZAF based at Piva, Bougainville, in November 1944. It features a faded 4-tone USN scheme, and the numerals are slightly out of register as shown in a photograph of the actual aircraft. The model was also touched up and faded according to actual colour swatches from weathered RNZAF aircraft. The harsh conditions of its operational theatre meant that paintwork quickly faded and aircraft assumed a patchy appearance. To achieve fading I mix up a very thin wash of varnish and various grey tints and then spray this onto the model so as to "bleach" colours in the same way as on the full size machine (i.e. more washing on the top of the fuseagle than the sides). The undersides were washed in a pale greyish-pink to mimic the effect of coral dust.

In constructing models with this level of detail a considerable amount of assistance is needed, and I would like to acknowledge that provided by the NZ Air Force Museum in Christchurch and also the Naval Aircraft Museum at Pensacola.

My latest project is a Messerschmitt Me 110 G-2: unlike my previous models, this one is being covered with lithoplate. As each major component is finished it is then covered in metal panels in the same manner as on the original. The technique has been described elsewhere by Alan Clark, who achieves finishes which must be seen to be believed.

The major difficulty with this technique is in replicating large spun pieces such as propeller spinners. On the 110, these were shaped out of a single piece of plate with continual annealing over a small Primus stove, and subsequent shaping. I have made myself a variety of hardwood shaping tools to assist with panel beating. Except on broad flat surfaces, I have found that metal tools are often too hard on the lithoplate. After some practice it proved possible to make a spinner in about half an hour. Lithoplate is also very good for cockpit detailing in that it provides a real metal finish to weather.

To expedite the sheathing process I first mark out all panel lines on the model. I cover each major sub-assembly as it is completed. I then cover the area to be plated with clear sheet and trace the panel lines onto the sheet with a fine line overhaed marker. The resultant elements are then cut out and serve as templates for the aluminium sheet.

RESIN CASTING: I cast a number of parts in resin, including propeller blades, most ordnance, and any parts which required more than one to be built, or which can be used on subsequent models. I have also used resin in lieu of glazing on some parts (e.g. odd shaped instrument panel glass). Although I still occasionally use polyester resin, for most parts I now use epoxy. I have tried a number of the fast cast resins, but unfortunately these set too quickly and thus suffer from numerous pin holes due to the lack of time for air bubbles to escape. It also seems to set without the high quality finish of other resins.

For making moulds I use a variety of Silicone elastomers. The main attributes which are important are the ability to take undercuts, viscosity, and resistance to attack by epoxy resin. Unfortunately I have found out (the hard way) that a number of products available overseas either have different names in Australia or else are made by different chemical companies. Product names are thus of limited use outside one's own country.

ALCORN POSTSCRIPT: Following a carrot-growers' conference during late August (1998) in Madison, Wisconsin, Kevin spent three days with us in Seattle. We squandered not a moment, what with visiting the Seattle Museum of Flight, the Boeing/Everett plant, discussing airplanes and modelling techniques, and general socializing. It was a Hoot!

DR. DENNIS COLLINS

Alan Clark suggested that I contact Dr. Collins, whose delightful 1/20th scale models of 'teens and '20s British air racers are featured herein. The main components of these were made in the traditional scratch builder's manner of vacuforming polystyrene sheet over carved wood forms. After trimming, the shells were mounted upon a plasticard skeleton. As evident from the photos, Dr. Collins machined numerous components, particularly in the engine area, using a UNIMAT lathe.

Dr. Collins was born in Plymouth in 1927. In 1937, as a diminutive Air Scout steward at Roborough airport, he had the inestimable pleasure of holding the wingtip of Alex Henshaw's magnificent Percival Mew Gull, an event which engendered a lifetime's love affair with aviation.

Following an education severely disrupted by wartime bombing, he served in the British Army in India from 1945-48. His education resumed upon return to Britain—without the bombs. He obtained a Bachelor's degree in Chemistry in 1952 from the University of London. Following a number of lectureships in pharmaceutical and organic chemistry, he received a PhD in research.

A short stint as Head of the Chemistry Department at the West Australian Institute of Chemistry in Perth during 1964-67 was fol-

This lovely harpsichord is an example of Dr. Dennis Collins' current scratchbuilt production.

lowed by the Vice Principalship of Chiswick Polytechnic: in turn followed by Principalship of Isleworth Polytechnic in West London, from 1969 until retirement in 1987.

With Jill, his wife since 1954, he now lives in the New Forest, Sway, Hampshire. They have three sons and a daughter.

Since retirement, he has concentrated upon the construction of "scratch built"...harpsicords! As can be seen from the accompanying photograph of one, these are doubtless worthy of Bach or Scarlatti.

Epilogue

To close out this tome, it seemed fitting to summarize the fundamental attributes of a truly worthy scratchbuilt model, which have been emphasized throughout.

WORKMANSHIP

This is the first criterion by which any model is judged. Despite the unusual dedication and time investment required of a scratchbuilt project, such models are not necessarily immune from lapses of basic modelling craftsmanship—even when produced by highly skilled and experienced practitioners.

Perhaps the commonest explanation for such a seemingly inconsistent situation is post-completion deterioration of some aspect of the model. For vintage biplanes, an all too frequent occurrence is loosening of rigging wires for a variety of reasons, including: faulty (weak) attachment; long-term distortion of plastic structure in response to rigging tension; relaxation (elongation) of tensioned thread; or stresses experienced by the model during handling and/or shipment, and by differential thermal contraction. Another post completion factor is long-term dryout of seams, which had been joined by liquid cement, and perhaps filled, but which had not fully dried before final model finishing. In some cases, these seams simply become visible through shrinkage: in others, they actually crack.

"But," you may ask, "should such flaws be considered lapses of workmanship rather than of long-term durability, or even of misuse?" The answer, I believe, is "yes," since they are design/constuction related.

However, scratchbuilders are also capable of such commonplace weaknesses as often bedevil kit models: visible seams (not from long-term shrinkage, but at completion); component misalignment; superglue smudges; uneven panel line scribing; overspray; visible decal film; etc. One explanation, perhaps—though no excuse—is sheer weariness towards the end of a long project.

CONFIGURATION ACCURACY

As has been stressed throughout this book, and especially in CHAPTER IX: MODEL RESEARCH AND PHOTOGRAPHY, no scratch built model is any better than the plans from which it was constructed (or any other model, for that matter). As Clark Macomber cautions, no plans, even from the most reliable of source, should be used without thorough verification against published dimensions and photographs. "Guilty Until Proven Innocent": follow the Inquisitor's example in this respect. Even drawings which are basically correct may contain a few detail errors which could undermine the authenticity of your model. As Clark further stresses: just because the drawings have appeared in some widely circulated publication doesn't *a priori* make them correct.

But, assurance of accuracy doesn't end with the basic plans. As a rule, these do not include interior features; or adequate details of such important components as engines, landing gear, canopies, and armament. For this reason, many supplemental sources must be consulted, including tech manuals, detail photographs, type monographs, or perhaps the real thing. But, even these should be viewed with a jaundiced eye. A widespread pitfall here is that many surviving, restored aircraft contain certain features which have been altered from the original. Another is that manufacturer technical manuals occasionally show features which were altered during production: or conversely, that your subject differed in certain respects from its factory configuration, through field changes, or even at modification centers.

I (Alcorn) have found that configuration research doesn't end until the model is complete.

PAINTING/ MARKING AUTHENTICITY

Why is it that modellers are generally far more conscientious over this aspect than Warbirders? Would we, for example, put AVG markings on a P-40N, whose camouflage colors are bogus and shiny to begin with?

In fact, most serious modellers are extremely cognizant of these aspects, sometimes to a fault. It is we, by and large, who have prompted the vast amount of research which has gone into this subject over the past thirty-odd years. But, pitfalls remain, aside from lapses of application workmanship.

Individual aircraft markings must be researched and accurately replicated, just as for structural configuration aspects. Whether it be the numbers, stripes, and logos of an early '30s Thompson Trophy racer, or nose art of an 8th Air Force B-17F, such markings require careful reproduction from scrutiny of the best photographs and descriptions available; as to shape, size, position, and colors. While for kits, a rich choice of high quality aftermarket decals/dry transfers often exists, the scratchbuilder is rarely afforded such luxury—he's lucky if he can even find appropriately sized national insignia for a military aircraft.

FINISHING CONSIDERATIONS

As Peter Cooke points out, the ultimate test of a model's realistic appearance is the ruthless scrutiny of a camera. Within the limits of our skills and modelling practicality, photographs of a model should look like the real subject. (Realistic bases and backdrops notwithstanding: this is the province of the dioramist and special effects photographer, which does not concern us in this context.)

Photographs—particularly, detail shots—often reveal construction/finishing flaws which have eluded its creator. Maybe there exists a sort of "can't see the trees for the forest" syndrome, when simply looking at the actual model.

"Scale effect": intensity reduction of overall and markings colors, is an important factor in realistic appearance: the more so the smaller the model scale. In fact, this effect is usually overlooked by modellers, who are intent upon painting their subject to match color chips.

Fading/Discoloration: For all but pristine, fresh from the paint shop subjects, some fading/discoloration has occurred, at least for the vintage aircraft with which this tome is primarily concerned. Several factors conspire to produce these effects, including sunlight, rain, heat, time of exposure, paint quality, and initial color. As has been so dramatically brought in the numerous fine books of color photographs from W.W.-II, camouflage colors often weather in remarkable ways; hues sometimes changing from, say, olive drab to russet. Again, though, as with configuration drawings, be skeptical: are we observing color shift on the actual aircraft, or of the 55 year old print/negative? Usually, other objects of (better) known color provide the clue: earth, flesh, leather jackets, uniforms, grass, trees, etc.

Weathering: Here, I refer to aspects other than paint fading/discoloration, namely: staining, as by engine exhaust, greasy hands, and oil leaks; abrasion, as by desert sand; peeling, as so often occurred with W.W.-II Japanese camouflage paint; scratching, as by tools and shoes; and spatter, as by mud and pigeons. The universal caution is: "Don't overdo it!" Nevertheless, any airplane in service displays some degree of weathering; from minimal when almost new, to maximal after a year or so in the Western Desert, New Guinea, or the Russian Front. Your primary guide should be photos of your subject aircraft, and of others of the same type in similar circumstances.

Surface Features: In Chapter IV: HOW I BUILT MY DE HAVILLAND DH9A, under the section FINISHING, I discussed the simulation of several kinds of surface features on such aircraft, namely: fabric wrinkling; plywood warping; side panel lacing; and wing rib/edge tapes.

Other HOW I BUILT MY... chapter authors, Peter Cooke and Alan Clark, in particular, described their techniques for application of panel lines and rivet detail, usually applied to thin skin over the underlying shell/form.

However, there is another aspect which I have never seen properly represented on a model, namely the actual indentations on the top skin of metal monoplanes, due to having been walked upon by pilots and maintenance personnel. Maybe this is because no one, at least to my knowledge, has been able to bring himself to so defile the lovely panelled and rivetted surface which he has labored so hard to achieve. This effect is, of course, usually accompanied by a certain amount of paint removal.

Patina: This is usually the final effect to be produced upon the aircraft surface, be it painted or natural metal. Sometimes it is achieved with the final color coat, thinned out and deftly applied. Other times, it is brought out through polishing, buffing, or even very fine sanding. Most commonly though, it is obtained with a final clearcoat having some matte properties, such as Testors Dullcoat or Polly Scale Clear Flat Acrylic (water-based).

Regardless of how obtained, scale realism should be the goal. The two patina extremes are all too often seen: showroom auto shine and full matte. Neither are appropriate for a real airplane, especially when scale effect is considered.

Rearwin "Speedster. This delightful model is evocative of those halcyon private flying days just before W.W.-II. The Rearwin company of Kansas City, Kansas, also built their own line of radial engines, under the "Ken-Royce" name—these being the names of the founder's two sons, both of whom were active participants in the firm. However, the "Speedster" was powered by a Menasco "Pirate"C4, of 125hp. Ron's model won First Place in the Scratch Built Aircraft category at the 1978 IPMS/USA Nationals.

Piper L4-H "Grasshopper". This militarized version of the J-3"Cub" was the aircraft of Lt.H.E. Brown of the 4th Infantry Division. This model won the Best D-Day Award at Cap Con 1994, Ottawa, Canada.

SURVIVABILITY

OK, so you've labored lo those many moons over your *magnum opus*. You want it to last for many more moons, right? *Deo volente*, it will last for many decades, or even centuries—to become part of the cultural baggage (i.e. burden) of your descendants, or of institutions. At any rate, what you don't want is for it to deteriorate before your very eyes. But, it can, and often does happen, unless one anticipates potential threats.

An obvious threat is deterioration of the construction materials. In Chapter XI, I warned of the long-term degradation of polystyrene plastic: the very stuff of our hobby. I then remarked that maybe it isn't such a threat once it has become incorporated in a model, and painted, inside and out. To be sure, though, certain other materials, including epoxy/fibreglass, are more intrinsically durable. Wood also should have superior durability, so long as it has been well dried before use and is properly painted—or covered by polystyrene sheet, which would be stabilized by glue on one side and paint on the other.

Although I discussed the threat of rigging deterioration above, under WORKMANSHIP, it is a key survivability issue.

Another aspect, which also should perhaps more properly come under the heading of "workmanship," is general robustness of the basic model structure. A common failing here, especially among scratchbuilders, is to construct an element so authentically that it is dangerously weak—landing gear being the most vulnerable elements in this respect. I should know: I have committed this error on numerous occasions, most notably on my A-20A. As a rule of thumb: make all retractable, oleo-strutted landing gear out of brass tubing, solder the components, and firmly anchor them into the model structure.

Survivability also depends upon environment. A fine model deserves to be on display: in the builder's (or purchaser's) home, or in a museum. However, under no circumstances should it simply repose upon a table top—nekked—exposed to the depredations of dust, dusters, cats, dogs, casual admirers, and marauding children. If it is worthy of the time invested, it is worthy of a proper glass-top case: or, of display in a modelling cabinet, among its peers. Even here, though, environmental dangers await their moment to strike. So enclosed, the greenhouse effect can melt down or distort a model in short order, if left exposed to direct sunlight. Another threat is motion—even impact—from a tabletop or other location where the tramp of Roman Legions (herds of kids). or even an unbalanced clothes washer can rock it asunder.

A locked, security-alarmed, bullet-proof case, with artificial light, in a temperature/moisture controlled, inert gas environment, mounted upon a steel base, whose stout legs are embedded into the Canadian Shield—that's the best.

SCRATCH BUILT! A CELEBRATION OF THE STATIC SCALE AIRPLANE MODELER'S CRAFT

John Alcorn/George Lee/Peter Cooke.

Written by three well known practitioners of the craft, SCRATCH BUILT! explains advanced aircraft modelling techniques in a lively and readable, yet thorough manner and includes many "how-to" photos and line drawings. Also included are superb portraits of over thirty scratch built models.

Size: 8 1/2" x 11"

144 pages, hundreds of b/w and color photographs; soft cover

ISBN: 0-88740-417-0 $24.95